INDIA-PAKISTAN RELATIONS

INDIA-PAKISTAN RELATIONS
THE STORY OF A FRACTURED FRATERNITY

M. P. Ajithkumar

Publications

KALPAZ PUBLICATIONS
DELHI-110 052

India-Pakistan Relations

Rs. 750

ISBN : 81-7835-493-4

Published in 2006 in India by
Kalpaz Publications,
C-30, Satyawati Nagar,
Delhi-110 052
E-mail : kalpaz@hotmail.com

Lasertype Setting by: Tact Computer Graphics, Delhi
Printed at: Salasar Imaging System, Delhi

With memory
in the feet of my father
the late
R Parameswara Kurup

Contents

Foreword

This book gives a detailed account of the relations between India and Pakistan from almost their birth in 1947 as independent states, till 2005. It covers the entire range of the Indo-Pakistan relations including the momentous times of 1971 when in the wake of the Indo-Pak war of that year, Pakistan, was partitioned following the liberation of Bangladesh (East Pakistan) which was "the result of a caesarian operation effected with India officiating as a willing midwife". The two states have been in a state of perpetual cold war ever since they became independent from British domination, and their relations have been seldom happy and invariably hostile. Their attitudes were conditioned by diverse factors—political, cultural, social and economic. With the Kashmir issue as the most thorny and intractable problem between the two countries, matters such as the tragic results of Partition, division of assets and liabilities, integration of states of Junagarh, Hyderabad and Kashmir, rehabilitation of refugees, canal water disputes, Sino-Pak agreement relating to transfer of Pakistan occupied territory in Kashmir to China, the wars of 1965, 1971 and 1999 etc. have worsened the relations. Little wonder that scholars of Indo-Pak relations have shared the view of Inder Malhotra that the matter "is vast, complex and is covered with a thick overlay of emotion, prejudice, preconceived notion, plain ignorance and deliberate misrepresentation"

Sri Ajithkumar has made an intelligent analysis of Indo-Pak differences, the efforts of Anglo-American powers to keep these differences alive and capitalize on them, the failure of the early rulers of India to realize the gravity of the issues and find timely and effective action to prevent them assuming alarming proportions threatening peace in South Asia and holding up the development of the country and the well being of its people and the reluctance amounting almost to refusal to adopt a tough line of approach to the entire problem so that an early solution could be arrived. He has done his best to provide a mine of information to students of Indo-Pak relations by citing authors and their publications, whose writings on different aspects of the subject he had read, reflected upon and produced this narrative which I am sure not only the academic community but the general public as well will read with pleasure and profit.

Sri Ajith has attempted to expose all significant matters relating to Indo-Pak differences without bias, but has not hesitated to present his own point of view whenever he found facts, values and reasons so warrant.

Cochin
20 August 2005

P. C. Menon
Professor of History
& Principal (Rtd.)
N. S. S. Colleges, Kerala

Preface

Historical truths differ from general belief or what is made to believe. The propagandist elements combined with general ignorance have kept truths far away from being known to the common folk with the result that deliberately spread untruths and half-truths remain unchallenged. They have made their inroads into the academic groups who are some times not ready to get at the truths and enlighten the public on what really happened in our nation's past. In most cases there are only dilettantish approaches to the past realities, a clear picture of which would have solved many riddles usually held as insoluble.

Developments in both national and international affairs proved that many untoward situations of present politics are the bitter fruits of history. It was this bitter fruit of painful realities that India drew from her dealings with Pakistan. More painful is that though she has been endowed with adequate material and human resources to tide over any challenge she has always been at the loosing end. Though she won stupendous military victories against the aggressor she suffered diplomatic defeats at the end. What the army won for its nation the political leaders blasphemously waved off at diplomatic counters. This is indeed the misfortune that has been haunting our nation over the years since 1947.

If India was torn to pieces in 1947, the years that followed saw her being audaciously fooled both by her neighbouring state as well as by those who moulded her destiny over the past half a century. Her problems with Pakistan still remain unsolved, haunting her in the forms of terrorists infiltration, the proxy wars, the armed fights staged in Kargil and other places, isolated bomb blasts and sometimes sporadic outbursts of communal frenzy called *jihad*. Over the years India has had to sacrifice a lot of her men and material resources either to fight the enemy or to feed the migrants who made their way to India, escaping Pakistan's oppressive rule. Governments, which came to power in India, have not handled Indo-Pakistan issues with the required seriousness, and the trouble continued like a cancer eating into the vitals of her national economy, peace and security. This is certainly an undesirable state of affairs about which our leaders and diplomats are bound to be more concerned than ever. Once it is settled for good, India can fast grow in the Asian region as an economic citadel. And if the modern generation of political leadership would turn mature enough to understand the realities of our nation's dealings with Pakistan and act as much wisely as to find remedial solutions to this long drawn issue it would be the greatest national fortune of this century. We may hope that such a generation of intelligent politicians would emerge.

My sincere thanks are to my teacher, P. C. Menon, formerly Professor of History and Principal, N. S. S. Colleges, Kerala, for his having patiently read the script, suggested necessary corrections and graced the book with a foreword.

M.P. Ajith Kumar

1

Introduction

History often offers solutions and provides the hindsight needed to correct past wrongs. It reminds us that no problems, which confront man, are insoluble and all human mistakes could be set right with the passage of time. A study of things and events would convince us that developments, past and present, are predetermined. Upholding his cyclical theory of history, the great saint and savant, Sri Aurobindo said that we return to the point from where we set out. Beginning is the end and vice versa and no nation or civilization can escape from the will of nature[1]. History has been witness to several dynamic and unexpected changes during the past five to six decades. The unification of the two Germanys, which was once believed an unrealizable dream, became a stark reality. The one time Leviathan USSR known for its strength and solidity is today in shambles. The British empire, which once boasted that the sun would never set on it, has been reduced to a small state of a few islands one of which, Ireland, is seeking separation from it. The formation of European Union has brought together the long time enemies, France and Germany. The Israelis, inheritors of one of the world's ancient civilizations are successfully fighting a battle for survival and progress against the onslaughts of several powers and forces.

Compared to the massive dimensions of the problems that the above countries had to face, the issue of Indo-Pakistan differences is so small and insignificant that with a little goodwill on either side they could be easily solved. If these twin states born to a common mother could shed their mutual distrust and misunderstanding and stand together, that would help bring peace to the subcontinent and facilitate the settlement of the many problems in the Asiatic region. Viewed from any angle, Indians and Pakistanis are the legatees of a common cultural heritage. Pakistan was carved out of India's northwestern zone, which was the heartland of her cultural continuity through the centuries. Modern archaeological and geological finds corroborated by the available literary evidences show that the river Saraswathi flowed through the above area. The excavations conducted by the archaeologists, especially the Pakistani group led by M. Rafique Mugal, former Director General of the Department of Archaeology of Pakistan, have brought to light the remains of a highly advanced urban, secular and indigenous civilization on the banks of this now lost river which was the life-line of the cultural and socio-economic progress of early north-western India[2]. This civilization had cultural and commercial contacts with several contemporary civilizations. The area attained great heights in political, cultural and socio-economic fields during the days of the Vedas and allied works. A thousand buds of thoughts bloomed there and the well-known archaeologist B. B. Lal holds that the Vedic people were themselves the authors of the civilization that flourished on the banks of Saraswathi and Sindhu. The lamp of India's cultural heritage was kept bright and burning down the centuries by the renowned university of Takshasila and the several Buddhist Viharas and Lamaseries of the north-west India which attracted students from far and near. Most of the distinguished scholars of ancient India were associated with the above university or hailed from its proximity. The noted Russian author Nikolai Notovich and the learned German thinker Faber Kaiser have stated that Jesus Christ had his spiritual education sitting at the feet of the Indian preceptors of the Lamaseri at Leh[3]. Panini the doyen of Sanskrit grammarians and Chanakya the great political scientist had by their life and learning hallowed the precincts of the University of Takshasila. To be a student of this prestigious centre of learning was the cherished dream of the seekers of knowledge of the times. The North-West had indeed been the cradle of Indian culture and civilization, the centre of its birth and nourishment.

But Pakistan and Pakistanis do not seem to attach any significance to this glorious past of their new homeland. Right from its birth all governments, which were set up in Pakistan have been following an anti-Indian policy for their survival.

Raising the India bogey has become the stock-in-trade of the rulers of Pakistan to divert the attention of their people from internal problems and escape from public wrath. The hate-India policy they have been following is well reflected in Pakistan's approach to all matters. While education has not been given the importance it deserves, those educated are so indoctrinated as to believe that they belong to an alien culture and have nothing in common with India. The entire curriculum seems drawn up to sow the seeds of deep anti-Indian sentiments in the minds of the new generations and make them look upon their next-door neighbour as their enemy number one.

Indo-Pak discord has all along been a threat to peace in the region and has been holding up the economic progress and the well being of the people of both the countries. Pakistan has been encouraging cross-border terrorism by providing all facilities to terrorists to undergo mercenary training and helping them to enter India to foster trouble of all sorts. Analytical studies into the causes of this longstanding bitterness between these two countries and the factors that have been perpetuating these differences, and possible solutions to them have become imperative necessities today. The changing scenario in Asiatic politics also demands a new approach to Indo-Pakistan relations. India and Pakistan have a great deal to gain, and chances of peace in Asia could be bettered if they could remain on friendly terms with each other.

This work seeks to provide the details of the various aspects of the mutual relations between the two countries born in the wake of the partition of the Indian subcontinent in 1947, during the most crucial period in their history stretching from their birth to the present.

References

1. Sri Aurobindo, *The Human Cycle – The Ideal of Human Unity – War and Self Determination*, Pondicherry, 1985, p. 2.
2. M Rafique Mugal, 'Recent Archaeological Research in Cholistan Desert', *Harappan Civilization* (Ed. G Possehl), Delhi, 1993, pp. 85-95. Also see Michel Danino, *The Invasion that never was*, Mysore, 1996.
3. Holger Kersten, *Jesus Lived in India*, New Delhi, 2001.

2

A Moth-Eaten Pakistan

The origin of Pakistan was one of the misfortunes of the 20th century. Born of the communal sentiment channeled to an ignoble end, Pakistan has been a problem state ever since its birth in 1947. As is well known, Pakistan had its source in the communal politics of the Two-Nation theory based on the Hindu-Muslim difference. Worst of all the undesirabilities, this fanaticism has been the inspiration for the continuity of Pakistan's political life too down the preceding decades. It has been stereotyped in many recent writings that the development of communalism was a phenomenon of the 19th and the 20th centuries in which the colonial policy of the English administrators aided and patronized Muslim fundamentalism as a counterpoise to checkmate the Indian patriotic enthusiasm spearheaded by the Indian National Congress. But this may not be taken in face value since the question of communalism in India can be traced back to the appearance of crescent on Indian horizon in the 8th century (AD) when the ideas of the Universal Empire and Universal Church had been gaining unprecedented currency. As a prelude to the later Islamic invasions of India, an Arab fleet headed by Imad-ud-din-Muhammad Bin Khasim, nephew of the Bagdad Governor, Al-Hajaj, stormed and captured the port city of Debal from its Hindu ruler, Dahir. Historians in their flights of fancy have dismissed it as a passing episode and an ephemeral incident in the history of India. But the spark this ephemeral happening left behind had set ablaze the centuries to come, bringing into Indian theatre Islamic invasions one after the other sworn to turn India, the Dar-ul-Harb into Dar-ul-Islam. This cancer of fanaticism was then a worldwide phenomenon. Having been tended to eat into the vitals of many civilizations of the time, it led to many undesirable developments in medieval Europe where the Cross and Crescent had been testing their mettle and might. It had its reverberations in the Crusades, in the conquest of Constantinople by the Turks who converted the Church of St. Sophia into Haga Sophia, in the Portuguese-Arab conflict in the Arabian Sea, in the Greek war of independence, in the Israel-Palestine issue, in the American designs in the Gulf regions, Afghanistan, and perhaps in future, if circumstances would take new turn, Pakistan too, in the diehard outfits like 'Al-Quaida' and all such 'Jihadi' terrorist wings[1].

That India has become a part of this theater of fanatical designs, and operations was the freak of fortune which was hell-bent to make her lay bound at the feet of the Central Asiatic conquerors, the Turkomans or the Mugals who fought relentlessly to silence the sentiments and cultural ethos of India. While the Khiljis and the Mugals were making their incessant warfare against the Hindu states of Mewar and later of the Marathas, the Bahmini, their Muslim counterpart was measuring sword against the Hindu kingdom of Vijayanagar in the far south, all to erase the non-Islamic entities from India and convert it into Dar-ul-Harb. Throughout the medieval period, India has presented the picture of a political melting pot with the native Hindus taking to swords to protect and preserve their age-old culture from an external proletariat sworn to subvert whatever it found non-Islamic. The medieval Indian literature is replete with the stories of the Rajput heroes defending their women and culture from the lust of the Khilji debauchery or Akbar's Din-Ilahi which helped him to have many wives, along with many such Muslims whose marriage with the Hindu women could bring many more converts to the Islamic faith. The battles of Khanua, Haldighat, the triumphant attacks the Chhathrapathi Sivaji unleashed against the bigotry of the Mugals and the shrill voice of the swords of Vijayanagar soldiers that resounded in the Doab of Raichur wax eloquent on the epic heroism of the Hindu-India relentlessly engaged in defending her timeless cultural heritage. Though the foundations of Mugal power was completely eroded by the resurgence of the Maratha-led Hindu nationalism the Muslim dominance got an edge over it with the defeat of the Marathas in the third battle of Panipat. Once again the history of India would have become the story of minority ruling the majority. But fate willed otherwise. It was left to the British to step into shoes of the Maratha and mould its destiny for the next three centuries.

The era of colonialism the European powers had inaugurated in India had brought about far reaching changes in the country's polity, economy and society. All of them followed the same colonial and commercial designs supported by their well-equipped naval forces and arrogant church manned by a ruthless missionary wing[2]. The Cross and military force competed in cooperation for territorial conquest and religious conversion leading ultimately to the establishment of alien supremacy in India. The Portuguese, the Dutch, the French and the English competed among themselves in this colonial expansion in India, and when the smoke and dust finally settled down England emerged successful. The battles of Plassy and Buxar, the Anglo-French tussle, and the wars they fought with the Marathas and Mysore enabled the English to set up their complete political supremacy in India. Throughout these times the British were zeroing in only on how to extent the boundaries of their dominion in India, and as a consequence they did not begin to play on the communal chessboard of Indian politics. As matters stood then the pursuit of such a policy was uncalled for because India in the early days of British rule was not strongly united or held together by any sense of a unifying patriotic ideology. They started the policy of 'divide and rule' only when it became a political imperative to perpetuate their empire in adverse situations of the anti-imperialist struggles and national movements for independence. Consequently, till the outbreak of 1857 the British bestowed little attention on the communal divisions in the country.

The British did not view the 1857 Revolt as India's national movement, but as a sepoy mutiny or as an effort to reestablish the dead Mugal Empire. The British had sensed in the decision of Bahadur Shah to breath life into the corpse of the deceased Mugal Empire, a revival of Muslim polity, which would pose a threat to the imperial interests of Britain in India. Any unity of Indians, based on politics or religion, would only turn anti-British was a fact well known to the British. Accordingly, they designed their strategy in such a way as to check any such move. Playing with the over-smouldering embers of communalism, they thought, would suit their mounting political ambition. They began to move the pawns judiciously on the communal chessboard of Indian politics, playing one community against the other. Initially they pursued a policy of neglecting the Muslim community and appeasing the Hindus, thinking that the latter could be relied upon when threatened by any Muslim move against them.

The period after 1857 saw the emergence of new organisational trends in Indian political life. People began to think in terms of an all India organization, which alone would help the Indians wrest freedom from British hands. The ideological background of the patriotic movement was already prepared by the socio-religious movements of the 19th century. The teachings of Swami Vivekananda, Swami Dayananda Saraswathi, Ram Mohun Roy, Bankim Chandra and Sri Aurobindo, and the movements of modernisation among the Muslims, Sikhs and the Parsis, helped India a great deal in its progress towards enlightenment and patriotic awakening. Coupled with this new awakening was the rapid growth of revolutionary activities with the result that troubles were brewing in various parts of British India. These new developments seemed to sweep the British existence in India in a sudden flood of popular upsurge, and the government was becoming alarmed over the complaints it was receiving about the popular dissatisfaction and the isolated terrorist outbreaks in the various parts of the British India. Naturally the government had to devise something new to appease the Indians and to keep them loyal to the English. This they did in their characteristic subterranean style.

Allan Octavian Hume, an English Civil Service officer, who worked in India during the horrible days of 1857, was aware of the clouds that were gathering. He had received through his official correspondence from all over the country an intimation of "the imminent danger of a terrible outbreak owing to the economic sufferings of the masses and the alienation of the intellectuals". William Wedderburn writes in his biography of A O Hume:

> "Innumerable entries referred to the secretion of old swords, spears and matchlocks, which would be ready when required. What was predicted was a sudden violent outbreak of sporadic crimes, murders of obnoxious persons, robbery of bankers, looting of bazaars. In the existing state of the lowest half-starving masses,

it was considered that the first few crimes would be the signal for hundreds of similar ones, and for a general development of lawlessness, paralysing the authorities and the respectable classes and that ... a certain small number of the educated persons, at the time desperately, perhaps unreasonably, bitter against the Government, would join the movement, assume here and there the lead, give the outbreak cohesion and direct it as a national revolt"[3].

Wedderburn says that the ill-starred measures of reaction, combined with a brutal police repression during the viceroyalty of Lord Lytton had brought India to the verge of a catastrophic outbreak. Hume therefore felt the need of founding a forum, which would be a "safety valve for the escape of great and growing forces, generated by our own action". Therefore, in consultation with a several British officials, Hume ventured on the new scheme of appeasing the discontented Indians through his wily tactics, which found expression in the founding of the Congress as an efficacious 'safety-valve'. Lord Dufferin, the Viceroy aided and advised Hume in this move. Hume had indeed, at the outset, no idea to make the Congress a political platform, but only a movement for social reform, and it was Dufferin's advice that convinced him of the desirability of making it a political forum. Dufferin was desirous of making the new organisation Hume had in mind, an Indian counterpart of the Opposition in the British Parliament. He told Hume that "there was no body of persons in this country who performed the functions which Her Majesty's opposition did in England ... It would be very desirable in their interests as well as the interests of the ruled that Indian politicians should meet yearly and point out to the Government in what respects the administration was defective and how it could be improved"[4]. In short what the British wanted in India was a body of Indians who would correct the policies of the government in such a way as to make it popular, and thereby to perpetuate their rule in India. At the time of its birth it never aimed at an independent India as it did later. It was born to make India a perpetual slave of England though it turned out to be otherwise by virtue of fate, in the years to come.

The pro-British nature of the organization was reflected in the mindset of the dignitaries associated with its establishment. Its first session, which met at the Gokuldas Thejpal Sanskrit College in 1885 was an assemblage of the wealthy landlords and moneyed class or whose interests were with the British. W C Bonnerjee, well known for his pro-British interests, was readily chosen to be the first President whose address overflowed with encomiums for "the many and varied benefits accruing to the country from the benign rule of the British". It was also not unnatural that the meeting of such a pro-British body started with prayers for the health and long life of the British Queen. "The second President of the Congress, Dadabhai Naoroji, exclaimed with warmth and pride, that they were laying the second foundation stone for the British Empire"[5]. Surendranath Banerjea proved more loyal than the king himself. Presiding over the 1895 session, he prayed for the perpetuity of the British Empire in India. In 1902 he had it that the highest aspiration of the Indians was to be admitted into the great confederacy of self-governing states under the auspicious motherhood of England. In fact the Indian National Congress was a safety valve to ventilate the growing discontent and anti-British feelings of the Indians.

Congress which went on with its three-pronged programme of Prayer, Petition and Protest, was rightly disparaged a political mendicant with its leaders genuflecting before the British for favours and goodwill. That a group which was proud of enjoying the privilege of being entertained with garden parties arranged by the British would not do anything good to India was well revealed by its shameless loyalty to the British and admiration for British institutions, and the concessions Indians got thereof. No wonder it became the target of criticism of many unbending nationalists like Sri Aurobindo who disparaged the Congress as "a blind led by the blind" into a ditch[6]. The criticisms were too severe that the moderatism the Congress followed became a worn out idea that was pooh-poohed by the majority of the new generation. Enamoured of the new ideology of firebrand patriotism propagated by the European philosophers of nationalism like Joseph Mazzini and the Irish freedom fighters, the rising generation began to worship the motherland as a deity, and followed the teachings of the new ideologues who raised nationalism to the state of a religion. They heard from one of their new thinkers that the Mother, Motherland and Mother-Goddess were equally sacred. This faith the writings of Bankim Chandra exuded, imparted a new philosophical foundation to the idea of nationalism. The concept of the 'santans' (children) of Mother India Bankim depicted in his '*Anandamath*' fired the patriotic imagination of the youth, and his song 'Bandemataram' became the rallying cry of the patriots facing British bullets and gallows[7]. The reverberation of the idea of unbending nationalism Bankim gave the Indians was soon to take the entire India on a wave of patriotic upsurge strengthened and sublimated by the new lions of Indian national life, like Lala Lajpat Roy, Bipin Chandra Pal, Bal Gangadhar Tilak, Sri Aurobindo, C R Das and others. With them infusing a new life and vigour into the inert and inarticulate body politic of India, the Congress started taking to the path of leonine fight, extremism and proud patriotism. The idea of cultural nationalism came to have a theoretical and practical framework. The call for 'Swaraj', 'Swadeshi' and National Education took the nationalists to new ways of freedom struggle. The concept of 'Swaraj' took the Calcutta Congress by storm, while 'Swadeshi' swept the whole Bengal, setting it move on the path of attaining independence. Indeed with the famous Surat split national movement flourished outside the precincts of the Congress under the leadership of Tilak, Sri Aurobindo and the like extremists. Gone was the time of slavish political policy, which the early leaders of the Congress practised. Thus, the organisation born to safeguard the British Empire in India now turned out to be an arrogant and uncompromising enemy sworn to drive Britons out of India. The weapon boomeranged on its makers.

In cultural awakening and patriotic activities of India Bengal played the lead role. Its geography, climate and cultural background made it an epitome of India. It was imaginative, poetic, artistic, heroic, and endowed with all the qualities required to make a national community. Indeed India's nation soul owes a good deal to the sacred soil of Bengal, which bristled with all sublimating ideas and philosophical outpourings. It gave India the luminaries of her national life like Sri Ramakrishna Paramahamsa, Swami Vivekananda, Bankim Chandra Chatterji, Sri Aurobindo, C R Das, Maharshi Debendranath Tagore and his illustrious son, Rabindranath. The works of Iswarchandra Vidyasagar, Michel Madhusudan Dutt, Syam Sundar Chakravarthi and a host of others enriched Bengal with their literary effort while those like Barindra Kumar Ghose, Rash Behari Bose and a group of firebrand patriots turned it revolutionary. All this made Bengal a beehive of nationalist activities and a hotbed of national discontent that transformed it into a place of people who hated alien rule. Naturally the ideas of Swaraj and Swadeshi began to sweep entire Bengal, which was soon to unleash the tempest of patriotism throughout the length and breadth of the Indian nation. No wonder Bengal became a thorn in the flesh of British bureaucracy, which knew that it was a time bomb strong enough to destroy their Indian empire in the near future.

This scenario so unnerved the British authorities that they were determined to erode the foundations of the national movement in Bengal where the people irrespective of Hindu-Muslim differences were sworn to liberate India from alien rule. Lord Curzon, the Viceroy acted in the characteristic colonial style. The divisive policy was applied to do away with the solidarity of the Bengalis. He resolved to partition Bengal under the pretext of administrative convenience. He explained that the province had become too unwieldy to be managed by a single administrative unit, and that the only way out was partition. Though judiciously couched, the evil design behind the scheme was not a secret, and naturally it met with stiff opposition from all quarters of Indian public and even the English media. The 'Englishman', the orthodox Anglo-Indian daily in Calcutta, and the Bengal Chamber of Commerce, which represented the European traders heavily came down upon this move. The whole atmosphere turned tense with protest meetings and anti-partition agitation, which convinced Curzon of the strength and solidarity of the Bengalis. Yet he would not desist from his move and was determined to crush all opposition before it was too late, by effectively destroying the unity of the Bengalis. He now projected the much more comprehensive plan of dividing Bengal into two separate provinces – the whole of northern and eastern Bengal with Assam, forming the province of Eastern Bengal and Assam, and Western Bengal with Bihar and Orissa, constituting the province of Bengal[8]. To camouflage his wily tactics Curzon upheld the convenient excuse that this was aimed at relieving the Governor of Bengal of his administrative burden. But Sir Charles Stevens who had served in Bengal in various capacities including that of holding the office of the Lieutenant Governor laughed at this contention[9]. Because while this plan would lessen the burden of the Lieutenant Governor of Bengal by about three and a half million people, four and a half million people from Orissa districts and states would be added to his charge[10]. By doing this, Curzon argued, he was favouring the petition of the people of Ganjam district and a 'prayer' from Raja Baikunthanath of Balasore that "all districts and states" speaking Oriya language be united and placed under one common administration. But Stevens countered this and remarked that Curzon did not respect the very same sentiments of the Bengalis whose identity the scheme would undo. The evil design behind this was obvious. "In East Bengal the Muslims, politically less advanced and more loyal to the British than the Hindus, would be in a majority, while in Bengal the Bengalis would form a minority by the inclusion of Behar and Orissa. Thus, the Bengalis would be divided from their kith and kin; the Bengali Hindus, hated and dreaded by Curzon for their advanced political ideas, would form a minority in both provinces; and a thin wedge would be driven between the Hindus and Muslims of Bengal. It was undoubtedly a master-plan to destroy the nascent nationalism inBengal"[11]. The suggestion of Stevens was sensible and desirable, and if accepted would have avoided the birth of an Islamic state in India[12].

As said already, the scheme aroused untold public indignation. Entire Bengal was agitated. It was in a ferment of patriotic outburst. Swadeshi and anti-partition slogans rent the air. The people of the affected area organised more than 500 protest meetings during December 1903 and January 1904 alone. They expressed their solidarity and proclaimed their unity by organising rallies and meetings in which '*tilak*' was applied on each other's forehead and '*rakhis*' were tied on one another's wrists. Bengal fraternity was a feeling of mind that nobody could crush. Sir Henry Cotton who retired after having served in Bengal for long wrote in the *Manchester Guardian* of 5 April 1904:

> "The idea of the severance of the oldest and the most populous and wealthy portion of Bengal and the division of its people into two arbitrary sections has given such a shock to the Bengali race, and has roused such a feeling amongst them, as was never known before. The idea of being severed from their own brethren, friends and relations ... is so intolerable to the people of the affected tracts that public meetings have been held in almost every town and market place in East Bengal, and the separation scheme has been universally and unanimously condemned".

He described the partition of Bengal as the "most arbitrary and unsympathetic evidence of irresponsible and autocratic statesmanship". The Maharaja of Meimensing and Salimullah Khan, the Nawab of Dakka equally denounced the partition of the province. The latter disparaged it as a 'beastly arrangement'.

But Curzon was determined to divide the province, and he had it approved by the Legislative Council on 20 July, 1905 at Simla with only the official members present. Official notification to this action was issued so as to make the operation of the Act an accomplished fact on 16th October 1905. The people of Bengal were however adamant to defeat the scheme of Curzon. On the day it became effective people observed mourning throughout the province. As narrated vividly by Henry Nevinson in his 'The New Spirit in India':

> "On that day... thousand and thousands of Indians rub dust or ashes on their foreheads; at dawn they bathe in silence as at a sacred fast; no meals are eaten; the shops in cities and village bazars are shut; women refuse to cook; they lay aside their ornaments; men bind each other's wrists with a yellow string as a sign that they will never forget the shame; the whole day is passed in resentment, mourning, and the hunger of humiliation. In Calcutta vast meetings are held, and the errors of the Indian Government are exposed with eloquent patriotism"[13].

Even John Morley the new Secretary of State admitted in the House of Commons that, "nothing was ever worse done in disregard to the feeling and opinion of the majority of the people concerned". Even the so-called moderates scoffed at it. According to Surendra Nath Banerjee:

> "We felt that we had been insulted, humiliated and tricked. We felt that the whole of our future was at stake, and that it was a deliberate blow aimed at the growing solidarity and self-consciousness of the Bengali-speaking population... The partition would be fatal to our political progress and to that close union between Hindus and Muhammadans upon which the prospects of Indian advancement so largely depended"[14].

He pointed out that "it was openly and officially given out that the Eastern Bengal and Assam were to be a Muhammadan province" and that "the creedal distinctions were to be recognised as the basis of the new policy to be adopted in the new province"[15]. It was widely criticized. In fact Curzon's draconian scheme met with an all-round chorus of disapproval.

But Curzon was typical of the English manipulators, whose subterranean methods put the Bengalis at poles apart. Official machinery was pressed into operation to gather support for the government decision. Every known trick of the trade was employed to realize it. Official patronage was liberally used to enlist Muslim support to the plan. Nawab Salimullah Khan of Dakka who had earlier disparaged it as a 'beastly arrangement' later became a sworn supporter of the plan with the British having lavished on him a loan of about 100,000 Dollars with no strings attached. Having been the beneficiary of the British, Salimullah endorsed the government view that the partition was greatly beneficial to Muslims who had so far been mistreated by the Hindus. This resulted in the Muslims coming out overwhelmingly in support of partition. Reports say that Salimullah organised counter meetings to cow down the meetings of the swadeshi agitators. Many Congress workers who led the Swadeshi agitation were massacred by the Mohammadans in the notorious Comilla outbreak, which was incited by Salimullah. The bands of hooligans ravaging the streets, shouting *'Alla-ho-Akbar'*, and attacking the people and breaking into the houses of the Hindus was a daily phenomenon. Led and instigated by the Nawab "the rowdy elements of the Mahommedan population broke into lawless riot, attacked Hindus wherever they found them, broke into shops and private houses and assaulted students, pleaders, and other respectable Hindus, attempting even in some cases to enter the woman's apartments"[16]. Yet this was justified by the Anglo-Indian bureaucracy and the journalists who not only desisted carefully from raising voice against it but also careful in reporting it as an example of Hindu aggressiveness and comparative Muslim moderatism[17]. It was a combined operation the British and the Muhammadans were unleashing against the anti-partition agitators. The Bengal Governor, Sir Bampfylde Fuller thought that violence and intimidation, and Gurkha police and Regulation lathis are the very best means to suppress the nationalist agitation. Sri Aurobindo wrote in *Bande Mataram*: "At present the bureaucracy have two strings to their bow – general Morleyism with the aid of the loyalist Mehtaite element among the Parsis and Hindus; and occasional Fullerism with the aid of the Salimullahi party among the Mahomedans"[18]. The outbreak at

Comilla happened under the very nose of the administration with the connivance of the police of the Nawab and the British law-enforcing authorities. But nobody including the Anglo-Indian journalists voiced against the Muslims attacking the Swadeshi agitators[19]. Indeed the British authorities were silently enjoying the scene of India's national agitation being sabotaged and if possible suppressed by the anti-national forces. As the workers of the Congress were adamant on getting the partition plan annulled, so was the Muslims in seeing Bengal partitioned in expectation of the British promising that the new province would be a Muslim paradise. The Muslims came to regard the new province with the same emotional attitude, which bound them to the idea of Pakistan later. The more the Hindus were seeking the annulment of partition, the more were the Muslims convinced of their conflicting interests.

The whole of India rose as one against partition. Notwithstanding this, Curzon stuck to his tough stand. To him partition was "a settled fact". But the gravity of the movement was more than what the British could imagine and control. And after a long-drawn agitation, it was unsettled. Realising the folly of its obstinacy, the authorities abrogated the partition by means of an announcement by King George V at the Delhi Durbar on 12 December, 1911[20]. It was in fact the retreat of a Government which miserably failed in executing what it arbitrarily decided, an imperial dream shattered on the rock of national intransigence. But the havoc the partition scheme did to India's national unity was so irreparable that it proved to be an earliest major move from the part of the British for India's future disintegration.

Exploiting Hindu-Muslim difference at all levels of public life was an important characteristic of British rule, and the bureaucracy tried its best to practice this policy as the intelligible and the most practical to perpetuate their domination in India. The poisoning of Indian brain or the brainwashing of many true nationalists by the British rulers in the interest of British imperialism was a regular feature of the then rule. Their wily tactics succeeded in converting some of the early nationalists into diehard separatists. The story of Sir Syed Ahmed Khan who is generally held the doyen among the nationalist Muslims is the best example. A man of noble presence, he was endowed with all the qualities seldom found among the usual run of Islamic followers. His sole aim was to free the Muslim community from its economic and intellectual shackles. And he even resorted to woo the British administration to this end. Already a faithful servant of the British Raj, he was interested in demonstrating Muslim loyalty to British rule which he successfully managed through publishing stories of 'loyal Muhammadans' who risked their own lives to protect British officers and their families in the days of 1857 Revolt[21]. He had tried to prove that Hindus were the instigators and Muslims, the victims of the Revolt. He interpreted the Islamic doctrines and drew upon the theory of medieval Sultanate and Mugal jurisprudence to prove that Islam makes no bones about supporting a government like that of the British. He even disparaged some of the Ulemas who issued 'Fatwas' which were instrumental in instigating the Muslims to revolt against the British administration. He did all these with the expectation that the British would shower some favours on the Muslim community. But when it appeared that his pro-British policy would not effect the desired gains and that the British had not forgotten the Muslim stand during 1857, Ahmed Khan changed his mind. He knew that the only way to secure benefits for his community was to unite with the Hindus. He saw that, being a favoured community, Hindus were provided with education and employment while the Muslims were deliberately ignored. Therefore, Ahmed Khan thought that the only way for them was to join forces with the Hindus[22]. A sagacious politician as he was, he took up the two-pronged programme of Hindu-Muslim unity on the one hand and the reform of the Muslim society on the other. He believed that anglicisation would be the best answer to the problems of the Muslim society. He even saw British conquest of India as a 'historical necessity', and once explained this point through a homely metaphor:

> "At a time when the British rule established itself, India was... left a poor widow, and she stood in need of another husband, which husband she herself chose in the English nation in order to fulfill the commandment of the gospel that the twain shall be one flesh"[23].

And he looked forward to that day when the Muhammadan community would emulate the English systems and styles of life and imbibe the western oriented scientific approach descending from the academic traditions of Oxford and Cambridge. This hope of life motivated Ahmed Khan to found the Muhammadan Anglo-Oriental College at Aligarh where he entertained the services of English Professors in expectation that the institution could cultivate 'a class of persons Muhammadan in religion, Indian in blood and colour, but English in tastes, in opinions, and in intellect'[24]. True this aroused an almost universal chorus of disapproval from the Islamic world with even Jamalad-din Al-Afghani, the founder of the 19th century pan-Islamic movement condemning the Aligarh movement as the 'root of corruption'[25]. But this would not deflect Ahmed Khan from his chosen path of uplifting his people. Whether it was the adoption of English systems, or unity with the Hindus or the both, Ahmed Khan would warmly welcome anything provided that it would help the all-round progress and prosperity of his community.

Though a firm believer in the virtues of the British Raj, he was fearless in exposing its shortcomings too. He was a sincere admirer of the nationalism of Bengal and its people whose intellectual brilliance and progressive outlook deeply appealed to him. One of the most respected leaders of his time, Ahmed Khan envisioned a strong India based on Hindu-Muslim brotherhood. This father of communal harmony, while addressing an audience on 27 January 1884 at Gurdaspur said:

> "We [i.e., Hindus and Mohammadans] should try to become one heart and soul, and act in union. In old historical books and traditions you will have read and heard, we see it even now, that all the people inhabiting one country are designated by the term One Nation. The different tribes of Afghanistan are termed One Nation and so the miscellaneous hordes pouring Iran, distinguished by the term Persians, though abounding in variety of thoughts and religions, are still known as members of One Nation...Remember that the words Hindu and Mohammadan are only means for religious distinction– otherwise all persons whether Hindus or Mohammadans, even the Christians who reside in the country, are all in particular respect belonging to one and the same nation".

Later at a gathering of the Indian Association at Lahore, he said:

> "I heartily wished to serve my country and my nation faithfully. In the word nation I include both Hindus and Mohammadans, because that is the only meaning I can attach to it... These are

the different grounds upon which I call both those races which inhabit India by one word, i.e., Hindu, meaning to say that they are the inhabitants of Hindustan"[26].

According to Ahmed Khan all Indians, irrespective of their religious differences, could be called Hindus by virtue of their belonging to Hindustan.

The progress of the Hindus or Muslims was no matter to the British, but they were greatly worried over the unity of the two, which in every way would adversely affect their interests. So they started playing cleverly, turning one community against the other. They pretended to outwit even the Muslim leaders in their love and concern for the Muslim community. While addressing the students of the Aligarh College, its Principal, Theoder Beck said: "Your people, the Muhammadans are not flourishing as are the other subjects of Her Majesty Queen Victoria", and he put before them a grand scheme to uplift them. Naturally he began to find for himself a place of considerable importance in the good books of the Muslim community. Gradually Beck gained ascendancy over the mind of the aging Ahmed Khan who allowed himself to be indoctrinated with reactionary political ideas. Not only Beck, but all his successors as principals, addressed themselves to the task of disrupting Hindu-Muslim unity. This had the results the British expected, and by a sudden freak of fortune Ahmed Khan who attempted through his nimble antics and gyrations to style himself as an ambassador of Hindu-Muslim unity, reversing all his political convictions overnight, returned to his old moorings. Addressing a gathering that represented the brain and muscle of the Muhammadan community on 28 December 1887, he complained against competitive examinations on the ground that India did not consist of one nation[27]. This speech benefited him beyond measure. He was "honoured and created a Knight Commander of the most exalted order of the Star of India three days after the speech"[28]. Even A O Hume himself condemned this speech, which, he believed, was instigated by the Viceroy, Lord Dufferin[29]. Beck excelled in engineering from behind the curtain the Muslim protest against Charles Bradlaugh's Bill of 1889 which envisaged the introduction of democratic and representative institutions in India. He aimed at an Anglo-Muslim collaboration to keep the Muslims on the British side with the result that the Hindu-Muslim unity Mr.

Ahmed Khan once waxed eloquent on could be buried for good. This resulted in the formation of the Anglo-Muhammadan Association with Beck as Secretary. With himself at the helm of this newborn collusion, Beck could now effectively avoid any likelihood of the principal communities sharing a common platform. The Aligarh School founded with the lofty motto of enlightening and modernising the Indian Muslims became the citadel of separatism and diehardism, and as Aga Khan very aptly wrote, " the independent sovereign nation of Pakistan was born in the Muslim University of Aligarh". Suffice it to say that the role of Aligarh, which thrives safely in free India, was plainly negative during the pre-independence era.

It would of course be historically untrue to write off the entire Muslim community as anti-Indian with none of them having made any contribution to Indian nationalism. The community, no doubt, did give its contributions to India. But the only thing is that their role could have been much more impressive. It is interesting to note that even the foreign Muslims' noticed the callous indifference of the Indian Muslims to India's national cause. Most of them were of the opinion that the Indian Muslims should have participated in the national fight against the British. Maulana Azad says:

> "They [Arab and Turkish revolutionaries] expressed their surprise that Indian Muslims were either indifferent to or against nationalist demands. They were of the view that Indian Muslims should have led the national struggle for freedom and could not understand why the Indian Muslims were the camp followers of the British"[30].

Thus from the early days of the freedom movement in India the British were sabotaging any move for a Hindu-Muslim concord which they thought would be fatal to their imperialist interests in India. And it can be said that Hindu-Muslim differences would not have gathered so alarming a dimension as it did, had not the British policy makers found in India's communal situation a welcome pretext for carrying on their policy of negativism to its illogical conclusion.

The exploitation of communal difference was taken to further heights by Lord Minto, who in close collaboration with Lord Morley, incorporated communal representation in the new councils created under the Minto-Morley reforms. Not only did this reform fail to take India a single step towards independence but it wrought untold havoc upon the national movement by infusing separatist tendencies into Indian politics. The subterranean movements the British made to play the Muslim community against the Congress were highly dramatic. Prior to the 1909 Reforms the British rulers had entered into an 'unholy alliance' with the leaders of a section of Muslims in North India. The Muslim deputation led by H H Aga Khan which waited upon Lord Minto, the Viceroy on 1 October 1906, claimed separate electorate for the Muslims. This deputation, says K M Munshi, was a "command performance" planned by Sir William Archbold, Principal of Aligarh College, and Dunlop Smith, Private Secretary to the Viceroy among others[31]. Minto had readily granted Aga Khan's demands. The latter wrote later in his memoirs:

> "Lord Minto's acceptance of our demands was the foundation of all further constitutional proposals made for India by successive British Governments and its final, inevitable consequence was the partition of India and the emergence of Pakistan"[32].

The Minto-Morley Reforms thus gave a permanent shape to the policy of "counterpoise of native against native" initiated by Lord Curzon. "Indians were politically divided into communal compartments, to thwart the growing national unity. The seed of Pakistan was sown"[33].

The feeling of Indian Muslims that they did not belong to the nation they lived in was concretised with the emergence of the Muslim League. Aided and inspired by Lord Curzon, it was founded under the patronage of Salimullah, the Nawab of Dacca. Born on 30 December 1906, this organisation had Aga Khan as its first president and he held that office till 1912. As is well known, the idea behind the founding of the new organisation was the communal unity of the Muslims as a bull-work against the growing nationalism spearheaded by the Congress, though in its early days it worked as a moderate group and adhered to constitutional methods and progressive activities. The sole motto of the Muslim League, its leaders said, was to promote among Indian Muslims "feelings of loyalty towards the British Government ... to promote political and other rights of the Indian Muslims and to place their needs and aspirations before the Government in temperate language". The League, as already noted, was not at all a reactionary body in its early phase and could contribute some of the greatest patriots to India. It held an "idea so close to that of the Congress, that it remained a separate party only in name"[34]. For instance, Muhammad Ali Jinnah, its leader was a staunch nationalist in his early days. It is interesting to note that this true advocate of nationalism founded on Hindu-Muslim unity, strongly came out against the Gandhian support to Khilafat lest it should evoke separatist feelings among the Muslims, which would be fatal to the idea of national integration. In the League's Lahore meeting of 1924, Jinnah who was its President waxed eloquent on the universal demand that India should be given a "full-fledged Dominion responsible government". But it should be noticed that the League with its birth graced by Salimullah Khan, the turncoat of 1905 could not cast aside its separatist idea inherent in its composition and walk straight down the path of national agitation for independence.

Despite the lukewarm attitude of the League to the nationalist cause, Congress persisted in its policy of cultivating its cooperation to make a united demand for national reforms. However, much disintegrating was the League's demand for separate electorate, the leaders of the Congress would concede it since they thought that the Muslims themselves would sooner or later ask for its abrogation. Indeed Gokhale accepted it in 1909, and Tilak, in 1916. According to M R Jayakar, Lokamanya's acceptance was based on the hope that the communal electorate would only be temporary and the Muslims themselves would give them up[35]. Jinnah also thought that the Muslims, if appeased with more representation, could be brought back to the national mainstream. While giving evidence before the Select Committee in 1919, he was asked whether he really spoke as an Indian nationalist. He emphatically replied, "I do". When asked further, he told Major Ormsby Gore that, "nothing will please me more when that day [the day of Hindu-Muslim unity which would abrogate the communal electorate] comes"[36]. Indeed Jinnah dominated the Congress and the League and played the key role to get the idea of Communal Electorate accepted by both the organizations. The League's promise to work with the Hindus for freedom in return for the Congress endorsing the scheme of separate electorate for Muslims "with weightage far in excess of their numerical strength" gave high hopes to the Congress. Supporting the Congress-League Pact at the Congress session at Lucknow, Tilak said:

> "It has been said that we, Hindus, have yielded too much to our Muslim brothers. I am sure I represent the sense of the Hindu community all over India when I say that we could not have yielded too much. I would not care if the rights of self-government are granted to the Muslim community only. I would not care if they are granted to the lower classes of the Hindu population. Then the fight will not be triangular, as at present it is"[37].

The Congress-League cooperation gathered unprecedented tempo and the practice of holding the meetings of both the organisations simultaneously in Lucknow was continued with many of the Congress workers participating enthusiastically in the meetings of the League. A jubilant Jinnah said:

> "The main principle on which the first all-India Muslim political organisation was based, was the retention of the Muslim communal individuality strong and unimpaired in any constitutional readjustment that might be made in India in all the course of its political evolution. The creed has grown and broadened with the growth of the political life and thought in the community. In its general outlook and ideal as regards the future the All-India Muslim League stands abreast of the Indian National Congress and is ready to participate in any patriotic efforts for the advancement of the country as a whole"[38].

Jinnah now exuded an air of optimism. Though he was highly critical of the separate electorate, he was optimistic in that he could lead the Muslim masses into the nationalist camp. "The Lucknow Pact was hailed by the Hindus as well as the Muslims. No one could then foresee that the Pact was to blossom as the two-nation theory"[39].

The Lucknow Pact of 1916 may well be acclaimed as a memorable event, which was expressive of the great sincerity with which the Indian nationalists tried to bring the minority to the mainstream of the freedom movement. The Congress-League scheme endorsed the principle of separate electorate and extended it to Punjab and Central Provinces[40]. The concession given to the Muslims was indeed beyond what was due, and as V B Kulkarni observes, it is impossible to think of a set of concessions more far reaching than this. And yet the pact, although it signalled, as Prof. Coupland remarks, "a triumph for Indian nationalism" failed in its purpose because neither communalists nor the British Government was happy about it. Edwin Montague records a typical diehard Muslim reaction to it. A "delightful old man with a beautiful beard and a fine profile" told the Secretary of State that although he had studied Koran and all its commentaries he could find no "sanction for the Congress-Muslim scheme in them"![41]. Notwithstanding all this undue concessions, the authors of the Montford Reforms received representations from almost all Muslim associations, demanding further increase in the number of seats allocated to the Muslims. The reforms document played its part in sniping at the Lucknow Pact by raising a series of objections. It was laughed at as an 'unworkable machine', it being needlessly generous to the Muslim community. Yet the same reform made no bones about extending the evil of separate electorate fully in line with the Lucknow Pact[42]. Thus, by an adroit manoeuvre, both the Government and its Muslim supporters sidetracked the Congress demand for self-government. These types of failure resulting from treacherous political manipulation became the standard pattern for all the later attempts to forge Hindu-Muslim concord.

Dr. K K Sarma has recently opined in an article that the highly adored Father of the Nation, Mahatma Gandhi, himself was to a good extent responsible for the creation of Pakistan[43]. Dr. Ramesh Chandra Majumdar goes further, even to question the very epithet, 'Father of the Nation' bestowed upon Gandhiji[44]. According to them the Mahatma's enthusiasm in supporting the Khilafat was a folly that made the communal politics of India most violent and vulnerable. The Khilafat, as the term itself reveals, had no connection with Indian affairs, and was an institution that sprang up from an issue totally alien to India. It sourced off from the British decision to enforce on Turkey the Treaty of Severs, which sought to deprive Turkey of its control over Armenia, Smyrna and Kurdistan, leading to the ultimate dismemberment of the Turkish Caliphate. The Turkish Sultan, the highly revered Pope of Islam happened to be on the anti-British front in the First World War. Defeated in the war, Turkey had to eat a humble pie with many of the peace terms dictated threatening even its existence. This country, ruled by an effete Sultanate, had been aptly described by the Czar of Russia as the sick man of Europe, which had unlawfully held a number of non-Turkish races under its hegemony. Already not in the good books of the international powers, she was about to be effaced form the world map with its Caliphate buried for good[45]. Naturally this would affect the interests of the Muslims the world over with the result that the Khilafat movement was organised worldwide. The Indian Muslims who were in a ferment right from the beginning of the First World War were worried of the proposed dismemberment of the Turkish Caliphate, and were ready to contribute their due to the world Khilafat movement[46]. In December 1918, both the Indian National Congress and Muslim League had met in Delhi with Dr. Ansari as the Chairman of the League's reception committee. He denounced Sharif Hussain of Mecca for revolting against the Caliph. He demanded the maintenance of the integrity and independence of the Muslim states, and the restoration of the 'Jazirat-ul-Arab' (Arab region) containing the holy places of Islam to Caliph. The Congress Reception Committee Chairman, Hakim Ajmal Khan also supported the sentiments of Dr Ansari. Maulana Muhammad Ali and his brother Shaukat Ali, with a large Muslim following approached Gandhi for help to lead the mass movement against the anti-Turkish policy of Britain. Without noticing that the Khilafat was totally an extraterritorial affair, Gandhi threw in his lot with the Muslim cause as he saw in it an opportunity to bring the Hindus and Muslims on a common platform. Writing in *Young India* on 11 May, 1921, he had it that the Khilafat question gave the Hindus and Muslims the opportunity of a lifetime to unite. "If the Hindus", he wrote, "wish to cultivate the eternal friendship with the Musalmans they must perish with them in the attempt to vindicate the honour of Islam". To Gandhi this was a means for attaining national unity and independence. But the irony behind the matter is that the very Ali Brothers whom Gandhi supported audaciously declared that they were Muslims first and Indians only secondly[47]. With the premonition that the Mahatma's move to support the Khilafat cause would only mire India in grave danger, many national leaders abstained from it. Their apprehension regarding Gandhi's decision to slapdash to mix Indian national politics with a foreign imported issue based on communal fundamentalism was indeed noteworthy. Srinivasa Sastri wrote "I fear the Khilaphat Movement is going to lead us into disaster". Bala Gangadhar Tilak abstained from it though he did not openly oppose the Gandhian move[48]. Jinnah also held with admirable realism that the fate of distant Turkey was none of India's concern, and "warned Gandhiji not to encourage the fanaticism of the Muslim religious leaders and their followers"[49]. Making a foreign issue the plank of Indian national movement, Jinnah knew, would give the Indian Muslims a foreign identity. Jinnah realized that once the Khilafat would die out its leaders would leave the platform of Indian independence struggle. Indeed this advocate of the Hindu-Muslim unity did not like Gandhiji supporting a foreign issue to win Muslim support for Indian national movement. But all these wise counsels proved ineffective before the intransigence of Gandhi who was as obstinate as a mule in his support to the cause of Khilafat. The death of Lokamanya at this critical juncture was an added misfortune. With Tilak gone, Gandhi became the undisputed leader of Indian politics.

But the policy behind the support Gandhi gave to Khilafat, which was an extraterritorial issue, needs further explanation. The sincerity and goodwill that made him save the Muslim brothers was no doubt a noble sentiment. But it is also relevant to think whether England's treatment of Turkey was a greater degradation and humiliation to India than England's treatment of Indians during a century and a half or even the Jallianwallabagh atrocity[50]. Besides, Gandhi supported an issue as well as a group of Indian Muslims symbolising Islam's dishonour rather than the honour as he mistakenly used to say[51]. Again the Indian Muslims had never in their past been sympathisers of the Turkish Caliphate. Even Aurangzeb, the most orthodox of the Muslim rulers of India, had not acknowledged the Sultan of Turkey as a spiritual head. According to the renowned historian Sir Jadunath Sarkar, "the theory that the Muslim ruler of Turkey is the spiritual head of all Muhammadans, is a creation of the late nineteenth century, and merely a result of the growth of a political pan-Islamic movement as a natural reaction against the steady absorption of all sovereign Muslim States by the Christians"[52]. No Indian Muslim was thus either ideologically or politically wedded to the Turkish tradition. All these notwithstanding, Gandhi was mad after the Khilafat which he treated at par with the Home Rule or the principle of Swaraj. Thus, fully prepared to fight for a foreign cause to which the sentiments of only a small group of Indian Muslims were wedded, Gandhi embarked on the full tide of the Non-Cooperation Movement which had become almost one with the Khilafat.

The timing of the Non-Cooperation-cum-Khilafat was apt. Because it was at this critical juncture that the proposed visit of the Prince of Wales was to take place. Gandhiji issued instructions to boycott the Prince's visit. Lord Reading, the Viceroy became unnerved at the disgraceful prospect of England's Heir apparent riding in full splendour through the empty streets of the Indian cities. Therefore, he decided to pay a heavy price for the friendship and cooperation of the Indian people. Now it was decided to call a Round Table Conference of all the political leaders at Calcutta wherein the Viceroy himself would represent the British Government. He agreed to grant full provincial autonomy and discuss the possibilities of a Diarchy at the centre. The same offer was given to C R Das who was then spending his life at the Alipore jail. Gandhiji at first was prepared to accept the offer, but according to Kanji Dwarak Das about half a dozen Maulavis induced him to change his mind[53]. The reason for this extraordinary decision was that though Reading had offered amnesty to all the political prisoners, he kept reservations regarding the release of the Ali Brothers who were convicted under certain provisions of the penal code, which placed them in a different category from the others[54]. Gandhiji's decision was most unfortunate. According to Subhash Chandra Bose, "C R Das, was beside himself with anger; 'the chance of a whole lifetime has been lost', he said"[55]. Of course as K M Munshi says, the speculations about what might have happened if Reading's offer had been accepted is of no avail today. But it is necessary for historical judgement. Had Gandhi accepted that offer India would have got Dominion Status before 1939 without having had to partition it. But fate willed otherwise. The man in whose hands destiny had entrusted India's future acted so frantically at such a critical juncture that it was ill-fated to be partitioned. Despite the fact that such a great figure as Gandhi took up the cause of the Khilafat in India it did not add to the popularity of the movement. It was a big blunder as was looked both in national and international politics. First of all the people of Turkey themselves were indifferent to the movement which was given a deathblow thanks to the rise of Mustafa (Kemel) Pasha to power. Kemel had hated the Otoman Empire outright and dismissed it as a "crazy structure based on broken religious foundations". Having secularised the whole state in 1924, he abolished the Khilafat, disparaging it as a stinking relic of history. Kemel was furious at the intrusion of Aga Khan in the affairs of his country and took the opportunity of unearthing the history of His Highness! This 'emperor without an empire' who floated safely on the vast ocean of India's national movement without having had done anything for the nation's cause was however not given an easy go by the Turkish statesman. Ataturk's attack was vehement and uncompromising. "He is", declared the Turkish leader, "a special agent of the English"[56].

But these were not matters of concern to the Indian Khilafatists to whom the movement was just a comic affair banking on the illiteracy and credulousness of the Muslims. The Caliphate, which though appeared most illogical and outdated, and hence uncalled for in the land of the Caliph turned out to be a major issue in India when it got the support of Gandhi. The movement's illogicality was amply testified to by the leader Muhammadali himself. In his early days he openly scoffed at the idea of the Indian Muslims being affected by the events in the Muslim world outside India or entering into an agreement with the Hindus to bring pressure upon the British. But the firebrand speeches and activities of Muhammadali during the Khilafat days in favour of the Congress-Muslim pact was an outright negation of his early views. Nonetheless he got Gandhi to dance to his tune. And as Nathuram Vinayak Godse very aptly pointed out, even though all the previous attempts at the Hindu-Muslim concord had abruptly failed Gandhi was still "stubborn in the pursuit of his phantom of Hindu-Muslim unity"[57]. He even openly supported Muhammad Ali's invitation to the Amir of Afghanistan to invade India and capture it from the anti-Muslim British and said that in such a situation it would be the duty of all Muslims to assist him actively[58]. Even the renowned poet of universal humanism as Rabindra Nath Tagore himself doubted the national outlook of a majority of Indian Muslims, and believed that most of them were Muslim nationals rather than national Muslims. It was his firm conviction that at the time of a war between India and a Muslim nation they would denounce India in the name of Islamic brotherhood. Later in 1924, he openly pronounced this in an interview to a press representative. *The Times of India* thus wrote in an article on 18 April 1924:

> "...another very important factor which, according to the poet, was making it almost impossible for Hindu-Mohammadan unity to become an accomplished fact was that the Mohammadans could not confine their patriotism to any one country... The poet said that he had very frankly asked many Mohammadans whether, in the event of any Mohammadan power invading India, they would stand side by side with their Hindu neighbours to defend their common land. He could not be satisfied with the reply he got from them. He said that he could definitely state that even such men as Mr. Mohammad Ali had declared that under no circumstances was it permissible for any Mohammadan whatever his country might be, to stand against any other Mohammadan".

But these were of no consideration to the Mahatma. Supporting the idea and conspiracy behind the Afghan invasion, he had it that "I cannot understand why the Ali Brothers are going to be arrested as the rumours go, and why I am to remain free. They have done nothing, which I would not do. If they had sent a message to Amir, I also would send one to inform the Amir that if he came, no Indians so long as I can help it, would help the Government to drive him back"[59]. If the Amir would have invaded India, it could be vouched from the statement of Gandhi himself that he would have been in the forefront of the Afghan army, his walking stick in hand, leading from the borders of India, the Jihadis sworn to convert India into an Islamic country!

But the British knew how to strike when the iron was hot. They saw Gandhi stubborn and shifted the assault away from the wrong side. Determined to get rid of the Non-cooperation-Khilapfat menace, they were ready to resort to foul means if the fair would not suffice. The customary double-dealing served their end of wooing the Muslims. A slight tilting of scale in favour of the Muslims would help them win the situation, they knew. Everything went dramatic, producing the mesmeric effect upon the Muslim community. Lord Reading published a telegram, which he is reported to have sent to Montague in England wherein he urged the need of the evacuation of Constantinople, continuing the Sultan's sovereignty over the holy places and the restoration of the Otoman Thrace including the sacred Muslim city of Adrianople and the unreserved restoration of Smyrna[60].

The publication of this telegram without proper sanction was illegal. But it had its desired effect. The League became pro-British overnight. This change of Muslim attitude can well be summed up in the words of Hasrat Mohani who said that the reason for their quarrel with the Government was that it was anti-Islam, and now that it supported the Islam they should support it. He was for dropping the Non-Cooperation Movement altogether. Indeed such a change came not as an accident. It was not altogether unexpected, taking the time-tested stand of the Muslim League. The Muslims have always kept themselves aloof from the national movement. Here too they did the same. They "kept the Khilapfat movement distinct from the Congress all along; they welcomed the Congress support but they did not merge with it"[61]. And it may not be a surprise that when the Muslims saw their demand met with by the British, they abandoned the Khilafat issue, turned their back upon Gandhi and went their way taking the wind out of his sails. The mad cow, which Gandhi thought could be milked for Indian nationalism, kicked at his face again in its characteristic style. Yet this would not offer Gandhi any moral for his future nationalist activities as could be made out from what he did during the days of the post-Khilafat scenario troubled with Hindu-Muslim riots born of the divorce following the Congress-Khilafat honeymoon. Communal conflicts broke out in various parts of India, especially in the Malabar belt of Kerala where the Moppilas massacred and mass-converted the Hindus[62]. The Hindu-Muslim relations thus continued to deteriorate, but Gandhi was still haunting the hallucination, and "like a proverbial gambler ... increased his stake"[63]. We may look to how Nathuram Godse accused Gandhiji's attitude to the Malabar rebellion:

> "The Mahatma who had brought about all this calamity on India by his communal policy kept mum. He never uttered a single word of reproach against the aggressors nor did he allow the Congress to take any active steps whereby the repetition of such outrages could be prevented. On the other hand he went to the length of denying the numerous cases of forcible conversions in Malabar and actually published in his paper *Young India* that there was only one case of forcible conversion. His own Muslim friends informed him that the forcible conversions were

numerous in Malabar. He never corrected his misstatements but went to the absurd length of starting a relief fund for the Moplahs instead of for their victims; but the promised land of Hindu-Muslim unity was not yet in sight"[64].

Along with the Moppila outbreak the attempted emigration of some 18,000 illiterate and credulous Muslims to Afghanistan in August 1920, revealed the dangers of harnessing religious bigotry to political ends[65]. The Khilafat thus ended in smoke, picking up the over-smouldering embers of communalism. It bifurcated the Indian society beyond all the possibilities of rendezvous and reunion. Naturally this could result only in political and territorial segregation.

Political cornering of eminent persons and the nourishing of the personality-cult by forming party cliques which preferred personal interests to national, has been the bane of Indian National Congress and the nation it piloted for the last one century. This cheap tactics always blocked the nation's fortune to avail itself of the intelligence and service of many of its visionaries in its onward march to progress and self-reliance. Sometimes it boomeranged too upon the national cause. Even Gandhiji himself erred in this regard. At least some of the historians agree that Gandhiji's greatest blunder and India's gravest misfortune was in the alienation of Muhammad Ali Jinnah from the main stream of Indian national movement. Jinnah had been in his early days a staunch nationalist untouched by the malice of fanaticism. In almost all decisive moments of the national movement, Jinnah proved himself highly patriotic. He stood shoulder to shoulder with Tilak during 1916 Lucknow Pact, and in their views regarding Gandhiji's arbitrary decision to take the issue of the Khilafat to India. Progressive and unorthodox in approach and attitude to things and events, Jinnah loathed the worn out traditions and customs of the Muslim society. Having had his forensic skills honed in London's Inns of Court, he had been a believer of western democratic ideas. He was not to an inch inspired by Islamic religion, nor had he read a single line of the Koran. "He drank and ate pork, which are un-Islamic" and "seldom visited mosque and knew no Arabic and little Urdu", and had in his forties even "went outside his religion, to marry a Parsi girl of eighteen"[66]. A strong ambassador of Hindu-Muslim unity, he scoffed at the idea of Pakistan presented to him by Rahmat Ali from Hyderabad as a boy's impractical scheme, which is undesirable and uncalled for. He looked upon Gokhale as the "wisest and ablest of the moderates", whom he liked to emulate in his future career. Speaking at a meeting of the Muslim League in 1916, he declared that he had always been a Congressman to the letter and "no lover of sectarian cries". Belonging originally to a Hindu stock, he was the beloved 'Jinnah Bai' to his friends and fellows in Gujarat. Yet it was the same Jinnah who made the uncompromising call for Pakistan.

Jinnah was an ambitious man who confined himself to an exclusive and affluent way of life. As one who came from the upper class he had least consideration and affection for the common man. He even thought it undesirable to give membership in the Congress to those below matriculation level of studies. He was by all means a political aristocrat, proud, arrogant and uncompromising in his views and convictions. In matters of personal dignity and pride Jinnah would not tolerate even the slightest humiliation and negligence[67]. Gandhi's policy of eliminating any body whose views he would consider as disagreeable to him from the official chairs of the Indian National Congress was a curse of Indian politics. Indeed the way in which Gandhi gave undue weightage to Nehru and others jarred on Jinnah's sense of pride. This policy of Gandhi-Nehru group frustrated Jinnah so much that he almost called off his political activities in India. Speaking to Louis Fisher, Jinnah once said that owing to the disappointment he had on account of this "he decided to stay in England. He did not even go back to India to sell his possession, but sold them through an agent and remained in England until 1935"[68]. Writing 'In Memory of Jinnah' in the *London Economist*, 17 September, 1949, a correspondent who knew Jinnah well, stated that while Jinnah was practicing law in London, someone reported to him that Nehru whom he despised and hated had imprudently said at a private dinner party that "Jinnah was finished". An "outraged Jinnah packed up and sailed back to India at once to 'show Nehru'... To Cleopatra's nose as a factor in history one should perhaps add Jinnah's pride"[69]. Thus withdrawn and isolated, Jinnah became arrogant to the point of being discourteous. Having developed contempt and hate for "Mr Gandhi", Jinnah zealously guarded his prestige by becoming the undisputed leader of the anti-Congress Muslim

League[70]. Of course it is relevant to ask whether it suited a true nationalist to turn anti-national owing to personal ill-will and irritabilities felt against someone else and to take to a radically opposite stand to what he did so far. The answer is a big 'no'. But it is also to be noticed that everybody associated with the national movement may not necessarily be a highly enlightened one, rising up to the level of believing in nationalism as a religion. Jinnah, no doubt, had no such philosophic height of mind, the type Mahatma Gandhi claimed to have had. But where was that psychic height and philosophic approach of Gandhiji which is said to have been so broad as to accommodate even his enemies? Indeed it is the essential quality a nationalist or a public figure calls for, a quality, which Gandhiji did not appear to have had at a time its need was most urgently felt. Had the leaders of the Congress shown prudence, intelligence and magnanimity at such a decisive juncture, Indian politics would not perhaps have lost one of its highly competent leaders such as Muhammad Ali Jinnah. But that it happened otherwise was a great national misfortune, which had taken India far beyond all the readjustments and rapport based on religious harmony.

On 8 November 1927, the 'All White' Simon Commission was announced. The exclusion of Indians from this Statutory Commission was denounced by all sections of Indian society. According to Tej Bahadur Sapru this avoidance could "only mean a complete want of confidence in the judgment and capacity of the Indians to serve on the Commission which is to determine the future Government of their country"[71]. He alleged this as a denial to the Indians the right to influence the making of their constitution with the result that it inspired no confidence and commanded no public support. No wonder, the Commission was received with black flag demonstration by the mob raising the slogan 'Simon Go Back' wherever it went in the country. Indian leaders of all political parties accepted the challenge thrown by Lord Birkenhead "to put forward their own suggestion for a constitution to indicate to us the form in which in their judgment any reform of the constitution may take place". This was followed by the Nehru Report of 14 August 1928, which rejected the separate electorate for the Muslims and provided them with reserved seats[72]. But by now Jinnah the nationalist, who was eulogised as the ambassador of the Hindu-Muslim unity had taken to the opposite ground. In a special session of the Muslim League that met on 28 March 1929 he came down heavily on this report, and formulated his Fourteen Points. He offered to join the Hindus in the struggle for freedom provided the Muslims would be conceded Master-race privileges as compared to the Hindus. He envisaged a federation of Hindu and Muslim majority provinces and effective representation for the Muslims, separate electorates, the right of a community to veto a resolution in the legislature unless three-fourth its members in the legislature supported it, one-third membership for the Muslims in all cabinets, both central and provincial, and in central legislature, and adequate Muslim representation in services and self-governing bodies[73]. Jinnah thus spearheaded the communal feeling he once hated most. "The form of the future constitution" he said "should be federal with residuary powers vested in the provinces". Such a demand could be met only by discarding the policy of centralization, which had begun way back in 1773 when the Regulating Act was passed.

It is said that during this time Jinnah believed in the efficacy of the parliamentary system of government. But his Fourteen Points, which had designed a team of ministers representing the sectional interests, were its outright negation. In fact the issue loomed large in 1937 when the Congress took over office in the provinces under the Act of 1935. "Its refusal to accommodate fully the Muslim League's claim for a place in the Congress Ministry in the United Provinces led to a mighty uproar and the eventual partition of India"[74]. Whether or not Jinnah realised the grave dangers involved in his demands, they were bound to strike at the progress of the parliamentary system of government, and lead to the eventual creation of a separate homeland for his coreligionists.

On 7 September 1931, Gandhiji attended the Round Table Conference in London with the objective of securing transfer of power to India. In an assembly of what Nehru called "vested interests–imperialist, feudal, fanatical, industrial, religious, communal ..." it was natural that "the leadership of the British Indian delegation should usually fall to Aga Khan". When Gandhiji invited him to make some united demand on the British, Aga declined it on the ground that the recognition of the communal claims was the precondition to everything[75]. The Round Table

Conference thus ended with Aga Khan successfully bringing the issue of India's independence to an impasse. Following this deadlock, Ramsay Mc Donnald declared the Communal Award, which envisaged separate electorates for numerous other communities. This aimed at the further division of the Indian people into innumerable compartments. The British had already damaged the Hindu-Muslim relation beyond repair, and now they were designing new wily tactics to put the strong national community of the Hindus at sixes and sevens by driving a wedge between the Caste-Hindus and the Harijans. Having sensed the evil design behind the Communal Award, Gandhiji started 'sathyagraha' to bring the Harijan leaders to an agreement with the Congress and the mainstream national movement. This resulted in the signing of the Poona Pact of 25 September 1932 between the leaders of the Harijans and the Congress. But such an adjustment with a non-Hindu group as the Muslims was rather utopian. An agreement for the freedom of the motherland with an organization whose sentiments were not wedded to India was more difficult than squeezing oil out of sand. The League would not change its stand.

The passing of the Act of 1935 was of disastrous consequence. The election that followed to the provincial legislatures in 1935-37 put the League in frustration whereas the Congress won a landslide victory. The League's totally unsatisfactory performance in the election wounded Jinnah further and he was looking for an opportunity to see the Congress genuflecting. However, the victory of the Congress helped it form ministries in Bombay, Madras, Central Provinces, Bihar and Orissa, and North-West Frontier Province, and a coalition ministry in Assam. It thus controlled eight out of eleven provinces. Even in the Muslim majority provinces of Sind and North-West Frontier Muslim League could draw only a blank, while in Punjab, a key Muslim province, its score was confined to a single seat. Its total gain out of 485 Muslim seats amounted only to 108 with the result that in none of the eleven British Indian Provinces, the League could form responsible governing units. Again in the United Provinces, the Congress victory to some extent, was due to the support of the Jamiat-ul-Ulema-i-Hind, which hoped that the League and the Congress would cooperate in forming a ministry in the province. But the later refusal of the Congress to accommodate the League in the ministry aggravated the situation further[76]. According to Maulana Azad "the mistake of 1937 was bad enough. And the resulting frustration and resentment of the League leader were at the root of his subsequent attitude towards the Congress, and furnished the driving force for the partition movement".

Jinnah fired the first salvo in the Lucknow session of the Muslim League in 1937. He accused the Congress leaders of "alienating the Musalmans of India" by an "exclusively" Hindu policy, which he alleged, was reflected in the activities of the Congress ministries[77]. He had such a host of complaints. The National Song, 'Bande Mataram' which he himself had been singing for the past fifteen years as an active member of the Congress, now offended his Muslim sentiments! The Tricolour flag that once flaunted over the Khilafat rally was not acceptable to Jinnah then. Also the League held up the view that all those Muslims who stood outside its fold were mere 'quislings' and not the true representatives of their community. Added to this, the longstanding controversy over Hindi and Urdu was now inflated into a major Muslim grievance. Jinnah who was sworn to see the communal demands satisfied by all means, had completely ruled out as utopian the likelihood of any Hindu dominated administration turning accommodative to the Muslims. No wonder when following the outbreak of the Second World War, the Congress ministries resigned owing to the dejection from the British denial of Indian demands, Jinnah and his followers celebrated 22 December as the day of 'Deliverance' from Congress 'atrocities'.

The stand of the British administration too aggravated the situation. Its refusal to have any kind of rapprochement with the Congress sterilised the prolonged talks between the Viceroy and Gandhiji in the beginning of 1940. And a jubilant Jinnah went on victoriously opposing whatever the Congress would propose. He opposed the Congress' demand for the formation of a Constituent Assembly, remained callously indifferent with the question of complete independence and would not even opt for Dominion status during the war. The British had a real contempt for Jinnah who was never a man with popular support. Yet they knew that he could be utilized as a counterpoise to the national demands of the Congress. To them Jinnah was just a missile to strike the enemy, and this they did judiciously. Besides, there were other Muslim organizations with mass following of the community who would not join hands with the Muslim League in its demand for Pakistan, and instead would oppose the idea of partition. Therefore they knew, acceptance of the demands of either the Congress or the non-League Muslim outfits would be an impediment to the British design of prolonging their rule in India. Already in 1939 the Viceroy wrote to the Secretary of State, "I feel it wiser to be patient with Jinnah and endeavour to lead him into the direction which we desire"[78]. At the international level too the British were trying to woo the Muslim communities and pamper the pan-Islamic sentiment with a view to draw the Muslim countries to their side. With this aim in view they even started in London a center for Muslim religion and culture under the auspices of the Royal Central Asian Society. All these British moves sufficiently convince us that their policy was of using Jinnah as a ploy for the prolongation of their rule in India. This British policy had its high influence even on Maulana Azad, the man of much publicised nationalism and secularism. In his presidential address to the Indian National Congress at Ramgarh in March 1940 he presented an altogether new thesis on the position of the Muslims in India: "In the texture of Indian politics, nothing is further remote from truth than that Indian Muslims occupy the position of a political minority. The Muslims in India number between 80 and 90 millions... The powerful bonds of Islamic brotherhood and equality have protected them to a large extent..." He had also taken much pride in the strength of the Muslim community in India, and he exhorted them to cast aside their feeling of being a minority. This speech of Azad got wide press coverage and won the admiration of the Muslim League. Asked about the League's reaction to Maulana's speech M K Dehlavi observed: "There I must confess I was most agreeably surprised and I am glad to discover that our lost brother Maulana is, after all, a Muslim at heart and politically, not only that but a pan-Islamist. He has made an authoritative admission, as the duly elected and accredited President of the Congress, that the Muslims in India are a nation and not a minority"[79]. This was the case of a secular Muslim like Maulana Azad, leave alone that of Muhammad Ali Jinnah.

In the very same year in which Muslim League accepted the 'Pakistan Resolution' at its session held on 23 March 1940, Jinnah threw a veritable bombshell in Indian politics through his Presidential address. He said:

> "The problem of India is not inter-communal but manifestly of an international character... It is extremely difficult to appreciate why our Hindu friends fail to understand the real nature of Islam and Hinduism. They are not religions in the strict sense of the word, but are, in fact, different and distinct social orders. It is a dream that the Hindus and Muslims can ever evolve a common nationality and this misconception of one Indian has gone far beyond the limits, and is the cause of most of our troubles and will lead India to destruction if we fail to revise our notions in time. The Hindus and Muslims belong to two religious philosophies, social customs and literature... To yoke together two such nations under a single state, one as a numerical minority and the other as a majority, must lead to growing discontent and final destruction of any fabric that may be so built up for the government of such a state".

Jinnah very strongly put it that "Musalmans are not a minority as it is commonly known and understood... Musalmans are a nation according to any definition of a nation, and, they must have their own homelands, their territory and their state".

The League confirmed the thesis of Jinnah, which later came to be known as the Pakistan Resolution. And by 1942, when the Cripps Mission arrived in India, the League was fully committed to the idea of Pakistan[80]. The Cripps proposal, though was coldly received, satisfied the demand for Pakistan, providing for the secession of any province desirous of opting out of Indian Union[81]. This secessionist element inducted into the proposal was highly criticized by many national leaders and patriotic outfits. The Hindu Mahasabha criticised the Government's assurance to the minorities, which it held as highly alarming to the Hindu community. It said, "Any attempt to cut at the root of indivisibility of India as a political unit could not fail to evoke an undying opposition form Hindudom as a whole". Nehru lambasted it saying that "the whole background is one of division and the real political and economic issues have been relegated to the background". Commenting on the proposal as a "postdated cheque on a fast crashing bank", Gandhiji told Cripps: "Why have you come with such proposals? I would advise you to go back by the first available plane". Gandhiji objected to the proposals mainly on the grounds that they envisaged the balkanisation of India into three parts, granted veto to the minorities, promised only a Dominion Status instead of complete independence and left the ministers with no voice in the defence of the country during the war.

But to the Congress, Gandhiji was no more a man of importance, and what he had to say about the future of India had fallen on deaf ears. It kept aside Gandhiji and carried on talks with Cripps. Rajendra Prasad thus remarked:

> "The declaration thus concluded the right of secession to any province of British India from All-India union and practically accepted the demand of the Muslim League for the creation of Muslim states independent of the Indian union. The Congress Working Committee did not reject the offer, as it could have done, on the ground that it contemplated a break-up of the Indian unity. On the other hand it made it clear that it cannot think in terms of compelling the people in any territorial unit to remain in an Indian Union against their declared and established will, but pointed out that any break-up of that unity would be injurious to all concerned. It rejected the offer on the ground that the offer kept the defence out of the sphere of responsibility and reduced it to a farce and nullity".

It is clear that the British had plans to balkanise India, and the contrast between the wavering Congress and the steadfast Muslim League in regard to the partition of India proved fatal. Above all, Jinnah was callously indifferent to the call of a united India even though the Congress leaders were bound to clarify their stand and come to an agreement with the League. All efforts for any Hindu-Muslim concord dashed themselves on the rock of Jinnah's intransigence. Besides, Jinnah knew that Britain, caught in the World War, would concede any demand he would make. Now the author of Fourteen Points the first of which had demanded that "the form of future constitution should be federal", saw no more use for such a provision. Already in 1939 the Working Committee of the League had it that the party was "irrevocably opposed to any federal 'objective' which must necessarily result in a majority community rule under the guise of a democracy and a parliamentary system of government". It further explained, "such a constitution is unsuited to the genius of the peoples of this country which is composed of various nationalities and does not constitute a national state". Now that the League had passed the Pakistan Resolution too, Jinnah and the League were not to have any rethinking on the matter. Pakistan was to Jinnah a settled fact to which Cripps offer gave a further boost.

With this new thesis as the plank of future dealings, the League adopted the doctrine of 'two nation' and demanded separate 'Homeland' for the Muslim 'Nation'. Jinnah who was once an unbending nationalist now became arrogantly anti-national. This former ambassador of Hindu-Muslim unity became its most implacable foe. Thus he wrote to Gandhiji in September 1944:

> "We maintain and hold that Muslims and Hindus are two major nations by any definition or test of a nation. We are a nation of a hundred million, and, what is more, we are a nation with our own distinctive culture and civilization, language and literature, art and architecture, names and nomenclature, sense of values and proportion, legal laws and moral codes, customs and calendar, history and traditions, aptitude and ambitions – in short, we have our own distinctive outlook on life and of life. By all canons of international law we are a nation".

Now that communalism grew more in importance than nationalism, this assertive definition by its supreme exponent, however unbalanced and untenable it might be, was accepted as the gospel of truth. And the argument that this situation was the result of the erroneous policies of Gandhi and Nehru snowballing for the last three decades and the wily tactics of the British bureaucrats had now become just a subject of history. The giant had by now grown to an uncontrollable dimension and would not be satisfied without its bloody share.

When the Congress asked the British to 'Quit India' first so that the Hindus and Muslims could fight out their constitutional problems by themselves, the League raised the slogan 'Divide and Quit'. Jinnah now condemned Rajagopalachari's formula, as offering "a shadow and husk, a maimed, mutilated and moth-eaten Pakistan". He was not prepared to accept Rajaji's suggestion of having a plebiscite taken of all the inhabitants of the North-West and North-East India to decide the issue of separation from Hindustan[82]. The Desai-Liaquat Ali formula, which provided equal representation to the Congress and the League was conveniently transformed by Lord Wavel into an equality between Muslims and caste-Hindus. The communal zeal of the League became uncompromisingly arrogant with the Cabinet Mission Plan stating in unequivocal terms that it would get the grouping of provinces it demanded for the projected Pakistan. But the mission's rejection of the League's demand for partition put Jinnah in a dilemma; he found no way out of the plan. However he saw it in Nehru's unfortunate statement that "the Congress was free to modify the Cabinet Mission Plan as it pleased". This gave Jinnah an opportunity to reject the plan and declare, "the only solution for India's problem is Pakistan"[83]. The League was for no compromise and announced the rejection of the Cabinet Mission Plan on 27 July 1946. It moved further with the declaration that August 16th would be observed as the day of 'Direct Action' for getting Pakistan. Instead of joining the interim government the League decided to create a deadlock by 'Direct Action'. "What we have done today", Jinnah declared, "is the most historic act in our history... This day we bid good-by to constitutional methods... Today we have also forged a pistol and are in a position to use it"[84]. Writing in *The Statesman* from Calcutta on 5th August he stated: "Bloodshed and disorder are not necessarily evil in themselves, if resorted to for a noble cause. Among Muslims today, no cause is dearer or nobler than Pakistan"[84]. The cry for the Hindu blood by this prophet of 'goondaism' and street-fight was implemented by the mendacious Muslim hordes of Bengal with the full backing and support of the Muslim League Ministry under Mr. H S Suhrawardi. No sooner the League's procession moved by the street than the worst holocaust took place in Calcutta, leaving the whole city to the vultures. "The Direct Action", as Dr.R C Majumdar very aptly puts, "was merely a camouflage for an organised anti-Hindu campaign of loot, arson and indiscriminate murder of men, women and children in broad daylight with impunity"[86]. Maulana Azad says, the police of Suhrawardi "remained inactive while innocent men and women were killed"[87]. Left with no other alternative, the Hindus finally retaliated. Between the dawn of 16 August 1946, and the dusk three days later, the people of Calcutta hacked, battered, burned, stabbed or shot 6000 of each other to death, raped and maimed another 20000. The fragments of human corps lying scattered in the streets would have shuddered even such bloodthirsty criminals of history as Atila or Robespire and put to shame the cannibals of the bygone ages. But Jinnah could not have been anything except satisfied by the lessons that were inevitably drawn from it. For, he could prove with the most ruthlessness, the validity of his claim that in an independent India, Hindus and Muslims could not live together and he managed to convince the British and the Indian public, of this.

Though Jinnah pretended to be prepared to join the interim government, he still held the League's rejection of some clauses of the Cabinet Mission Plan, and would not join the Constituent Assembly, which was to meet on 9 December 1946. Nehru's scheme was to appoint fourteen ministers at the centre, six Congress, five Muslim League, three Christian and one Parsi. But Jinnah insisted that no Muslim should be appointed unless he was a member of the Muslim League. A conciliation based on any other terms would be to end only in a political impasse, Jinnah warned. But such a scheme could be worked out only by ignoring the political realities and situations of the time. Jinnah's logic would not fit in with the socio-political mathematics of the period concerned. "Two provinces had a Muslim majority: the Punjab and the Frontier. The Frontier had 93 per cent Muslims but it was represented by the Khudai Khidmatgars and not by the Muslim League. How could Jinnah and his party represent this province? But the basic anomaly was that the Muslim League wanted more than its share in the Central Government. What right did the Muslim League have to demand that the Congress should not allow any Muslim to represent it?"[88]. Naturally Jinnah had no other option than to have a dilly-dallying ending in an escapist denial. Shortly the working committee of the League met at Karachi and passed the resolution denouncing the composition and procedure of the Constituent Assembly as invalid and illegal. This showed not only the League's denouncement of the Cabinet Mission Plan but it's commitment to 'Direct Action' as well. The Congress therefore prevailed on the Viceroy to get the League off the interim government and warned that otherwise the Congress would withdraw from it. Either course was bound to plunge the country once again into a civil war of an all India dimension.

The take over of the Government in England by Clement Atlee was a bolt from the blue. On 20 February 1947, Atlee made the statement in the House of Commons that "His Majesty's Government wish to make it clear that it is their definite intention to take necessary steps to effect the transfer of power to responsible Indian hands by a date not later than June 1948". Aware of the likelihood of the Muslim League abstaining from the Constituent Assembly, Atlee added that in such a situation it would be left to the discretion of his Majesty's Government to "consider to whom the powers of the Central Government in British India should be handed over ... in the best interest of the people". To carry out the transfer of power Atlee announced that Admiral, the Viscount Mountbatten has been appointed Viceroy with effect from March 1947.

The League was not to desist from 'Direct Action'. Multan, Rawalpindi, Amritsar, Lahore, Bengal and North West Frontier Province witnessed shocking atrocities. According to official account 2049 persons were killed and 1000 seriously injured in course of a fortnight. And the Congress was left with no other alternative than to concede demands of the League to purchase peace. On 8 March 1947, the Congress passed a resolution, "envisaging the division of Punjab into two provinces so that the predominantly Muslim part of India may be separated from the predominantly non-Muslim part"[89]. It further pointed out, "the same remedy would hold good for Bengal if the circumstances in that province were similar"[90]. No doubt, the Congress could have desisted from such a drastic move, avoiding itself from being mainly responsible for the ultimate partition of India. But fate willed otherwise.

Another misfortune of India lay in the defiance the Congress had shown to its own Godfather, Mahatma Gandhi. Gandhiji was right when he said that the Congress workers garlanded his photograph but treated him like a sweeper. Now too his suggestion was looked down upon in negligence by his own followers. He had his panacea to solve the communal problem. He advised Mountbatten, during his first interview, to dismiss the executive council and give Jinnah the option of forming a government with members of his own choice. But it was not acceptable to his followers who were mad after power. To a generation clamouring for position and power the Gandhian ideas of renunciation and self-abnegation were rather worn out things unfit for the modern world. To them, even Gandhi himself was something uncalled for, leave alone his lofty ideals!. No wonder his suggestion was most unceremoniously rejected by the Congress. A saddened Gandhi with his words woefully neglected by his own followers, thereupon withdrew his proposals along with himself from politics, leaving all future negotiations to the Working Committee. Finding no alternative, and being convinced that "whether we like it or not, there are two nations in India", Sardar Patel accepted the idea of partition. Jawaharlal too was gradually reconciled to it. The killing in Punjab was too much, and the plan, Nehru said, "offered a way out of it". Also they expected that the "partition would be temporary, that Pakistan was bound to come back" to India. Of course, the Lucknow Pact was also signed with such an expectation. But its failure did not make the Congress avoid repeating another error. Maulana Azad says, Gandhi also was a changed man after his meeting with the Viceroy on 2 April 1947. Gandhi "was still not openly in favour of partition, but he no longer spoke so vehemently against it". Gandhiji said in a prayer meeting that "If both of us – Hindus and the Muslims cannot agree on anything else, the Viceroy is left with no choice" other than partition[91]. The Congress Working Committee, which met on 12 June 1947, accepted the proposals embodied in the announcement of 3 June. The resolution to accept the proposal was seconded by Gobind Vallabh Pant and Maulana Azad. The council of All India Muslim League, which met in Delhi on 10 June also approved of His Majesty's statement of 3 June[92]. Thus, the long-drawn communal question got its answer with the Pakistan proposal being accepted by all concerned. With the passing of the Indian Independence Act the unity of India became a thing of past[93].

This was the most heinous act in modern history that caused intense sorrow and sufferings to many. The division was effected with scant regards to even ordinary humanitarian considerations. First, both the parties ignored the grievances of the Hindus as well as the Muslims who would be left as minorities in the new nations. When this issue was raised, it was met with the most foolish, unbalanced, and disgraceful reply. "It was being openly said in certain circles that the Hindus in Pakistan need have no fear, as there would be 45 millions of Muslims in India, and if there was any oppression of Hindus in Pakistan, the Muslims in India would have to bear the consequences". Again, this statement, which was the most unbalanced, revealed some bare and bitter facts. Though the land was divided on communal basis 45 million Muslims, adequate enough to create yet another Pakistan was left in India. Besides, who would answer to the problems of the Hindus who would become minorities in Pakistan? It was well known what their fate would be in a land to be ruled by rank communalists known for total intolerance. But who would address to their impending disasters? A Jinnah who cried for the Hindu blood or a Nehru waiting impatiently for India's Prime Ministerial chair? But those who were enamoured of power and position wanted just a way out of the confronting realities however illogical and impractical the solution might be. And they guaranteed the lives of the Hindus in Pakistan with the lives of the 45 millions of Muslims in India! To put it blank, it meant nothing other than that the massacre of Hindus in Pakistan could be compensated by the deprivation of the lives of the millions of Muslims left in India. A very safe conclusion derived from the wisdom of the new generation of politicians destined to rule independent India! A few lines from Leonard Mosely would suffice to convince the folly of this conclusion.

> "Both sides had signed on 20 July, at Mountbatten's behest, a declaration that they would respect the rights of the minorities. But Mountbatten was right in suspecting that they did not know what they were signing. The Sikh policy was to exterminate the Muslims in their midst. The Muslims, with their eyes on the rich farmlands, were contend to drive the Sikhs out and massacre those who insisted on remaining. It is said to have to admit that in their deliberate disobedience of their signed pledges they were encouraged by the British Governor of the West Punjab, Sir Francis Mudie, who wrote to Mr. Jinnah on 5 September 1947: 'I am telling everyone that I don't care how the Sikhs get across the border; the great thing is to get rid of them as soon as possible,".

Even those living by the border themselves had a narrow escape, leave alone the tragic story of those who had to tread a long way from Pakistan's interior to India. Mosely says about what happened to the Hindus of the West Punjab: "600,000 dead, 14000,000 driven from their homes, 100,000 young girls kidnapped ... forcibly converted or sold on the auction block".

Mosely concludes:

"It need not have happened. It would not have happened had independence not been rushed through at such a desperate rate. A little patience and all the troubles might have been avoided ... Jinnah was dead within a year. A little patience. A refusal to be rushed".

India and Pakistan got nothing out of this division except a redoubled rivalry, which was to strain the bilateral relations in the years to come. "Pakistan turned into a Balkan state riddled with corruption and intrigue. The Congress crusade for an idealistic India diminished into a squalid fight for political supremacy"[94]. But there is the question of the national conscience of India. Dr. Ramesh Chandra Majumdar, India's nationalist historian asks, "whether Mountbatten or his critics were right" to the verdict of history? An imperialist nation and its people who had kept India, the land of one of the most ancient and renowned cultures, a slave for their economic gains and finally led it towards partition can never claim any favour from the verdict of history.

References

1. The statement of the Pakistan President Gen. Pervez Musharraf that Pakistan would be the next target of attack of the Western forces deserves special attention. He said that it is being speculated that Pakistan would become the victim of the bloodthirsty West after Iraq. He cautioned the Pakistanis to be aware of this impending danger, and be prepared to meet any such move. He said to his countrymen: "We will have to work on our own to stave off the danger. Nobody will come to our rescue... We will have to depend on our muscle". *The New Indian Express*, Kochi, January 20, 2003.
2. Proselytizing was the agenda common to all the European powers. Among them the Portuguese took the lead role in sending missionaries to convert the Eastern nations into Christianity. The story of St. Francis Xavier and the works of the Jesuit Society are well known. He came to India as the Portuguese King's Inspector of Missions and represented the Pope as a Legate. This missionary with the help of Portuguese traders gave material help to the poor fishermen – 'Mukkuvas' of the cost of Kerala and the Portuguese Governor of Quilon (Kollam) threatened them with reprisals if they would not accept Christianity. Xavier toured

the villages with these twin weapons, threat and material help, and converted many poor fishermen to Christianity. He was also an iconoclast number one. His letters to the Society of Jesus well reveal this. He wrote, "following the baptism, the new Christians return to their homes and come back with their wives and families to be in their turn also prepared for baptism. After all have been baptised, I order that everywhere the temples of the false Gods be pulled down and idols be broken. I know not how to describe in words the joy I feel before this spectacle of pulling down and destroying the idols by the very people who formerly worshipped them"(letter dated 8-2 - 1545). K M Panikker. *Asia and Western Dominance*, pp.45, 66; S D Kulkarni(Ed). *The Struggle for Hindu Supremacy*, p. 44; H J Coleridge. *Life and Letters of St. Francis Xavier*, Vol. 1, p.10. Not only in India but wherever the Europeans went as well, they used the religious propaganda to economically exploit the native people. Jomo Kenyata, the leader of the African national movement satirically commented, "when the Europeans came we had the land and they had the Bible. They told us, this is the book of God and asked to meditate with it. After years of meditation, when we opened our eyes we had the Bible and they had the land". That the missionary invasion was a part of the British strategy was proved with the British Prime Minister Lord Palmerston announcing two years after 1857 revolt, that it was in the interest of Britain "to provide for the diffusion of Christianity throughout the length and breadth of India". Joseph Cornelius Kumarappa, the well-known Gandhian economist once observed, "The Western military has four wings: the Army, the Navy, the Air Force and the Church". H V Seshadri. *The Tragic Story of Partition*, p.13.

3. William Wedderburn, *Life History of A O Hume*, pp. 80-81. Also see P N Chopra, 'The Genesis of Indian National Congress', *Journal of Indian History*, Vol.L. Part II. Serial No.149.
4. R C Majumdar, *History of the Freedom Movement in India*, Calcutta, 1971. Vol.I. pp. 345-346.
5. H V Seshadri, *op. cit.*, p. 18.
6. Sri Aurobindo, *Indu Prakash*, Bombay, 21 August, 1893.
7. Bankim Chandra Chatterji, *Anandamath* (Trans. B K Roy), Delhi, 2000, pp. 34-35.
8. R C Majumdar, *History of the Freedom Movement in India*, Vol. II, p. 4.
9. A K Majumdar, *Advent of Independence*, p. 31.
10. *Ibid.*
11. R C Majundar, *Op. Cit.*, pp. 4 - 5.

12. A K Majumdar, *Op. Cit.*, p. 32.
13. K R Srinivasa Iyengar, *Sri Aurobindo – A Biography and History*, p.191.
14. Surendra Nath Banerjee, *A Nation in the Making*, London, 1925, pp. 187-188.
15. V B Kulkarni, *British Dominion in India and After*, pp.109,110.
16. Sri Aurobindo, 'The Comilla Incident', *Bande Mataram*, 15 March, 1907.
17. *Ibid.*
18. *Ibid.*
19. Sri Aurobindo, 'British Protection or Self-Protection', *Bande Mataram*, 18 March,1907.
20. V B Kulkarni, *Op. Cit.*, p.110.
21. B R Nanda. *Gandhi – Pan-Islamism, Imperialism and Nationalism in India*, Bombay, 1989, p. 29.
22. Wali Khan, *Facts are Facts – The Untold Story of India's Partition*, New Delhi, 1988, p. 4.
23. Shah Muhammad, *Writings and Speeches of Sir Syed Ahmed Khan*, Bombay, 1972.p. 178.
24. Lelyveld David, *Aligarh's First Generation*, Princeton,1977, p. 207.
25. H A R Gibb, *Modern Trends in Islam*, Chicago, 1945, p. 58.
26. Wali Khan, *Op. Cit.*, pp. 3-4.
27. V B Kulkarni, *Op.Cit.*, p. 175.
28. Husain B Thyabji, *Badrudin Tyabji: A Biography*, Bombay, 1952, p. 198.
29. *Ibid.*, p. 200.
30. Maulana Abul Kalam Azad, *India Wins Freedom*, Madras, 1988, p. 7.
31. K M Munshi, *Pilgrimage to Freedom*, Bombay, 1967, p. 3.
32. *The Memoirs of Aga Khan*, London, 1954, p. 94.
33. K M Munshi, *Op. Cit.*, p. 3.
34. V B Kulkarni, *Op. Cit.*, p. 181.
35. V B Kulkarni, *M R Jayakar*, Delhi, 1976, p. 114.
36. K K Sarma, 'Gandhiji and the Partition of India', *Journal of Indian History*, Thiruvananthapuram, Vol. L, Part II, No.149, pp. 531-554.
37. D G Tendulkar, *Mahatma*, Delhi, 1988, Vol. I, p. 191.
38. *Ibid.*, p. 192.
39. K M Munshi, *Op. Cit.*, p. 8.

40. Tara Chand, *History of the Freedom Movement in India*, Delhi, 1983, Vol. III, pp. 438-439.

    The main proposals of the Lucknow Pact were:

    (i) Special or separate electorate for the Muslims in the Provincial Councils was according to the following proportion: Punjab-50%, United Provinces-30%, Bengal-40%, Behar-25%, Central Provinces-15%, Madras-15%, Bombay-33%.

    (ii) The Imperial Legislative should consist of altogether 150 members of whom 120 should be non-officials, and one-third of the elected members, Muslims.

    (ii) No bill or any clause of a bill, nor resolution introduced by a non-official member affecting one or the other community shall be proceeded with, if three-fourth of the members of the community, in the provincial or imperial council oppose the bill, clause or resolution.

41. Edwin Montague, *An Indian Diary*, London, 1930, p.118.
42. V P Menon, *Montague-Chelmsford Reforms*, Bombay, 1965, p. 54.
43. K K Sarma, *Op. Cit.*
44. R C Majumdar, Op. Cit., Vol. III, p. 55.
45. C D M Ketelbey, *A History of Modern Times*, Bombay, 1979, p. 443. Also see Bernad Lewis, *The Emergence of Modern Turkey*, London, 1965, p. 241
46. Tara Chand, *Op.Cit.*, Vol. III, p. 487.
47. The very same Muhammad Ali after some years (i.e., in 1924) delivered a 'Coup de Grace' to Gandhi's leadership, declaring that, however pure the Mahatma's character was, he could not in matter of religion be superior to "any Musalman even though he be without character". He declared: "Yes, according to my religion and creed, I do hold an adulterous and fallen Mussalman to be better than Mr. Gandhi". Ramgopal, *Indian Muslims – A Political History*, Bombay, 1964, p. 166.
48. Two days after the Khilaphat Committee (28 May, 1920), the Congress Committee met at Banaras where Tilak was present. But he did not appear to have actively participated in the AICC proceedings. While he sympathised with the Muslim sentiments over the Khilaphat, he seemed to have entertained grave doubts about making a religious and extraterritorial issue the plank of Indian freedom struggle. His wisdom was vindicated when, under Mustafa Kamal Pasha, the Turks themselves abolished the Caliphate and declared themselves a secular state. N G Jog, *Lokamanya Bal Gangadhar Tilak*, New Delhi, 1979, p. 22.
49. K M Munshi, *Op. Cit*, p. 22.

50. Gandhi failed to realise that the pan-Islamic idea, which inspired the Khilaphat question would cut at the very root of Indian nationalism. If the 'real sympathy and vital interest' of a large section of Indians were bound up with a state and society which lay far outside the boundaries of India with which it had no connections, they could never form a true unit of Indian nation. If a hundred million Muslims were vitally interested in the fate of Turkey and other Muslim states outside India they could have been hardly regarded as a unit of India. By his own admission that the Khilaphat question was a vital one for Indian Muslims, Gandhi himself admitted in a way that they formed a separate nation. The fact of the matter is that the Indian Muslims were 'in' India but not 'of' India. R C Majumdar, *Op. Cit*, Vol.III, p. 50.
51. Caliphate was a theocratic institution based on broken religious foundations, and was disowned by the people of Turkey themselves. Indeed they looked down upon this institution as the dishonour of Islam, which they wanted to brush aside safely into the dustbin of history. The people of Turkey never liked to keep with them this stinking institution on their onward march to a new era bristling with the new ideas of administration. Enamoured of the democratic form of government, Turkey wanted to establish a republic, which it came to have under the leadership of Mustafa Kamal Pasha. But the Indian Muslims still wanted the Khilaphat in Turkey! Interestingly they got Gandhi to support their comic acts.
52. B R Nanda, *Op. Cit.*, p. 211.
53. K M Munshi, *Op. Cit.*, p. 23.
54. *Ibid.*
55. *Ibid.*
56. V B Kulkarni, *British Dominion in India and After*, p.184.
57. Nathuram Godse, *May it Please Your Honour* (Gopal Godse.Ed), Delhi, 1989, p.73.
58. R C Majumdar, *Op.Cit.*, Vol. III, p. 97.
59. Nathuram Godse, *Op. Cit.*, p. 83.
60. Tara Chand, *Op. Cit.*, Vol. III, p. 504.
61. Nathuram Godse, *Op. Cit.*, p. 82.
62. It is the recent trend to interpret the Moppila revolt of 1921 as the war of independence and peasant revolt. But the notoriety and the fanatic colour of the revolt is revealed by the memorial of the women of Malabar to Lady Reading in which they describe the horrors they were met with owing to the fanatical outburst of the Malabar Muslims. The memorial laments on how the women were subjected to massacre and mass-rape, how the

temples were desecrated with destruction and pillage and how the Muhammadan 'mahdis' killed their children mercilessly. See 'Petition of Malabar Ladies to Lady Reading', C Sankaran Nair, *Gandhi and Anarchy*, Ottapalam, 2000, pp. 100-104. Kerala's renowned poet Kumaran Asan, himself an opponent of caste Hinduism and diehardism, lamented on "Eranad blood-white with the massacre of the Hindus by the cruel Muhammadans" in his poem '*Duravastha*' (i.e., the hardships of a Brahmin lady subjected to fanatical outbreaks.) Even he had called upon the Hindus to shatter the walls that divided them into various castes and sub-castes and stand united to defend the Hindu community from the attacks of 'Mlecchas'. "Change all your age old customs" and stand united, the poet exhorted the Hindus, "otherwise the customs would change you" perhaps into non-Hindus. The general public of Malabar had accused Gandhi's policy as the reason behind the outbreak. The victims of the tragedy cursed Gandhiji as having "scratched the rash". But, despite all the concrete evidences regarding the fanatical nature of the revolt, some leftist historians of Kerala through their hard-sweated history writing exercise pictured it as a part of the national fight against colonialism! The whole aim behind this inglorious mercenary writing was to get freedom fighters' pension for the Moppilas whose goodwill and vote-bank would in return help the leftist group to form government in Kerala. Wooing the Muslims, they know, would help them in elections to the state's Assembly. See Rolland E Miller, *Moppila Muslims of Kerala – A Study in Islam's Trend*, Delhi, 1976, pp. 110-120. Also see K Madhavan Nair, *Malabarkalapam* (Malayalam), Kozhikode, 1987.

63. Nathuram Godse, *Op. Cit.*, p. 73.
64. *Ibid.*, pp. 81-82.
65. V B Kulkarni, *British Dominion in India and After*, p. 184.
66. Louis Fischer, *The Life of Mahatma Gandhi*, Bombay, 1983, p. 511.
67. The incident that made Jinnah differ with Lord Wellington was not based on matters of opinion or ideology. Once as the Governor of Bombay, Wellington invited Jinnah for a party. Accompanied by his wife, Rutan Bai, Jinnah attended it. Lady Wellington looked at Mrs Jinnah disapprovingly of her attire. She asked the A D C to bring a shawl for Mrs Jinnah, since she would be feeling cold because of her "inadequate" dress. Felt insulted, Jinnah left the place immediately with his wife. And when Lord Wellington took over as the Viceroy of India later, Jinnah departed to England, leaving India for ever. See Wali Khan, *Op. Cit.*, p. 9.

68. Louis Fisher, *Op. Cit.*, p. 512.
69. *Ibid.*, p. 513.
70. K K Sarma, *Op.Cit.*
71. *The Tribune*, Lahore, 28 December, 1927.
72. *A Hundred Years of the Hindu*, Madras, 1985, p. 36.
73. K M Munshi, *Op.Cit.*, p. 25.
74. V B Kulkarni, *British Dominion in India and After*, p. 186.
75. Michael Brecher, *Nehru: A Political Biography*, Oxford, 1959, p. 180.
76. M A Azad, Op. Cit., pp. 170-171.
77. Jinnah's allegation was in fact a travesty of facts. Sir Harry Haig, the Governor of the United Provinces remarked that the Congress ministries "acted with impartiality and a desire to do what was fair" while dealing with questions related to communal issues. Also we have the testimony of Maulana Azad who was in charge of the parliamentary affairs in several provinces, Bengal, Behar, U.P., Punjab, Sind and the Frontier. He writes: "Every incident which involved communal issues came up before me. From personal knowledge and with a full sense of responsibility, I can therefore say that the charges leveled by Mr. Jinnah and the Muslim League about injustice to the Muslims... were absolutely false. If there had been an iota of truth in any of these charges I would have seen to it that the injustice was rectified. I was prepared even to resign if necessary on an issue like this". See Maulana Azad, *Op. Cit.*, pp. 24-25.
78. Wali Khan, *Op. Cit.*, pp. 17-18.
79. H V Seshadri, *Op. Cit.*, pp. 132-133.
80. In 1930 Sir Muhammad Iqbal in his presidential address at the League session had suggested the union of Punjab, Frontier Province, Beluchistan, Sind and Kashmir into a Muslim state within or outside the British Empire. In 1933 Chaudhuri Rehmat Ali developed the concept of Pakistan around which separatism and emotion gathered strength. See K M Munshi, *Op. Cit.*, p. 47.
81. A K Majumdar, *Op. Cit.*, p.47.
82. V P Menon, *Transfer of Power*, Madras, 1989, pp. 162-163.
83. K K Sarma, *Op. Cit.*
84. Leonard Mosely, *The Last Days of the British Raj*, Bombay, 1971, p. 23.
85. *Ibid.*, p. 27.
86. R C Majumdar, *Op. Cit.*, Vol. III, p. 643.
87. *Ibid.*

88. Wali Khan, *Op. Cit.*, p. 97.
89. R C Majumdar, *Op. Cit.*, Vol. III, p. 656.
90. *Ibid.*
91. But this decision to divide the nation was questioned by many militant patriotic organisations. The Working Committee of the Hindu Mahasabha met in Delhi and passed a resolution which declared that "India is one and indivisible and there will be no peace unless and until separated areas are brought back into the Indian Union and made integral parts thereof". The Mahasabha even exhorted the people to observe a nationwide 'Anti-Pakistan Day'.
93. K M Munshi, *Indian Constitutional Documents*, Bombay, 1967, Vol. II, pp. 228-239.
94. Leonard Mosely, *Op. Cit.*, pp. 282-286.

3

'Hate-India'—Pakistan's Trump Card

One of the many problems ailing Asiatic politics for the past few decades has been the troubled relation between India and Pakistan. Pakistan, right from its very inception, has not been able to live on peaceful terms with India, its nearest neighbour to whom it owes its birth and existence. That it should have always been so was in the logic of history. The roots of such a strained relation were inherent in its origin and composition. Indeed these inherent problems made her to be at odds with India. Rightly speaking, internal issues made her leaders frame such a foreign policy as to camouflage from the Pakistani public all domestic problems they were finding difficult to solve. Therefore, to have an analysis of Pakistan's foreign policy one must have a look at the country's internal politics and other related matters.

There has never been a country in history like Pakistan, whose domestic life has been as splintered as its territorial shape, and whose foreign policies were designed to suit its internal problems. Judged by any standard of territorial demarcation, Pakistan was undoubtedly a unique creation! This satirical comment made by a modern Indian writer does not appear baseless while viewed against the backdrop of Pakistan's political and geographical settings. Pakistan does not, writes Keith Callard, "possess a history of national unity, it has no common language nor a uniform culture, and it is neither a geographical nor an economic unit"[1]. There had never been a nation like Pakistan whose geographical unity was cut apart by a distance of more than thousand miles of territory belonging to another nation. If this had been the picture of geography Pakistan presented to an outsider, its internal administration had been more comic.

As is well known, Pakistan was brought into existence by the very man who once loathed communalism to the backbone. It was the offspring of a wounded pride. Even when fighting for Pakistan Jinnah would not know whether such a state would ever become a reality. Sri Prakasa, India's first High Commissioner to Pakistan made some surprising revelations, which were realistic. He said, he was authoritatively informed at Karachi, that "the greatest shock of Jinnah's life was the conceding and establishment of Pakistan. He really never wanted it; and when it had come he did not know what to do with it. He found it almost impossible to manage it"[2]. For, Jinnah himself confessed that his separatist campaign was only to wring large concessions for his community. Penderal Moon writes that "privately Jinnah told one or two people in Lahore that his resolution (on partition) was a tactical move"[3]. He also knew that a good number of Muslims did not like his move for Pakistan and that even when he was clamouring to get a state for the Muslims he never had behind him the support of the majority of that community. Many of the well-wishers of the community had indeed opposed the move. For instance, the Punjab premier, Sikender Hayat Khan and his Muslim followers disliked the demand for partitioning India. But Jinnah's euphoric slapdash culminated in the birth of Pakistan that proved a headache to its own founder, and a source of trouble to the otherwise peaceful Asiatic region. Jinnah also knew that the state he carved out of India with the butcher's axe was bereft of any ideological foundation. Besides, Jinnah also knew that a state based on communalism could reach nowhere[4]. The premonitions regarding the dark future of Pakistan was apprehended more by Jinnah than anybody else. In such a situation it was not unnatural that Jinnah would think in terms of following a change in the state policies. Therefore, soon after the birth of Pakistan Jinnah tried to reverse all the policies he followed. On 11 September 1947 he called upon the people of Pakistan to cast aside their "angularities" about belonging to the "Majority" and "Minority" communities. "You may", he said, "belong to any religion or caste or creed; that has nothing to do with the business of the state". But soon Jinnah realised the folly underlying this statement. He knew that such a statement would run counter to the tirades and the lifetime work he had undertaken thus far to see the birth of an Islamic state. Indeed no other leader in history might have been confronted with such a psychological riddle as Jinnah did. But being unable to escape from the mistakes of his creation, he could only justify them. Therefore, in a press interview on 24 October 1947 he asserted that, "the Two-Nation theory is not a theory but a fact. The division of India is based on that fact". It being too late for him to correct his ways, he sought to assuage his mental anguish by unjustly attacking Indian leaders. About Jinnah's state of mind at this time Campbell Johnson writes: "It is clear that Jinnah living in almost total isolation both from his followers and the outside world, is a far from happy man who is trying to exorcise his fears by nourishing his hatreds". He writes further that Jinnah "kept on harping on the masochistic theme that India was out to destroy the nation of his making and his attitude to every personality and act across the border was coloured by the general assumption"[5]. This poisonous attitude of Jinnah was handed down to later generations of Pakistani administrators with the result that most of them in their policy towards India took to the stereotyped track. Addressing his countrymen from Lahore on 7 October 1947, Liaqat Ali Khan declared in a broadcast message: "Pakistan is not a shooting star that shines for a moment. Pakistan will not die". His barrage of verbal attack bristling with innuendos accusing the Indian leaders indirectly aired out that India could not do away with Pakistan. But such a tirade was uncalled for taking India's general attitude towards other states. For, the fear of an Indian attack on Pakistan by India, a nation bound fast to her traditions of peace and brotherhood, was preposterous. History records that India had never in her past, been on enemical terms with any of the foreign countries. But born out of the hatred of India and the Hindus, Pakistan had nothing except this anti-Indian tirade to depend upon for an ideological foundation. Naturally Pakistan went on with the 'Hate India' campaign as its usual stock-in-trade. It was a political gimmick rather than a defense imperative for Pakistan to be anti-Indian. The call to hate India proved convenient for Pakistani leaders to cover up their innumerable political and economic follies. They always managed to convince the Pakistani people that India is their enemy number one and that all problems ailing Pakistan could be solved if all scores are settled with India. They knew that by channeling the popular wrath raging against them and their reckless policies towards India, they could escape from their unpopularity. So long as the problems with India would remain unsolved their position would be safe in Pakistan, they thought.

Pakistan right from its birth was infected with political, economic and religious problems of horrible dimensions. It was not a united political entity, nor was it a sound economic unit. Pakistan had experienced total lack of cohesion among its various parts. Sind, Punjab and East Bengal were always at daggers drawn against one another. Pakistan's "territory cleft into two physically and culturally separate parts would have created difficulties even for a state blessed with far greater resources and much better administrative and political leadership". The case is imaginable when it comes to a newborn state with its poverty stricken economy and a group of inexperienced administrators[6]. The difference between West Pakistan and East Bengal could never be patched up. Ever since Partition the relations between the two wings of Pakistan were strained. Their physical features presented an extreme contrast. The East Bengal had a magnificent river system and was watered and fertilized by the Brahmaputra and the Ganga. It had flat alluvial soil, which comprised 90 per cent of the province, and was filled with cultivated fields stretching for "hundreds of miles interspersed with villages nestling amidst bamboo clumps, mango and jackfruit gardens and timber fuel trees. The monotony is broken by coconut, palm and betel-nut trees in the coastal district"[7]. With a tropical monsoon climate, the East Bengal had a rainfall varying from about 65 inches in Dacca to 160 inches in Sylhet. Though was only 54015 square miles in area, it had in 1965 a population of 50 million. Being one of the most thickly populated areas in the world with a density of 922 persons per square mile, the life of the people there was stricken with poverty, neglect and oppression. Following partition in 1947 the administration there was completely paralysed owing to shortage of civil servants. A large number of Hindu lawyers, doctors, university teachers and merchants had fled to India. Either the Punjabi civil servants or Urdu speaking Muslims who had migrated from India held many of the important positions in East Bengal administration. It is said that "over fifty per cent of the civil and criminal courts could not function owing to the shortage of judicial and executive officers"[8]. It confirmed the prediction of the British Governor of the undivided Bengal that, Bengal of the post-partition days would be a rural slum[9]. The dissatisfaction felt by the East Bengalis could not be easily done away with. Desperate poverty, political disenfranchisement, exclusion from important callings, and exploitation and aggrandisement on their resources by West Pakistan made them utterly indifferent to the Pakistani cause[10]. The pressure of population combined with abject poverty often drove them across the national frontiers in search of food and work. The East Bengalis were exposed to too much disability and affront with their place in the Army and Civil Service being appropriated by others. There were often head-on clash between Bengali and non-Bengali officers in matters concerning East Bengal. It is interesting to take note of the disagreements between Hamidul Haq Chaudhury, the Minister of Finance, Commerce and Industries in the government of East Bengal and Aziz Ahmad, the Chief Secretary. The Chief Secretary made most of the appointments without consulting the Minister concerned. "The Chief Secretary was a Punjabi, and all the key posts in the East Bengal Secretariat were in the hands of Punjabis or Urdu-speaking civil servants from outside Bengal"[11]. This made the local Bengalis totally frustrated. As one of the reports of the early period said: "A feeling is growing among the Eastern Pakistanis that the Eastern Pakistan is being neglected and treated merely as a 'colony' of Western Pakistan"[12]. While the foreign exchange earned from the East Bengal exports was used to carry out the development projects in West Pakistan, interests of the East Bengalis were neglected. Kingsley Martin, the famous British journalist wrote that in the East Pakistan, Dacca's resentment against Pindi was deeply rooted in the Bengali's dislike of being ruled by Punjabis or Pathans[13]. The impression of this journalist about the condition of East Bengal was one of extreme instability. The London *Economist* had pointed out in one of its articles that a planning commission economist estimated the income per head in East Bengal as 60 per cent lower than that in the West. Most of the new investments in capital and installations were concentrated in the West. Summing up, the report said that more than 90 per cent of the central government staff and armed forces hailed from the West. "This is 'two nations' with a vengeance and twelve hundred miles between them", it wrote[14].

There were of course progressive youth in the Muslim League desirous to see Pakistan taking to the path of modernisation and progress. Many young lawyers and students of East Bengal wanted to get into the Muslim League to pressurise the party to adopt a vigorous stand in support of their demands. They drew the attention of the authorities to recognise Bengali as one of the state languages. But their hopes were completely doused with the Pakistani administrators turning a deaf ear to their demand for reforms. Their indignation was further aggravated with the provincial government of East Bengal letting loose the police to fire at the Dacca University students agitating to get Bengali recognised as the state language. They even hoped for a Chief Minister who would uphold the Bengali cause. It was this Bengali sentiment that defeated the Muslim League in East Bengal in the elections of 1954 and put in power the United Front government under A K Fazlul Huq. This was followed by conflicts between Bengalis and non-Bengalis, which was reported to have left about 400 people dead. Raising the allegation that the Chief Minister was unwilling to meet the situation sternly his ministry was dismissed and Governor's rule was clamped on the state. It was alleged that Bengalis were seeking more autonomy amounting almost to complete independence. Appointing Iskander Mirza as the Governor, Prime Minister Muhammad Ali said, "the Centre will never allow this province to again incur the danger of disintegration". Seeing that there was little possibility of getting their demands met, many Bengalis became angry. It was indeed this frustration of the East Bengalis that made Suhrawardi to enlist the support of many a disenchanted Bengali in forming his Awami League Party. On 7 November 1964 Maulana Bashani, a prominent East Bengali, openly warned the authorities that "a lava was slowly boiling up" in the hearts of his people against the tyrannical higher ups. *Sangbad*, a Bengali language daily from Dacca, gave a clear picture of this West Pakistani attitude towards East Bengal. It wrote that whenever any claim was put forward on behalf of the just rights of East Pakistan in the cultural, political and economic fields, doubt was cast on the patriotism of the East Pakistanis 'enmasse' and a reign of terror was let loose. "Except for a few most of East Pakistan political leaders were branded at one time or the other as traitors"[15]. The daily further noticed that there was a wide gap in the rates of economic growth in the East and West Pakistan. And to remove this difference, the daily suggested, it would be necessary to stop all development projects in West Pakistan and divert all available resources to the East. It was to avoid break-away between the two wings that economists of East Bengal favoured two separate economies for the two wings. As already said, the people of East Bengal were different from the West Pakistanis. In tradition, language and culture the gulf was unbridgeable, and the two could be held together only on the basis of justice, fair play and equality in all walks of national life, particularly in matters of economic development. This bold Bengali daily even drew the attention of the Pakistan administration to the Muslim League's Pakistan resolution adopted at Lahore in March 1940, which envisaged that areas in which the Muslims were numerically in a majority, as in the north western and eastern zones of India, should be grouped to form 'independent states' in which the constituent units should be autonomous. The leaders of the Muslim League themselves had been well aware of the inherent and natural differences between these two areas. But instead of finding concrete solutions to such grave realities, Pakistani administrators attempted only to paper over the cracks with sulfur-hot fanatical slogans and untenable political gimmicks. Field Marshal Ayub Khan himself was not free from this usual Pakistani attitude towards East Bengal. He declared on 1 March 1962, "... if I were an East Pakistani, then, in order to get away from the cultural domination and grip of Calcutta I will change the script. That will give a tremendous psychological freedom to the people of East Pakistan from the forces of Hindu culture and influence"[16]. True, he was an astute politician having knowledge of the real import of the Lahore Resolution. But finding it difficult to apply any logicality in the moon-mad political situation of Pakistan where the leaders were interested only in securing power, he too thought it better to safeguard his seat in the administration by resorting to tricks, and followed the 'Hate-India' tirade coined and stereotyped by his predecessors to divert the attention of the East Pakistanis suffering for long from poverty and negligence which posed a serious threat to Pakistan's national unity and existence.

Among the various problems that affected the progress of the new born Pakistan was the long drawn head-on clash between the bureaucracy and politicians that had resulted in unending administrative troubles. Of course Pakistan did have a number of sagacious politicians who knew how to free the administration from the undesirable clutches of the bureaucrats. For instance, Prime Minister Liaquat Ali tried his best to politicise the bureaucratic system he inherited from Jinnah. But the domineering presence of Jinnah overshadowed the Prime Minister's efforts. Jinnah's death in September 1948 left Liaquat Ali all-powerful. His position as the Prime Minister as well as the President of the Pakistan Muslim League provided him ample powers to answer to the call for reform at the governmental level. An eloquent speaker who was logical and cogent in arguments, he commanded a popular appeal no other leader enjoyed. And in Pakistani politics troubled with the Punjab and Bengal problems he enjoyed the advantage that he belonged to neither of these places with the result that he could function as a safe intermediary between the various provincial interests in Pakistan, especially between the feuding Punjabi and Bengali Ministers[17]. But he too could not overcome the bureaucratic evils. Consequently like other Pakistani leaders he also went on with his 'courageous stand' against the alleged aggressive intentions of India instead of finding solutions for the many problems affecting his state. He could not "capture the popular imagination by offering a programme of economic and social reforms". Added to these were the conflicts of regionalism that proved a real headache to most of the Pakistani leaders. Prior to the integration of all parts of West Pakistan into the province of West Pakistan in 1955, Pakistan was a political melting pot with its different warring factions. In the west there were West Punjab, Sind and North-West Frontier Province while there were states like Bhawalpur, Khairpur and Baluchistan. There were the Tribal Areas in the North West Frontier Province, Baluchistan and Karachi, which were within the Central Government's jurisdiction. In addition, there was East Bengal, the province of innumerable troubles. And to bring about cohesion, and national unity among such a group of different nationalities called for extraordinary intelligence, broadmindedness and farsighted vision instead of nimble antics and gimmicks. Unfortunately none of the Pakistani leaders possessed these qualities, and they, one after the other, resorted to occasional tricks, which could only just paper over the cracks rather than find permanent solutions for the grave realities and impending disasters. Again the very idea of independence and national development in Pakistan was thrown to the winds when politicians who clamoured for a separate state for decades resorted to double dealings and inhuman practices to capture power, neglecting the urgent needs of this newborn state. Instead of caring for the needs of the new state they were concerned with the advancement of their selfish interests, which resulted in the complete disruption of the peoples' dream regarding a welfare state. To add to this, within four years of Pakistan's birth, two of its most prominent leaders, Jinnah and Liaqat Ali Khan died. The assassination of Liaqat Ali, the sagacious Prime Minister in October 1951 was a national misfortune. Consequently, politicians with no popular backing or even enjoying the support of their own parties filled in this political vacuum. Most of them were well placed opportunists and specialists in preaching separatism and disruption. Devoid of all ability, and least inclined to serve the national cause, they were interested only in capturing seats. Rafiusha Kahn says, often the members of the party in power made unashamed bid for power by using every conceivable political trick at their disposal. They intrigued, switched their loyalties over issues of no particular importance and frequently broke from the main party to form splinter pressure groups. In their scramble for power they made and unmade governments and within five years six governments and six Prime Ministers had fallen[18]. As V B Kulkarni very rightly observes, Prime Ministers followed one another in quick succession and retreated into obscurity with equal speed. Khwaja Nizamudin, Mohammed Ali, Chaudhuri Mohammed Ali, I I Chundrigar and Sir Pheroz Khan Noon who held the office of the Prime Minister for transitory period, flitted like phantoms across Pakistani horizon, gathering in some instances, greater unpopularity and odium on their return trip to the realm of anonymity[19].

Democracy thus being a comic interlude in Pakistan, it was in its logic of history that the army had often to take over its administration. On 8 October 1958 Major General Iskender Mirza, President of Pakistan abrogated the constitution and appointed General Ayub Khan as the Martial Law Administrator. Having watched with the "deepest anxiety the ruthless struggle for power, corruption, shameful exploitation of our simple, honest, patriotic and industrious masses, the lack of decorum and the prostitution of Islam for political ends", Mirza had no other option but to suppress these political bandicoots with military boots. Parliamentary democracy had turned to be so comic an affair that people lost all faith in it. President's proclamation recalled: "Recently we had election for the Karachi Municipal Corporation. Twenty nine per cent of the electorate exercised their votes and out of these fifty per cent were bogus votes"[20]. The Legislative Chambers often turned into wrestling arenas. Also Mirza at times criticised the unbalanced foreign policy, and went on condemning that against India, of course, they scream for war knowing fully well that they will be nowhere near the fighting line. But by making General Ayub Khan the Martial Law Administrator, Mirza paved the way for his own expulsion; he had to live a life of safe obscurity far away from his motherland.

True, the Martial Law Administration of General Ayub was better in many ways than his predecessors' pseudo-democracy. The third Five Year Plan (1965-70), which elicited the admiration of all the friendly nations, the Indus Water Treaty (September 1960) and the like measures were to herald the dawn of an age of progress and prosperity. The political observers took Ayub's early days of leadership as the prelude to a period of internal peace in Pakistan and friendly relations with India. But it ended soon, and the goodwill between India and Pakistan was short lived when it came to the issues of substantial importance like the treatment of minorities in Pakistan and the Kashmir question. Besides, Ayub could not control the fundamental fanaticism and superstition inside the country. There was still the economic disparity between the two wings of Pakistan, and the opposition to the Ayub regime was mounting day after day. Disparaged as the "government of the President, by the President, for the President", it was on the decline. His military regime betokened all the crudities of a rough and tough dictatorship, which had been questioned from all the quarters. On 2 April 1964, a member of Awami League advised the government to give adult franchise to its people before advocating the right of self-determination for the inhabitants of Kashmir. The Deputy Speaker of the National Assembly, Abdul Qasem challenged President Ayub on 17 April 1964 to oppose him in seeking the popular vote "from any constituency in the country on the basis of adult franchise"[21]. Thus as stated by some of the scholars in international studies, "the coup of 1958 brought about no fundamental departure in Pakistan political system... The power structure continued to be the same"[22]. The only major discernible difference was that the vehicle providing legitimacy to Pakistan's political system had changed. So far the politicians provided legitimacy to an essentially bureaucratic rule supported by the army. Now the army took upon itself the role of the legitimising agent. But the people's plight continued to be miserable, irrespective of the difference between an elected government and martial rule.

There was also the problem of the minorities, who were, as could be expected, a disgruntled lot. Their persistent efforts to integrate themselves into the national life of Pakistan always proved a failure. Downtrodden and neglected, they figured in the news only when a major calamity befell them or when they migrated to India in search of food and shelter. Even in the days of the parliamentary government, the members of the parliament other than the Muslims found it difficult to express their opinion in open. They had, says Prof. Callard, to contend with a substantial degree of suspicion and hatred towards the religion they professed. Even they stood against the separate electorate for the minorities. But to get a footing of equality for the non-Muslims in Pakistan was still utopian[23]. The constitution makers of Pakistan had even gone to the extent of driving a wedge between the outcaste and caste Hindus through the various legislative proceedings. Though the provisions for safeguarding the minorities and their representation in the legislature and services were written into the constitution, they were seldom taken seriously. Persecution of Hindus continued to be commonplace. In fact the tragedy of Noakhali in October 1946 was only a prelude to the savage attack unleashed later against the Hindus. The bloodshed became more ruthless in December 1963 when the news of the theft of the Prophet Muhammad's hair from Hazratbal shrine in Srinagar was afloat. The whole wrath turned against the helpless minorities. The otherwise controlled and suppressed press in Pakistan was allowed to publish the most inflammatory reports about the theft of the relic. The press went on publishing the same even after the recovery and restoration of the hair to the shrine[24]. The holocaust was untold. According to the testimony of an American Peace Corps nurse, published on 22 January 1964, more than thousand persons consisting mostly of women and children were killed in Dacca alone. The editor of the *Pakistan Observer* put the number of the massacred at 6000 and of the injured 3000. The destruction of the property amounted to Rs.25 million. Some broadminded Muslims strongly came out against the inhuman ways the minorities were dealt with. The *Pakistan Observer* reported that some including college students and Professors heroically protected the Hindus from being burnt alive and in this attempt twenty two of them perished in the flame of their coreligionists' fanaticism. The press of East Bengal including the dailies like *Sangbad*, *Ittefaq* and *Pakistan Observer* strongly criticised the persecution of their fellow countrymen. But these journalistic attacks turned out to be a cry in the wilderness. Left unprotected by the Government and callously exposed to the flames of fanaticism, these helpless people were left with the only alternative of fleeing to India. Mrs.Lakshmi Menon, Minister of State for External Affairs stated in Indian Parliament on 2 March 1967 that this exodus was due to the "organised large scale looting, arson, kidnapping and forcible occupation of their land by the members of the majority community with the connivance of the Pakistani Police and the village defense corps known as the Ansars"[25]. Rev. Girishchism who worked for the Bethel Mission in the Mymensing district told that he and his people had virtually lived under a reign of terror. A master plan had been prepared to "squeeze out" the minorities from his district, and for this the East Pakistani Rifles, the Ansars, and the "self-styled refugees" from West Bengal unleashed a combined operation [26]. The internal political uncertainties combined with the economic problems, the negligence of the East Pakistanis and the fanatic uproar resulting in the dastardly murder of the minorities had been the usual scenario in Pakistan. All these problems put Pakistan in a precarious set up. The interplay of forces at work within Pakistan since 1947 was so disruptive that it became a necessity for the politicians to hide their failures by diverting the people's attention elsewhere. Thus as already noticed Pakistan's hatred towards India was more a political gimmick than a national imperative. Sanghat Singh observes in his book *Pakistan's Foreign Policy*: "The foreign policy was tailored to suit Pakistan's domestic needs. It symbolised in particular the validity of her internal policies and served as useful distraction from her internal anxieties"[27]. While the priorities of the government should have been channeled to appropriate areas of national development, the government in Pakistan, like it does even at present, kept the population under tight wrap, reminding them time and again that India was the only enemy and not the unsolved problems within the country. Even the army which captured power from the corrupt politicians in 1958 soon discovered that the best way it could retain the grip would be the propaganda that the country's internal ills could be solved after settling its score with India. 'Hate-India' thus became the usual stock-in-trade to cover up the administrative failures from the people; anti-Indian sulphur-hot slogans became the craze of reckless fanatics. This being the state of affairs, Pakistan felt the need to find out a convenient bone of contention with India, which it saw in Kashmir.

A glance into the annals of Kashmir is of high significance and fascination to any student of Indian history and culture. It was so inextricably intertwined with the cultural life of the nation from time immemorial that any study of India's history without analysing the precious heritage of Kashmir would be incomplete. In culture, politics, economy and what not, the highly enchanting Kashmir had its deep impact on Indian life. Many a literary work from early times had sung on the beauty of Kashmir, which was held the geographical forehead of the nation. It was to India what the gem on the hood was to the snake. It was accommodative of many new streams of thought. Many systems of Indian spiritual tradition prevailed here. The practices of the Indian religions like Saivite cult, the Vaishnavite beliefs, the Sakthi worship, those thousand flowers of thought the great Master from Kapilavasthu had strewn all across the length and breadth of the nation's psychic plains have all converged in their spiritual bliss in the happy valleys of the dreamland that was Kashmir. Besides, it accommodated, if we are to believe the views of some recent writers, a host of alien thoughts too. The Russian scholar Nicholai Notovich, the German writers like Faber Kaiser and Holger Kersten and many Indian researchers believe that Jesus Christ visited Kashmir where he spent the evening of his life. The Ruzabal shrine, the Kashmiris believe, contains the mortal remains of Jesus Christ or the Hasrat Issa[28]. According to tradition

Kashmir had been the homeland of Indian religions where the ancient kings had many temples constructed in honour of their Gods. Kalhana speaks of king Asoka who constructed the temple of Asokeswara in the city of Srinagari and about his sons who prayed at Nandikshetra for salvation[29]. It was the arcadian homeland of Kalhana whose imaginations were stirred by its lovely valley, the flower-strewn meadows and the bee-loved glades. It had inherited the mighty flow of political tradition bristling with a host of rulers who had through their valuable contributions enriched the cultural potential of India. The foreign travellers like Chi-Mong and Huein-Tzang from China, and the Muslim writers like Al-Biruni and Al-Masudi are highly eloquent on the wonder that was Kashmir. Tarikh-i-Rashidi of Mirza Haider Dughlat is an eyewitness account of the Kashmir geography standing in perfect harmony with its Hindu temples and ancient sites, its history, politics and religion[30]. It had been subjected to many invasions including those of the foreigners down the history. During the British period it was ruled by the Dogra dynasty. Whatever changes might have been brought about by the various dynasties, which ruled Kashmir, it has continued to be an integral part of India and its national life all along.

But it was a misfortune that this heartland of Indian culture later became the bone of contention between India and Pakistan. The post-independence period proved most eventful in the history of Kashmir and Indian nationalism. The Indian Independence Act of 1947 saw that the sovereignty of Great Britain over Indian affairs had ceased. According to the Act two states of India and Pakistan would be born out of the British Indian dominion, and that all the native states would be free to join any one of them according to their choice, or remain independent from the day, the sovereignty of His Majesty over the Indian states had lapsed. Among the various states posing challenges to the movement for the integration of the native states with Indian Union, Kashmir ranked first. It continued to be the same throughout the history of India though there were strenuous efforts from the part of the successive Indian governments to Integrate Kashmir into the mainstream of India's political and socio-cultural life.

The provision of the 1947 Act that invested the native Princes with the right to merge their states into any of the newborn dominions was however a fall out with the principles of democracy.

This raised concern among the right thinking people and organisations committed to the democratic ideals. No doubt Indian National Congress was the first to come out strongly against this. According to the Congress the final authority to decide the dominion a native state was to join should be vested in the people and not with the rulers. But Muhammad Ali Jinnah and his League were wholly uninfluenced by such a consideration. He was only concerned with annexing large territories to his new dominion and would resort to any means suited to serve his end. He made no bones about instigating the rulers of Jodhpur, Jaisalmer and Junagadh to merge with Pakistan though their rightful place was in India, and for this he even quoted the provisions of the British enactment on the issue of accession. About Hyderabad, Jinnah made the most subversive observations. "Hyderabad", he declared, "is an independent sovereign state and it is for its duly constituted authority to accede to India or remain an independent dominion". He added that India should not resort to methods of force, coercion or violence to compel Hyderabad to accede to India, it being contrary to the high sense of morality, justice and fair play in dealing with a sovereign independent native state[31]. Yet the same Jinnah was not willing to take this stand in the case of Kashmir where the king Hari Singh was the real person to decide the dominion to which his state was to join. He saw no anomaly in taking up the principle of popular will rather than the king's right in deciding the future of Kashmir, and was even prepared to set aside his early view that consulting the people's wishes was a necessary precondition for Kashmir to join India or Pakistan. As an inducement to Hari Singh to join Pakistan Jinnah promised him "complete autonomy and independence in the internal administration of the state[32]". But such a move, the Raja of Kashmir knew, would make his state blood-soaked in communal frenzy and a stage for the reenactment of the riots going on in the neighbouring Punjab and North West Frontier. "In the existing conditions in the Punjab", writes Lord Birdwood who was by no means a friend either of India or the Kashmir Raja, "an open accession to Pakistan might well have resulted in the massacre and expulsion from the state of the Hindu and Sikh inhabitants"[33].But Jinnah and his friends were anxious to take possession of Kashmir. Moreover, Ramachandra Kak who became Kashmir Prime Minister on 28 June 1945 was known to be "closer to Pakistan" and had been hostile to any popular movement in the state[34]. True, even if Hari Singh would have got his state joined to Pakistan it would not have caused any discomfiture to India. But these things never dawned on the king of Kashmir whose only thought was to remain independent. It would be interesting to look into how Mountbatten reminisces on the Maharaja's state of mind about the future status of Kashmir:

> I said, "Hari Singh, you have got to listen to me. I'm an old friend of yours. You've got to make up your mind. I have come up with full authority from the present government of the future Dominion of India... I have come to tell you that if you decide to accede to Pakistan, they will think it a natural thing to do, because the majority of your population are Muslims. It'll not only cause no ill-feeling, but they'll give you all the support and help they can".

But Hari Singh objected to this plan and thought that the majority of the Kashmiri people would back him if he sought Kashmir's independence. So he said to Mountbatten, "don't forget that with Sheik Abdullah, who's madly pro-Nehru, most of my people would really wish to join India" and the Maharaja insisted on remaining independent. Indeed the Raja did not take to account the exact nature of Kashmir situation, which Mountbatten explained to him. Summing up the Kashmir situation, Mountbatten said:

> You can't be independent. I'm sorry. You are in fact, a landlocked country of a great size and not a very big population (only about seven or eight million inhabitants). You've got two rival countries, which are always going to be at daggers drawn: those are your neighbours. You're going to be pulled in to a scrimmage. You will end up by being a battlefield between the Hindus and the Muslims. That is what will happen to you. And you will lose your throne[35].

All these however fell on the deaf ears of Hari Singh who was obstinate in his decision regarding the future of Kashmir. He wanted to keep it to himself whatever might be the outcome. And wise counsel did not prevail.

This decision of the king of Kashmir was welcome to Jinnah who was eager to annex Kashmir to Pakistan. But Sheik Abdullah who was immensely popular with the Kashmiris, proved a thorn in Jinnah's flesh. Sheik's view of setting up a popular government was not acceptable to Jinnah. The Prime Minister of Pakistan, Liaqat Ali Khan made it clear that Pakistan would not like to have a referendum in Kashmir; and Jinnah could not think of the idea of a joint government of the Hindus, Sikhs and the Muslims in Kashmir[36]. Jinnah was out to annex Kashmir at any cost. But blaming Jinnah alone for the Kashmir problem would be an injustice. The Indian leaders also turned their back on the Kashmir issue since they had taken that state as a Muslim majority one. Asked by the Kashmiris when he visited the state in August 1947 whether they should join India or Pakistan, Mahatha Gandhi responded to it as a matter to be settled by themselves[37]. Sardar Patel, who spearheaded the movement for the integration of the native states to the Indian Union, also held more or less the same view. In fact his states ministry went out of its way and assured that "accession to Pakistan would not be amiss in India"[38]. Despite his deep attachment to Kashmir even Jawaharlal Nehru himself was indifferent to Kashmir's accession to Pakistan[39]. It was thus completely left to the Kashmiris to decide their future. Maharaja Hari Singh pleaded to Pakistan and India to maintain the status quo in their relations with his state till he could make up his mind on his state's future, and offered to sign a standstill agreement with both the dominions. Pakistan accepted the offer on 14 August 1947. But India showed no interest in the matter. Pakistan's move was however tactical and was aimed at persuading the state of Kashmir to join Pakistan. And it would have indeed been a blessing had its rulers been endowed with tact and patience. But the traditional Islamic methods of coercion and threat were considered the best means, and Kashmir soon became a victim of Pakistani invasion.

It is clear that even before the creation of Pakistan Jinnah had made up his mind to make Kashmir an integral part of the state he was planning to carve out. He had also hatched a plot for realizing his object even before the birth of Pakistan. He had convened a meeting at his residence (10, Aurangabad Road in New Delhi) to discuss the plan to occupy Kashmir. Professor Muhammad Ishaq Qureshi who was the right hand man of the Kashmir Muslim Conference chief, Chaudhury Gulam Abbas, has, in an article published in Nawa-e-Waqt, Lahore, stated:

> The Quaid-e-Azam (Mr. Jinnah) called him and the Working President of K M C, Chaudhury Hamidullah to Delhi. We met at his residence on 11 July 1947 at about 11 A M. We discussed the situation in Kashmir. Mr. Jinnah gave us some important instructions, which we carried out.

What were these instructions? It was known that Jinnah's Private Secretary Khurshid Ahmed had established a secret camp in a Srinagar Mosque and was busy organizing the fanatics to rise in rebellion at an appropriate time. His group was getting weapons from the Punjab Muslim League Chief, Nawab of Mamdot. A secret blueprint to organize a guerilla war was seized from him at the time of his arrest[40]. Mr. Jinnah had issued instructions to Mr. Liaqat Ali also. According to Qureshi, Liaqat Ali called him and Hamidullah for a meeting. A special messenger was sent to them in Srinagar. The *Nawa-e-Waqt* wrote:

> They reached Lahore on 21 September 1947 and attended a secret meeting convened by Liaqat Ali. Some Generals, NWFP Chief, Abdul Qayyam, Punjab Minister, Mian Iftekharuddin and Sardar Shaukat Hyat Khan along with Zaman Kiani (formerly of Azad Hind Fauj) were present at the meeting. (They) were taken into confidence about a plan to invade the state of Jammu and Kashmir from Muzafarabad and Shakkargarh-Sialkot side simultaneously. The plan was prepared by Liaqat Ali and his military and civil advisers.

A committee under the chairmanship of Mian Iftekharduddin was formed to draft a proclamation to be released at the time of invasion[41]. Professor Qureshi says, "I and *Pakistan Times* Editor, Faiz Ahmad Faiz were the members of the committee. We prepared the draft and sent it to the Prime Minister on October 1". In the meantime according to Qureshi, Khan Abdul Qayyam Khan and Nawab of Mamdot were "performing their duty" to supervise the preparations to invade the state through Muzafarabad and Sialkot sectors. According to him:

> an important part of the plan was to occupy Kathua that links the state with Pathankot by the Ravi bridge. Pakistan wanted to close this road to India. General Zaman Kiani and Brigadier Habibur Rahman along with Brigadier Majid Kiani were assigned to undertake this operation. They had set up their headquarters in Sialkot. Pakistan army had to advance from Shakkargarh situated only at 10 miles from Kathua border[42].

According to Qureshi the Tribal Lashkar occupied Muzafarabad on 22 October and entered Baramulla within three days, pushing the Dogras to the Srinagar airport. At that time the Maharaja's government had only a very small army and had not yet signed the instrument of accession with India. Qureshi says, "alas, the Pakistani army did not move on to the Eastern Sector. Otherwise it was easy to occupy Kashmir within a few minutes"[43].

Qureshi states that Jinnah invited him and Hamidullah to meet him in Lahore in the last week of October 1947. He was very much distressed over these developments. He was not told about the details. When Qureshi and Hamidullah met Liaqat Ali Khan he admitted that he had not told everything to Jinnah. "In fact Liaqat Ali's advisers had assured him that the army would occupy the state from Sialkot sector within a few hours and then Liaqat Ali would give the present of occupation of Kashmir to Mr. Jinnah on a silver plate".

This tribal invasion supported by Pakistani army was preceded by Pakistan's economic pressure on the King of Kashmir with a view to compel him to accede to Pakistan. Food supply and rail links were completely suspended[44]. Besides the tribal invasions, Pakistan also engineered an armed revolt in Poonch against the King of Kashmir. According to Mehr Chand Mahajan who took over as Kashmir Prime Minister in October and who later rose to become the Chief Justice of India, the raiders were recruited by the Pakistani Government "with the active help of the British Governor of the NWFP on all kinds of promises of gold, women, loot and what not"[45]. General Akbar Khan of Pakistan army led the tribals. Assuming the pseudonym of 'General Tariq' the old Moorish hero who defended Islam in Spain many centuries ago, Akbar Khan provided the invaders with arms, transport and various other facilities to overrun the state[46]. Besides, some other foreigners were also involved in the invasion. The Soviet writer I Andronov had it that an American called Russel K Haight disguised as a Pathan Tribesman spearheaded the lawless men. "In his Kashmir adventure", says Andronov "he was actually assisted by several resident agents of the British Intelligence Service and top-flight British representatives in India and Pakistan"[47]. No Kashmiri was involved in the invasion[48].

Bakshi Ghulam Mohammad one of the leaders of the National Conference who later became the Prime Minister of Kashmir gives an eyewitness account of the terrible disasters caused by the tribal invasions. He writes: "When on 25th October, 1947, Srinagar was suddenly plunged into darkness, we knew the invader must be near at hand. Nothing stood between this vast machine of conquest and rapine and the ancient and historic city–nothing but a band of brave Dogra soldiers under the command of Brigadier Rajinder Singh". This insignificant force which had been quickly rushed from Srinagar was reported to be encircled on all sides and running short of ammunition and supplies. He says, "Yet from the accounts that we got from the fleeing refugees during the preceding forty-eight hours, the Brigadier with his men had successfully held the invader at bay. But this situation was expected to change any moment considering that no fewer than ten thousand fully armed tribesmen, committed by Pakistan to mount this unexpected and sudden offensive against our state, would soon overwhelm all resistance"[49]. By the dawn of 26 October news spread like wildfire about the ravages the intruders were doing in the lovely valley, and that many people including some of the top officials had departed for Jammu. The crimes done by armed intruders went beyond all description, amounting almost to what Sewell told of the Islamic invasion of the city of Hampi centuries ago. They raped, murdered, burnt and looted at will, holding nothing sacred. Baramulla, a town of 14000 inhabitants was thoroughly striped of its wealth and women, and only 1000 persons were left alive to tell the story of the holocaust. Sheik Abdullah described these intruders as "criminals in history" and complained that they looted "everything and everyone" and dishonoured "even the holy Quran and converted mosques into brothels". He even invited the world Islamic community "to come and see for themselves what the invaders have done" in the state. True the Kashmir administration did its best to check the invaders like blowing up the bridges, posting armed volunteers at strategic points, preserving Hindu-Muslim-Sikh unity, and organising the headquarters of an Emergency administration and securing rifles and ammunitions from local police and supplying them to the fighting units. The people even collected whatever arms they could lay their hands on – old shooting guns, matchlocks, axes, ornamental swords and the like. In that precarious situation the people of Kashmir struggled hard to maintain the confidence of the terror-stricken refugees who poured into the city of Srinagar in a regular stream. "To maintain law and order, every mohalla in Srinagar was asked to raise a volunteer committee. Practically every youth reported for duty in these committees. Even the proverbially shy Kashmiri girls cast their 'burqas' to join National Volunteer Corps and receive military training. Others reported for duty as nurses in the medical aid centres we set up to tend the wounded and injured"[50].

But this was not enough to stem the tide of the ferocious tribals who abounded in number and were assisted by Pakistan government and army. In his state of desperation, the Maha Raja Hari Singh appealed to India for help on 24 October at the active behest of Prime Minister Mehr Chand Mahajan. But as the help from India called for its accession to Indian Union, the king of Kashmir signed the Instrument of Accession on 26 October. As already related, Indian Government was reluctant to interfere in the affairs of Kashmir. Thanks to Sheik Abdulla's effort Nehru agreed to send troops to Kashmir, and the situation was saved[51]. The editor of the British Weekly, *New Statesman* wrote: "There is no possible doubt that if India had not intervened ... Srinagar and the lovely valley of Kashmir would now be a devastated and blackened ruin". With the active assistance of Mountbatten India sent her troops to put out the tribal menace. On 27 October the first batch of Indian troops landed in Srinagar. Bakshi Gulam Mohammad writes:

> On 28th I rushed to the airport to meet the first batch of troops that were flown in by the Union Government in response to our request for military assistance. Unfortunately, no military vehicles were available to carry them to the front. So we arranged for some civil trucks and, under Colonel Roy, this small force rushed immediately to halt the invaders wherever they could be engaged. Colonel Roy was killed the same day near Baramulla, but not without forcing the main column of the invading forces to retreat[52].

He writes further: "From that moment onwards the tide began to turn in our favour and the whole of the Pakistani invading force was on the run. Its rout was achieved by the sacrifices and valour of the Indian Army fighting at the head of a people courageously defending their honour and freedom". An offended

Jinnah ordered his troops to march into Kashmir, but was soon forced to cancel his order due to the prompt intervention of Field Marshal Auchinleck, the Supreme Commander of the Indo-Pakistan army[53]. Mountbatten recalled the whole incident in an interview later. He said that Jinnah exploded with rage. He called General Messervy and told him, "This is going too far, we shall have to declare war. We will have to invade Kashmir and throw the Indians out"[54]. But Messervy warned Jinnah that this would entail severe repercussions and contacted Gen. Auchinleck who said, "You will not take Jinnah's orders to advance into Kashmir until he appreciates that the moment he invades, every British officer now serving the Pakistan army must be stood down before the order is given". This proved a shock to Jinnah, since it "stopped the war in its tracks". Mountbatten said, "Unlike the Indian army which had much more intelligent officers and could perhaps carry on, the Pakistan army couldn't carry on without the British officers. So when he [General Auchinleck] said they'd have to be stood down before the order was given that stopped them. Otherwise Jinnah would have given them the orders to go in"[55]. However, regular Pakistani troops moved into Kashmir in January 1948, just to retreat before the advancing Indian army. Thus the whole dream of Jinnah who was sure of winning Kashmir and had stationed himself at Abobtabad, expecting to ride in triumph into Kashmir and occupy the Maharaja's throne, was completely shattered[56].

One may doubt why the Pakistan army did not cross the Sialkot border. Liaqat Ali blamed his opponents while his opponents held him guilty for this lapse. Qureshi and his colleagues probably ignored the fact that the Pakistani invasion of this sector would have invited immediate retaliation from India, which at that time was able to strike at Lahore and Sialkot. Pakistani politicians and writers used to accuse Liaqat Ali of having committed a serious mistake by signing the ceasefire agreement. They claimed that Pakistan could have easily occupied the whole state of Kashmir, but for Liaqat Ali who "missed the easy catch". But many years after the incident Brigadier Shamsul Haq Kazi had exploded this myth. In an article published in *Nawa-e-waqt* on 8 February 1988, he wrote:

> The fact of the matter is that at that time Mujahideen Tribesmen and Pakistani army were facing defeat after defeat in all sectors. Indian Army had occupied Mendhar Valley and

> it had liberated the beleaguered city of Poonch by joining hands from both the sides. Now it was making brisk preparations to attack Mirpur and Mangla via Kotil. Our reserve army was reduced to only one Brigade. It was a very dangerous situation. Liaqat Ali, by bluffing the enemy as well as the Pakistanis, got ceasefire to save the prestige of his country[57].

This makes one think clear on the need of high statesmanship on the part of our rulers, because it was Nehru's miscalculation about the situation that induced him to agree to the ceasefire. While the Pakistan Prime Minister was aware of the actual situation and the possibility of a Pakistani defeat, his counterpart in India was totally ignorant of the outcome of the operations of Indian army in Kashmir! Indeed this proved one among the many comic scenes in the history of the relations between the army and politicians. Kashmir, from all historical points of view, had been an integral part of India. But Indian leaders never responded in right time to the call of that state. And even when the Government of India started to take some interest in its affairs it was too late, and left the military operations incomplete. Though the Indian Union took great strain to fight the tribals and threw the Pakistan army out, military operation proved fruitless owing to the lack of political farsightedness. Pakistan-Occupied-Kashmir was left untouched and was not incorporated into the Union of India. Jamna Das Aktar, the noted journalist who was at that time in Uri later said that the senior military officers had "expressed their deep resentment". "They deplored India's agreement to vacate the Pir Kanthi Peek. They said that Indian army was in a position to liberate the rest of the state within 15 to 20 days. It was due to this mistake that we lost the whole of Gilgit and other Northern Areas". In fact this was a case of unintelligent administrators destroying the gains of gallant military officials. And this type of triumph without result became the standard pattern for all the subsequent Indian victories over Pakistan and the final armistice.

The signing of the treaty of Kashmir's accession with India by Maharaja Hari Singh was fully in conformity with the provisions of Indian Independence Act of 1947, relating to the Indian native states and their accession to successor dominions. The discretion to decide this issue was vested in the rulers of the native states. It was this discretion the king of Kashmir exercised when he signed the accession with India. But Pakistan had been audacious enough to violate the very Act that provided legitimacy to its own birth by attempting to do away with the independence of Kashmir when its king wanted to have an independent existence. It is also true that Kashmir would have been an independent kingdom, but for the Pakistani invasions, which frightened the Maharaja and made him feel the necessity of seeking Indian help and signing the treaty of accession as a precondition to it. Thus by all the canons of law and logic Kashmir became a part of the Indian Union by the accession. By sending its troops to Kashmir, India was only attempting to safeguard its geographical boundary, though Pakistan, overriding all the standards of international politics and logic of diplomacy, made frantic attempts to grab Kashmir and annex it to Pakistan. And so far as a nation is concerned to defend its borders from foreign aggression is a moral and constitutional duty it was bound to perform. It was this duty the Government of India discharged in 1947.

As noted before, had not Nehru who was unaware of the successful progress of India's military operations in Kashmir agreed to a ceasefire the entire state could have been liberated. This was indeed a great blunder the Prime Minister of India committed. This was a prelude to a host of blunders the Government of India committed in later times. The first one done by the Prime Minister Nehru had boomeranged upon India, creating unending problems in the years to come. He took the Kashmir issue, which India could have easily settled herself, to the world forum and made it an international question, attended to with selfish motives and most often with utmost negligence and callous indifference by its members. Many national leaders had warned Nehru against taking it to the United Nations. Mahatha Gandhi had cautioned that by taking the Kashmir question to the United Nations, which was a forum of vested interests, India would get only "Monkey Justice". Sardar Vallabbhai Patel who was more adept than anybody in working out the mechanism of national integration also saw no propriety in going to the UN. He was confident that all intruders, Pakistani and other, could be thrown out by the Indian troops, especially after they had gained an upper hand over the aggressor. But it was a national misfortune that Nehru defied even Gandhiji's advice.

Susceptible to Mountbatten, and without thinking twice, Nehru filed India's complaint to the U N on 31 December 1947. This hasty and unwise step resulted in perpetuating problem that still haunts India. Because from this date onwards Indo-Pak problem developed into a political game the superpowers could play in their own interests. Right from the beginning of the proceedings the Security Council did not view the Kashmir question in the light of the Indian complaint, and treated Pakistan as a legitimate claimant to the disputed state. India's reasoned plea to judge the case on merits was brushed aside. A body with vested interests could not act otherwise. H V R Iyengar in one of his articles referred to his conversation with a foreign Ambassador in India. The Ambassador had it that India's approach to the Kashmir question was "amateurish". "You are", he said "behaving like babes in the wood; you don't realize that those boys in the Security Council are a tough bunch. Do you think that their primary interest is justice? ... Don't forget that this is international politics! Each one of them is playing his cards on the basis of his long-term interests"[58]. And as V B Kulkarni observes, the Security Council's policy of equating the aggressor with the aggrieved party frightened justice so much that it spread its wings and flew off that world forum[59].

Desirous of bringing out a peaceful settlement of the issue, India brought the complaint under Chapter 6 of the U N Charter instead of 7 pertaining to the question of aggression. And a ceasefire, as mentioned earlier, became effective on 1 January 1949 [60]. Pakistan dismissed the Indian charges and put forth a series of counter charges covering the whole range of Indo-Pakistan relations. It however admitted that some "independent tribesmen and persons from Pakistan" might have been involved in the Kashmir aggression. The Security Council under its resolution of 21 April 1948 set up a five-member Commission for India and Pakistan (U N C I P) to mediate in the matter. After its tour of the subcontinent the U N C I P suggested a three-phased programme as resolution including the provision for ceasefire and withdrawal of troops by both the sides. Its third part recommended for holding a plebiscite, which India accepted. But Pakistan rejected it[61]. The Council therefore, appointed General Mc Naughton of Canada as an informal mediator, and as he failed in his bid, appointed Sir Owen Dixion of Australia in his place. Dixion's mission too met the same fate like that of his predecessor. He observed that the only alternative to settle the dispute over Kashmir between India and Pakistan is partition and allocation of some means of autonomy in the valley rather than an overall plebiscite[62]. He however condemned Pakistani crossing into Kashmir as "inconsistent with international law". In October 1950, the general council of Jammu and Kashmir National Conference resolved to constitute an assembly to decide on the future of that state. Disturbed over it, Pakistan pressed the Security Council to oppose this move. Accordingly, the Security Council adopted a resolution on 30 May 1951, asking India to desist from taking any constitutional step pertaining to Kashmir and asked for a bilateral arbitration, and provided for the appointment of a new mediator, Frank P Graham of the United States. Having failed in his mission, Mr. Graham finally suggested the desirability of a bilateral negotiation[63]. Consequently during 1953-56 the Prime Ministers of both the nations attempted twice for direct negotiations to find a possible resolution to the Kashmir issue. The meeting of the two Prime Ministers at Delhi in August 1953 resulted in a joint communiqué, which referred to the desirability of a fair and impartial plebiscite and provided for the appointment of a plebiscite administrator by the end of April 1954. But the policy of reconciliation could hardly stand the attack of the intolerant Pakistani press, which unleashed its tirade against Nehru's suggestion to select the plebiscite administrator from one of the smaller nations. Besides, the cold war between the superpowers also had its impact on the developments in Kashmir. Pakistan having come in handy to meet America's need for an anti-Socialist ally in the Asiatic region against USSR and Communist China, USA had initiated a policy of wooing her and arming her to the teeth. And naturally India became a beneficiary of the declared support of the USSR[64]. The armed support Pakistan got from the USA did away with the possibility of demilitarizing Kashmir. Later Mr. Mohammad Ali reverted to his old position and reiterated that Pakistan would refer the question to the UN. The Pakistani decision on 1 July 1955 to join the Turko-Iraqi Pact, which was the prelude to the Bagdad Pact, sealed off the possibility of further negotiations. Above all, the statement of G B Pant, India's Home Minister that hailed the decision of Kashmir Constituent Assembly to unite the state with India as the "verdict of the people which could not be disregarded" indicated the new trend of India[65].

When H S Suhrawardi took over as the Prime Minister of Pakistan on 12 September 1956, he whipped up the hate-India campaign and the Kashmir Issue. Already in opposition to India over such international issues like the Suez Canal dispute and the Hungarian problem, Pakistan announced its decision to take the Kashmir question to the Lake Success. Mr. Firoz Khan Noon, Pakistan's Foreign Minister urged an early meeting of the Security Council to discuss Kashmir. His letter to the President of the Security Council stated that the Indian Prime Minister's declaration that he was opposed to a plebiscite and the decision to constitutionally 'integrate' the state of Jammu and Kashmir with India and the mounting unrest both outside and inside Kashmir had combined to create an explosive situation constituting a serious threat to peace in the region. It was thus "essential that the early action should be taken to implement the 1948 and 1949 resolutions of the UN Commission for India and Pakistan, in favour of a free and impartial plebiscite under the UN auspices", he pleaded[66].

Mr. Feroz Khan Noon opened the debate on Pakistan's letter in the Security Council on 16 January 1957. Marked for acrimonious comments against India, his speech condemned India as an aggressive nation, which unlawfully and unethically occupied many Muslim states in India whose rightful position should have been with Pakistan. About Kashmir, he said that a state whose majority had been Muslims had no choice other than to accede to Pakistan, but having done the unrighteous occupation of that state India had been interpreting the Treaty of Kashmir's accession arbitrarily in her own interest, and that plebiscite was kept pending owing to India's refusal to demilitarize the area. He also added that in the Indian occupied part of that state civil liberty had become extinct, and nepotism and corruption wide spread. And he requested the Security Council to ask India to refrain from endorsing the changes introduced in the constitution of Kashmir, make it binding on the parties to accept the conduct of a plebiscite, withdraw forces from the state and to induct a Plebiscite Administrator[67]. In the Council Mr. Noon had the silent support of the Mr. Henry Cabot Lodge, the member from the US who reminded the Council about his statement that steps were being taken to integrate the state of Jammu and Kashmir into Indian Union by 26 January, with the new constitution coming into effect.

The Government of India had deputed Mr. V K Krishna Menon to present the Indian case in the Security Council. His speech of January 23-24, 1957 spread over almost 8 hours maintained that the real issue in Kashmir was the invasion and violation of its territory by the Pakistanis. Mr. Menon had it that on 26 October 1947 the Maharaja of Kashmir had submitted an Instrument of Accession, which had been accepted by India. He went on to state that this invasion, since Kashmir had already become lawfully a part of Indian Union by the Treaty of Accession signed by its King, was nothing short of an act of aggression against India. He refuted the Pakistani charge that the Indian troops in Kashmir were the force of aggression and asserted that the Indian forces there were to protect that part of India from the foreign invaders. Mr. Menon also pointed out the Pakistani defiance of the UNCIP resolution of 13 August 1948 which provided for the withdrawal of Pakistani troops and nationals from Kashmir and the restoration of the unity of that state, and a subsequent discussion between India and Pakistan and the restoration of normalcy to determine fair and equitable conditions ensuring the freedom of expression of the popular will in the state. Pakistan was indeed flouting the will of the world forum, which represented the will of the international community, Mr. Menon reminded the Council. He called the attention of the UN to the Pakistani threat of war against India and the concentration of her troops on the Indian border. He made it clear that the situations in the Indian and Pakistani occupied areas of Kashmir were entirely different. In the POK the condition was so worse that 45000 Muslim refugees had returned to the Indian areas from Pakistan lest they should be subjected to arrest without warrant and ruthless shootings, he pointed out citing the memorandum presented to the Pakistan Constituent Assembly by the Kashmir Muslim Conference. He also ruled out the necessity of a plebiscite since Kashmir by now had presented a different scenario, and strongly protested against the Joint Draft Resolution submitted by Australia, Columbia, Cuba, USA and the UK (24 January 1957) which reaffirmed the need of a plebiscite in Kashmir under the auspices of the UN[68]. Coming out strongly against the moral background of the resolution, Mr. Menon observed that it was not the constitution of Kashmir and the Constituent Assembly that made Kashmir an integral part of India. It was the Act of Accession in 1947 that gave legal recognition to it, and the Council was not competent to challenge Kashmir's accession to India, he asserted. In conclusion he said that the attitude of his Government to the resolution on hand would be not different from the response to the previous resolutions[69].

On the night of 24 January 1957 the Security Council adopted the resolution. With the exception of USSR, powers like Australia, China, Columbia, Cuba, France, Iraq, Philippines, Sweden, the UK and the USA favoured the resolution. When the Security Council met again on 15 February 1957 the four-power resolution supporting the Pakistani cause and demanding for the plebiscite and the sending of the UN force to Kashmir was presented by Australia, Cuba, the UK and the USA. But this too was vetoed by the USSR[70]. Therefore on 21 February, the Council adopted an amended resolution, asking its President Gunnar Jarring of Sweden to propose some ways that would promote the settlement of the question. After having visited India during March-April 1957 Mr. Jarring returned with no tangible result. However, relying on the Jarring Report, the Council passed the resolution that would speed up the implementation of the UNCIP resolution of 5 January 1949. India categorically rejected this proposal put forth by Frank P Graham[71]. Afterwards nothing important happened. Both the nations went on harping on mutual hatred and complaints.

With the advent of Gen. Ayub Khan to the headship of Pakistani administration it seemed that all hatred was a thing of past. The Government of Pakistan adopted gestures of friendship with India and naturally India took it as a promising prelude to friendly relations with her next-door neighbour. Preparations were on the high anvil for the meeting between the heads of both the states. The meeting between Jawaharlal Nehru and Gen. Ayub Khan in 1959 drew world attention and was hailed with an almost universal chorus of approbation. The Indian Prime Minister's visit to Pakistan to sign the Indus Water Treaty and his friendly visit to various places inside that country resulted in a joint communiqué of 23 September 1960 which covered all aspects of Indo-Pakistan relations. The Kashmir issue, which so far was a stumbling block in the way towards any kind of meeting between the two countries proved no more a precondition to bilateral talks. Now Pakistan's Foreign Minister, Mansur Quadir observed that while a Kashmir solution was necessary, Pakistan was desirous of solving all other issues along with it[72]. This joint communique stated that the two countries "agreed to give further thought ... with a view to finding a solution," Ayub's invitation to the Prime Minister of India to visit Islamabad and the latter's acceptance of it were hailed "Good news from Lahore"[73]. The President of Pakistan waxed eloquent on the need of a strong India in Pakistan's interest so as to undertake an economic collaboration[74]. There was indeed a great expectation among the Indians and the world nations when for the first time the Government of Pakistan had shown signs of making a determined effort to promote friendship and good feelings with India.

But these friendly gestures did not have any longevity, and the warmth with which it started shortly proved transitory owing to the many new developments in the domestic affairs of Pakistan. Ayub's military regime like that of all the other military administrators of Pakistan plummeted in popularity. Pooh-poohed both by the Pakistani public and the international community as a "Government of the President, by the President and for the President", the Ayub administration sought for some sulphur-hot issues to feed his people who got fed up with the usual gimmicks. Besides, it was also realized by the Pakistani administration that any kind of developing friendship with India would fail her in earning the goodwill of China. It is interesting to know that after Ayub Khan issued a number of jarring statements against India, Pakistan and China came closer than ever to each other. On 15 January Mansur Quadir disclosed that China had agreed in principle to the demarcation of its border with Pakistan. Presumably it was in the Kashmir area, for nowhere else did Pakistan and China meet geographically. This very well smacked the Pakistani attempt to please China by sharing with her a portion of the loot she took by aggression from India, the Azad Kashmir[75]. As a convenient way out of the mess in which he faced innumerable problems, Ayub renewed with greater enthusiasm the 'Hate-India' campaign and referred to the Kashmir problem which he described as "a time-bomb never very far removed from the flash point"[76].

Naturally there was an atmosphere of mutual hatred that led to a warlike situation, and slogans of 'Jihad' to liberate Jammu and Kashmir were heard everywhere in Pakistan. On 2 February 1961 K M Kurshid, the President of Azad Kashmir, and on 7 May 1961 Jammu and Kashmir Muslim Conference passed resolutions extending full support to a holy war to be launched to save Kashmiris. Kurshid went so far up to the audacious extent, stating that his government was not bound by any commitment of even Pakistan Government in this regard[77]. The Working Committee of All Jammu and Kashmir Muslim Conference decided August 1962 as the right time for Jihad and decided to recruit 10,000 trained Mujahids (volunteers) within three years[78]. The Pakistan Government's decision to liberate Jammu and Kashmir was reiterated by President Mr. Ayub Khan himself who told the members of the Pakistan Institute of International Affairs on 25 August 1961 that "the present ceasefire line is just like a grip around our neck"[79]. Muhammad Zafrullah Khan, Pakistan's UN representative also hinted at the likelihood of an impending disaster, when he spoke at the Security Council on 27 April 1961. These tirades were compatible with the Pakistani violations of the ceasefire line in Jammu –Kashmir and Jammu-Sialkot sectors as many as 473 times. But India's leaders did not desist from warning the Pakistani authorities of serious consequences if an unnecessary war would be forced on her. Prime Minister Nehru stated in no uncertain terms that Pakistan's further violations of the ceasefire line in Kashmir would prove "disastrous to that country" and threatened an "all out war"[80]. Krishna Menon talked boldly about the "liberation" of Azad Kashmir, illegally occupied by Pakistan[81].

But Jihad turned out to be a paper tiger when it began to backfire on Pakistan itself. Several factors forced the Pakistan Government to withdraw from the holy war. The war euphoria of Pakistan however had little effect on India, which was not worried at all over the call for Jihad. Instead this only strengthened India's determination to resort to an 'all out war'. Though Pakistan always used the Kashmir gimmick to camouflage its own internal insecurity and administrative disruption, it was clear to its leaders that India's military ability could easily dwarf her in an armed conflict. Besides, the people of Azad Kashmir themselves were on the verge of a rebellion owing to the rigorous policy of the Center which had resulted in K M Khurshid himself tending to be independent of Pakistan. As Pakistan never liked the Kashmir issue drifting out of its court and assuming an independent nature, the plan for thc Jihad was finally abandoned. To save its face with regard to the Kashmir issue the Government of Pakistan issued a press-note on 24 May 1962, which read:

> Of late some individuals have been making statements settling the dates for private action for the liberation of Kashmir. They know perfectly well that liberation will not come by the kind of futile actions of which they are giving advance notices to the other side. If any law and order problem gets created by any statement, it will be dealt with as such[82].

Pakistan now started wooing the US President, John F Kennedy to mediate in the Kashmir issue and the latter "affirmed the desire of the United States to see a satisfactory solution of the Kashmir issue". However, the Prime Minister of India reiterated the Indian stand on the Kashmir question and offered to talk to the President of Pakistan about Kashmir without any precondition and solve the problem by making the ceasefire line the boundary. But the Ayub administration responded very coldly to this suggestion. However Kennedy did not drop his expectations and was "going to continue efforts" to solve the issue, and the name of Eugne Black, the President of the World Bank was suggested to mediate in the matter. Nehru, who did not welcome this proposal warmly, pointed out the desirability of a direct negotiation instead of third party mediation. Though the Indian High Commissioner in Karachi was making brisk arrangement for the meeting between Nehru and Ayub, the latter responded very coldly as he saw no point in visiting India[83]. Fully prepared to bully India by allying with the big powers, Pakistan started diplomatic overtures with China by signing the border agreement. Notwithstanding that Pakistan shared no boundary with China except in Kashmir, which she had grabbed from India, a move for this was started on 3 May 1962. With no ethical conscience, both the powers announced their decision to negotiate and demarcate the boundary. Though India warned Pakistan of "grave consequences", China, giving scant regards to the Indian warning, informed India of its refusal to recognize India's sovereignty over Kashmir.

With the programme of direct negotiations having proved utopian there were again rumblings on Kashmir in the UN. Bilateral talks held simultaneously too yielded no fruits. The fourth round of talks held at Calcutta did not succeed owing to the issue of Pakistan's boundary agreement with China[84]. Nehru made it clear that India could not reconcile itself with the boundary agreement between China and Pakistan over "the areas illegally occupied"[85]. But Pakistan with its arrogance boosted up from the Chinese friendship paid scant respect to the Indian viewpoint. Pakistan started violation of the ceasefire line in Kashmir. "Kashmir must be liberated if Pakistan is to have its full meaning", Bhutto cried openly, and Ayub hinted at the likelihood of his nation signing a military pact with China in case the former could not keep pace with the growing India. And the pact was entered into between Pakistan and Peking in August 1963, which opened Canton and Shanghai to Pakistan's international airlines[86]. India on the other hand, went on with steps that would further integrate Kashmir with her. The pattern of Kashmir's representation in Indian Parliament, which was through nomination by the State's Assembly was abandoned in favour of direct election by the people. In 1963 the people of Kashmir as well as the minorities in West Pakistan and East Bengal witnessed a great holocaust when the news was afloat about the theft of Prophet Muhammad's hair from the Hazratbal shrine near Srinagar[87]. The news aroused deep indignation among the Muslims of Pakistan and Kashmir who held the Government of India responsible for the theft. The terrorism they let loose was of course contained by 1964, and on 3 January the relic had mysteriously come back to Hazratbal shrine. But this had no impact on Indo-Pak relations.

In February 1964 the Kashmir drama was reenacted in the Security Council. Pakistan once again brought the issue to the UN, raising complaints against the decision of the Jammu and Kashmir Constituent Assembly to bring in some changes in the State's constitution, which would lead to the further integration of it with India. Pakistan was represented in the Security Council by her foreign Minister, Mr. Zulfiqar Ali Bhutto who later became its President. Indian representative to the Security Council Mr. MC Chagla reminisces on the behaviour of his Pakistani counterpart in the UN as follows:

> There probably never has been another case in which a man holding such an important portfolio displayed in his speeches such complete absence of a sense of responsibility as Bhutto did. He was incapable of sober, dignified speech and could indulge in mob oratory of the worst type. At the Security Council meetings he ranted as though he was addressing a crowd in Hyde Park rather than so august a body as the Security Council. He had great fluency with the language, and that, unfortunately, led him to be carried away by the flow and exuberance of his oratory. His words very often had no relevance to the issue under debate or even to truth or admitted facts. He could be grossly rude and discourteous if it suited him, and he had no respect for the standards to be observed in a solemn debate affecting the destinies of two vast countries. He was inconsistent and thoroughly unreliable; and if cornered on any point, he would seek escape by flying off at a tangent to something wholly different or irrelevant[88].

Addressing the Security Council on 5 February 1964, Mr. M C Chagla pointed out that Pakistan's claim over Kashmir owing to the Muslim majority there held no water and he refuted the claim that Pakistan was the sole protector of the Muslims in Kashmir. He reiterated that Indian Muslims are a part of the cultural fabric of India and pointed out that "Ours is a secular state and an egalitarian society, where everyone enjoys equal opportunities and the equal protection of law. We have no official religion… We have no first-class or second-class citizenship. Before the law everyone is equal". He also added that:

> Pakistan's perpetual harping on a plebiscite in Jammu and Kashmir is not the outcome of its faith in democratic principles. I should have thought that democracy, like charity, begins at home, and before Pakistan preaches to us how we should ascertain the wishes of the people of a part of our country she should first make at least a beginning in establishing democratic institutions at home. I need hardly say that since the state's existence it has never sufficiently trusted its own people to permit them to participate in a general and direct election for the creation of legislative and parliamentary bodies.

He pointed out that Pakistan had been making complaints regarding India's changing stand with regard to Kashmir, "and yet she has given away to China, in the boarder agreement, over 2000 square miles of Kashmir territory". Pakistan had no right or title to this region and yet she had been generous at another country's expense, Chagla pointed out. He strongly came out against Mr. Bhutto's submission before the Security Council to apply the principle of self-determination in Kashmir. He had it that it was for the people of Kashmir to determine whether they should continue as part of India or Pakistan. The king of Kashmir as well as the National Conference, which was the major political party, had taken a decision on this matter prior to Kashmir's joining India. "The principle of self-determination cannot, and must not, be applied to bring about the fragmentation of a country or its people" he said, and drew support for this stand from history, citing the case of the bloody war the United States had fought to prevent the whole of the south of the U S "from seceding and constituting itself into an independent country"[89]. He lambasted Pakistan's reactionary and obscurantist policy. Fanatic in all its relations with its own people as well as its neighbour, Pakistan Mr. Chagla said "would have the hands of the clock set backwards, and would go back to the days when countries permitted only one religion and persecuted those who followed another faith .." Citing the historic role Kashmir has been playing down the millennia as an integral part of India and a "repository of Indian culture and heritage", he asserted that "the people of Kashmir are the blood of our blood, and flesh of our flesh" and Jammu and Kashmir was "one of the sixteen states of the Indian Union"[90]. Concluding his speech on 18 May Mr. Chagla made a strong appeal to Pakistan:

> India is an example of a society where inter-communal harmony exists. My appeal to Pakistan is, 'Do not interfere with this experiment. Let the experiment go on, because the future of the world depends on inter-communal societies succeeding'.

But the Security Council deliberations reached nowhere, and left the Kashmir issue unsolved. As Chagla himself opined, discussions in the Council that started in fanfare ended in fiasco. Seven members of the Council suggested that the U N Secretary General might join the talks between India and Pakistan as a good moderator. But the USSR and Czechoslovakia opposed this suggestion, and supported the Indian stand. Finding no breakthrough, the Security Council left the Kashmir question to be settled bilaterally between India and Pakistan, offering the mediation of the office of the Secretary General only if both the parties wanted its help. Thus the deliberations in the Security Council proved unrealistic, and a futile exercise, which saw the finale in the mere summing up of the President which was just a statement containing the facts of the debate.

Indeed from the Security Council debate India won nothing, except that by taking the Kashmir question to the UN it was transformed into an international issue with the result that India lost the opportunity of settling it all by herself. The ball, which she could have played without third party intervention, was now out of her court. The lack of political and national insight that led the issue to be brought to the world body could not be compensated with anything else. Many were the political errors that made India miss the drink when it was between the cup and the lips. First, though India had won the battle in 1948, she could not settle the Kashmir dispute at gunpoint. Second, India should not have taken the issue to the UN where it became the toy for the world powers to play with. India had a political elite whose diplomacy and farsightedness could have been depended upon in times of high crisis. But that the new elite that was in the saddle, was gullible enough to be misled by interested parties was a great national misfortune. It was indeed in defiance of the advice and suggestions of the veteran leaders that Jawaharlal Nehru took the issue to the world forum, which, as was predicted by Mahatma Gandhi, could give India a 'monkey justice'. The Kashmir problem, solely a creation of Jawaharlal Nehru, thus continued unsolved among the many troubled legacies India's first Prime Minister left to posterity.]

References

1. Keith Callard, *Pakistan: A Political Study*, London, 1957, p.11.
2. *The Hindustan Times*, 16 September 1962.
3. Penderel Moon, *Divide and Quit*, London, 1961, p. 21.
4. In a conversation with Sri Prakasa, Jinnah turned to him "rather affectionately" and said: "Just as your grandfather had got so many Muslim friends, so perhaps I might tell you that for myself I have only Hindu friends". *Hindustan Times Weekly*, 9 September 1962.
5. Alan Campbell Johnson, *Mission with Mountbatten*, London, 1951, pp. 217-230.

   In January-February 1948 when India was mourning the death of Mahatha Gandhi, Jinnah arranged a banquet session at Karachi, and invited Sri Prakasa. But the offer was politely declined. Again when tributes were given to the Mahatha in the Pakistani assembly, Jinnah could not find appropriate words to refer to Gandhiji. When the other speakers called Gandhi 'Mahatha' it was impossible for Jinnah to do so. Sri Prakasa writes: "So he referred to Gandhiji as merely 'he' and said that he served his community as he thought best". *The Hindustan Times Weekly*, 27 October 1963.

6. Sayeed, Khalid. B, *The Political System of Pakistan*, Boston,1967, p.60.
7. Russel Andrus and Azizali F. Mohamed, *The Economy of Pakistan*, London, 1958, pp. 13-15.
8. Khwaja Nazimudin's address as the Governor General, *Constituent Assembly (Legislature) of Pakistan Debate*, II, No. 2 (11 December 1948).
9. Alan Campbell Johnson, *Op. Cit.*, p.65.
10. V B Kulkarni, *British Dominion in India and After*, p. 385.
11. Sayeed, Khalid. B, *Op. Cit.*, p. 64.
12. Constituent Assembly of Pakistan Debates, II, No. 1 (24 February 1948), pp. 6 - 7.
13. *New Statesman*, 16 February 1968.
14. 'Carpenter in Trouble', *The Economist*, London, 5 October 1963.
15. 'Pakistan News Letter', *The Times of India*, 28 November 1961.
16. *The Hindustan Times*, 29 March 1962.
17. Sayeed, Khalid, *Op. Cit.*, pp. 64-65.
18. Amitava Mukherjee, *India's Policy Towards Pakistan*, New Delhi, 1989, p. 6.
19. V B Kulkarni, *Op. Cit.*, p. 359.
20. *Ibid.*, p. 360.
21. *Indian Express*, 18 April 1964.
22. Amitava Mukherjee, *Op. Cit.*, p. 7.
23. Addressing Pakistan's Constituent Assembly, the leader of the Congress party, Siris Chandra Chattopadhyaya declared on 24 August 1945: "I do not consider myself a member of the minority community, or of this or that community; I consider myself one of the seven crores of Pakistanis. I do not want any special right. I do not want any privilege. I do not want reservation of seats in the legislature. I say, frame the laws for me which affect everything equally". But it fell on deaf ears. Pakistani rulers still looked down upon him as belonging to a separate 'nation'.
24. The press of West Pakistan specialised in preaching 'Jehad' (Holy war) against India. The *Dawn* was the most notorious for this

fanatical propaganda. *Dawn*'s tirade against Acharya Vinoba Bhave was very much diehard in nature. An erudite scholar of deep Piety, Bhave wrote on many religious systems, including an appreciative commentary on the tenets of Islam. But Dawn could not reconcile itself to the thought that a Hindu should venture to write on Islam. Demanding that the Acharya should not be allowed to enter East Bengal with his 'Bhoodan Movement', the paper editorially asked on 6 August 1962, "whether a man who has been guilty of such an unforgivable crime against Islam should be allowed to set foot on Pakistan's sacred soil".

25. V B Kulkarni, *Op. Cit.*, p. 373.
26. *The Times of India*, 4 March 1964.
27. Amitava Mukherjee, *Op. Cit.*, p. 3.
28. Holger Kersten, *Jesus Lived in India*, New Delhi, 2001. Quiet near to the Hazratbal shrine is the Musa's tomb, which, the scholars opine, consists the mortal remains of the Prophet Moses. They identify the Bendipur on the river Jhulum with the Bethpur of the New Testament to where Jesus Christ had his final departure after crucifixion in search of the lost tribes of the Israelites.
29. *Rajatarangini*, I. 106, 107, 108, Kalhana's Rajatarangini edited by R S Pandit, New Delhi, 1977, p. 21
30. Ramesh C Dogra, *Jammu and Kashmir*, New Delhi, 1986, pp. 38-39.
31. V B Kulkarni, *Op. Cit.*, p. 383.
32. V B Kulkarni, *Pakistan: Its Origin and Relations with India*, New Delhi, 1988, p. 214.
33. Christopher Birdwood, *Two Nations and Kashmir*, London, 1956, p. 41.
34. *Ibid.*, p. 46.
35. Larry Collins and Dominique Lapierre, *Mountbatten and Independent India*, Delhi, 1998, p. 52.
36. V B Kulkarni, *Pakistan: Its Origin and Relations with India*, p. 216.
37. Pyarelal, *Mahatha Gandhi: The Last Phase*, Ahmedabad, 1958, Vol. III, p. 355.
38. Alan Campbell Johnson, *Op. Cit.*, p. 223.
39. H V Hodson, *The Great Divide*, London, 1969, p. 443.
40. *Organiser*, Vol. XLI No. 39, 29 April 1990.
41. Mian Iftekharduddin, a crypto communist, was the President of the Punjab Congress who joined the Muslim League on the eve of partition. He started *Pakistan Times* in Lahore in August 1947.

42. In his autobiography, *Atish-e-chinar*, Sheik Abdullah says, Pakistan's mistake was that it did not mount an offensive form Sialkot side to take Jammu.
43. *Organiser*, *Op. Cit.*
44. D C Jha, *Indo-Pakistan relations*, Patna, 1972, p. 49.
45. *Bhavan's Journal*, 5 December 1965, p. 29.
46. V B Kulkarni, *Pakistan: Its Origin and Relations with India*, p. 219.
47. *Ibid.*
48. Prem Nath Bazaz, *Kashmir in the Crucible*, Bombay, 1969, pp. 136-137.
49. Bakshi Ghulam Mohammad, 'Those Momentous Days', *Illustrated Weekly of India*, 12 August 1962.
50. *Ibid.*
51. Mehr Chand Mahajan, 'Inside the Story of Abdulla's Role in Kashmir's Accession to India', *The Sunday Standard*, 10 May 1964. He writes: "It goes to the credit of Sheik Abdulla that it was at his instance and pressure that India agreed to send its army to Srinagar to confront the raiders, but only after accepting the accession of the state to India, as declared by the Maharaja". But there is also another story that Nehru accepted the accession of Kashmir to India only after forcing on the king of Kashmir some conditions. Most important of them was to involve Sheik Abdulla in the administration of Kashmir with the result that Abdulla became the Prime Minister of the state on 6 March 1948. Having realised the likelihood of a constitutional deadlock, Mahajan tendered his resignation already.
52. Bakshi Gulam Mohammad, *Op.Cit.*
53. Campbell Johnson, *Op. Cit.*, pp. 226-363.
54. Lt.Gen. Sir. F W Messervy was GOC-in-C, Northern Command, India, 1946.
55. Larry Collins and Dominique Lapierre, *Op. Cit.*, p. 60.
56. Campbell Johnson, *Op. Cit.*, p. 225.
57. *Organiser*, *Op.Cit.*
58. H V R Iyengar, "How adolescent can we be?", *Indian Express*, 21 May 1965.
59. V B Kulkarni, *Pakistan: Its Origin and Relations with India*, p. 225.
60. Karunakar Gupta, *India in World Politics*, Calcutta, 1969, p. 23.
61. Pakistan knew that a plebiscite would give a verdict in favour of India since India had the support of Sheik Abdulla and his National Conference. In September 1949, Sheik Abdulla expressed his full

confidence in winning a majority even in the Pakistan occupied Kashmir if the government of that country agreed to withdraw its troops from there.

62. Text of Dixion's report in Doc. S/1791, 17 September 1950. Security Council's Official Records (SCOR) quote in D C Jha, *Indo-Pakistan Relations*, p. 51.
63. D C Jha, *Op. Cit.*, p. 52.
64. Karunakar Gupta, *Op. Cit.*, p. 185.
65. *The Hindu*, 19 July 1955.
66. Keesing's Contemporary Archives, Vol. XI, p. 19381.
67. K K Misra, *Kashmir and India's Foreign Policy*, pp.215-216. Mr Noon's accusations held no water indeed. In the case of Junagad and Hyderabad they had Hindu majority, besides their geographical position being landlocked on all the sides by the Indian territories. Jinnah of course made all possible tirades against these states joining the Indian Union though as an astute politician he knew well that these areas lying far away from Pakistan and landlocked by the Indian areas could in no way be one with his state. It was also equally foolish to think about two Pakistani administered areas lying in the heartland of India. Even East Bengal located far away could not be controlled by Pakistan, and it went out of its hands shortly, leave alone Junagad or Hyderabad! But the case of Kashmir was different. The accession of that state to India was in accordance with all legal norms. It was in conformity with the Indian Independence Act of 1947 that gave credibility even to Pakistan, Kashmir took its decision to join India. Besides, the major political party of Kashmir, National Conference, too supported the accession of that state to India, a scenario absent either in Junagad or Hyderabad. More over it is to be noticed that the deadlock of demilitarization in Kashmir was not fully owing to India's intransigence. According to the resolutions of the UNCIP (13 August 1948 and 5 January 1949) the first state bound to withdraw all its forces was Pakistan. Pakistan declined this and the US-Pak military alliance smashed for good all the possibilities of demilitarization.
68. The text of the Resolution:

    "The Security Council, having heard statements from the representatives of the Governments of India and Pakistan, concerning the dispute over the state of Jammu and Kashmir, reminding the Governments and authorities concerned of the principle embodied in its resolution of April 21,1948, June 3,1948, March 14,1950, March 30,1951, and the United Nations Commission for India and Pakistan resolutions of August 13,1948, and January 5,1949, that the final disposition of the state of

Jammu and Kashmir will be made in accordance with the will of the people expressed through the democratic method of a free and impartial plebiscite conducted under the auspices of the United Nations:

"Reaffirms the affirmation in its resolution of March 30,1951;

"Declares that the convening of a constituent Assembly as recommended by the General Council of the All Jammu and Kashmir National Assembly, and any action that Assembly may have taken or might attempt to take to determine the future shape and affiliation of the entire state or any part thereof; or action by the parties concerned in support of any such action of the Assembly, would not constitute a disposition of the State in accordance with the above principle;

"Decides to continue its consideration of the dispute". See *Asian Recorder*, 1957, Vol. VIII, No. 6, p. 1283- UN Document S/3778.

69. Mulk Raj Anand (Ed), *V K Krishna Menon's Marathon Speech on Kashmir at the Security Council*, Allahabad, 1992, pp. 130-184.
70. K K Misra, *Op. Cit.*, p. 245.
71. D C Jha, *Op. Cit.*, p. 54.
72. *Ibid.*
73. *The Hindu*, 22 September 1960.
74. Ayub Khan's interview with Prem Batia, *Times of India*, 25 September 1960.
75. *Dawn*, 16 January 1961.
76. D C Jha, *Op.Cit.*, p. 60.
77. Statement of Kurshid in *Dawn*, 22 May 1961.
78. *Dawn*, 21 May 1962.
79. D C Jha, *Op. Cit.*, p. 62.
80. *The Hindu*, 20 July 1961.
81. *Ibid.*, 8 January 1962.
82. *Dawn*, 25 May 1962; *The Hindu*, 26 May 1962.
83. *Pakistan Times*, 23 March 1962.
84. *Times of India*, 13 March 1963.
85. Ajay Saxena, *India and Pakistan*, New Delhi, 1987, p. 74.
86. *Ibid.*, p. 75.
87. The relic (the *Moe-i-Muqaddas*) had been sent to Kashmir by the Mughal Emperor Aurangazeb and was kept in a glass tube to be ritually exhibited ten times a year.
88. M C Chagla, *Roses in December*, Bombay, 1994, p. 393.
89. *Ibid.*, p. 397.
90. *Ibid.*, p. 398.

4

Rumblings from the River

Pakistan's relations with India have always been marked with acrimony and irritabilities with the result that it could not take to an amicable approach in whatever matters dealing with India. A fit case to be described as the sick man of Asia, Pakistan could not get on with India without inhibitions and unrest. In regard to the Kashmir issue it was true that India could not reconcile herself to the unreasonable demands of Pakistan, but even when there was any positive response from the Indian side for some possible agreements the latter would only turn its back upon its neighbour.

This negative attitude of Pakistan was reflected in the canal water dispute too, which created much rumbling. The issue could have easily been solved had it been with any other nation bereft of internal collision and administrative disruption. Pakistan, locked in internal feuds, political sabotaging, the long military rule and a democracy which was a very short comic interlude between two long periods of military rule, lacked a stable polity and a strong economy with the result that it could not be a nation behaving normally to its neighbour. However much India would yield to the demands of Pakistan, it would go on with its characteristic dillydallying to evade any possible agreement with India.

The waters of the Indus system proved the only source of irrigation, which could help both India and Pakistan improve their food self-sufficiency. But unfortunately it became another bone of contention between the two nations right from 1947 onwards. A bilateral understanding could have helped them reach a compromise on the matter. But the political rivalry as well as the mule-like obstinacy of Pakistan brought matters to a critical situation.

The partition had left with India only a small strip of land irrigated by the Indus. Since most of the western rivers could not be relied upon, Pakistan wanted to depend on some of the eastern rivers. India too wanted to draw water for her agricultural development from the eastern rivers like Ravi, Beas and Sutlej. It would have also been possible for both the nations to develop an adequate and mutually benefiting river system, but for the political reasons that strained their relations. All the mutual deliberations regarding this, being preconditioned by irritability, proved abortive. Above all, Pakistan was very keen in finding out convenient excuses to keep itself away from any understanding with India. As the head-works of some canals fell within the Indian boundary all calamities in Pakistan like draughts and floods were interpreted by Pakistan as due to India's mischief. The acrimonious exchanges between the two countries brought about the interference of the World Bank, which submitted its proposal on 5 February 1954. Accordingly the lion-share of the waters of the three rivers, Indus, Jhelum and Chenab, would go to Pakistan while a small volume of it would go to Kashmir. The entire waters of the eastern rivers would be available for India after a transitional period of five years, the time by which Pakistan would construct link canals. The proposals also prevailed upon India to help Pakistan by bearing the construction cost of the link canals required to replace supplies from India 'to the extent of benefit derived by her therefrom'. This scheme was beneficial to Pakistan, and involved heavy sacrifices to India as it would be binding on her to give up her rights to the Chenab waters which would help her irrigate the deserted tracts of Rajasthan. It would also place on India's shoulders a heavy financial burden amounting to a sum between Rs. 50 crores and 60 crores[1]. Though India knew well of the financial burden the plan would force on her, she agreed to the proposal. But an agreement with India proved a climb-down to Pakistan, which only nurtured the feelings of the 'Jihad' against her neighbour. Nonetheless as the World Bank scheme held out to Pakistan so many favours, after a short term of enactment of the usual antics and gyrations, the Prime Minister of Pakistan declared on 22 March 1954 his conditional acceptance of the proposal, demanding some more time for further technical studies! Under fresh negotiations in June 1956, the World Bank suggested that besides bearing the cost of link-canals in Pakistan India should bear the cost of providing storage facilities for the water drawn from India. Pakistan's response to this too was very cold though India was prepared to meet it, and still continued to supply canal water to Pakistan on ad-hoc agreements. As per the suggestion of Nehru who visited the USA in December 1956, the World Bank fixed 31 March 1957 as the deadline to close the negotiations[2].

But Pakistan had no desire to settle the water dispute and had mixed it up with the Kashmir question. Speaking to the *Associated Press of America* in Karachi on 1 June 1957, Suhrawardi said, "canal waters and Kashmir are the two prongs of India's grip on us". The cheap and baseless grumbling of Suhrawardi had gone up to the extent of casting doubt on the Indian Government's ability to compensate for the link canals envisaged by the World Bank. 'Fight' was his byword whenever he spoke of India and made unnecessary squabbles over the issues India never even imagined of. Therefore he said, "If India decides to cut off the water, Pakistan would be within her rights to fight for the supply of waters, but the stopping of waters will be greater aggression than our fighting"[3]. As India's Minister for Irrigation and Power Mr. S K Patil had stated in the Lok Sabha on 25 July 1957, "there had been a good deal of propaganda by and on behalf of Pakistan, aimed at misleading the world opinion by suppression and distortion of facts". In a broadcast from New Delhi on 28 July Mr. Patil confirmed that during the last three years Pakistan had constructed link-canals capable of replacing nearly five million acre feet of water which would really reduce her dependence on Indian supplies to only five per cent of her requirement[4]. Also Mr. Patil informed the World Bank and Pakistan that India would not wait any more than the coming five years, the time by which the Rajasthan and Sirhind 'feeder' canals would be completed and would draw water from the eastern rivers.

Pakistan of course confirmed its acceptance of the World Bank proposal of 1954 in New Delhi on 7 August 1957 on the condition, that India should pay for link canals and storage. However the customary reluctance still prevailed. India's plan of diverting water through her newly constructed Sirhind and Rajasthan canals was described by Pakistan as "a threat to Pakistan's political and economic security" and its implementation as "an act of aggression against Pakistan"[5].

Having viewed the circumstance seriously, Illiff, Vice President of the World Bank made his trip to India in January 1958, to prevail on India and Pakistan to reach a consensus. Following this the Nehru-Ayub meeting held at Palam led to the settlement of the canal water dispute. The tripartite meet of India, Pakistan and the representative of the World Bank paved the way for the settlement of the issue. On 22 September 1959 India's Ministry of Irrigation disclosed that an agreement was reached to sign a bilateral water treaty[6]. The US also expressed its decision to finance the Indus Water Treaty Project[7]. And Eugen Black, the President of the World Bank, made it clear on 7 April 1960 that India and Pakistan accepted a settlement in principle[8].

The Indus Water Treaty signed at Karachi on 19 September 1960 heralded a new period in Indo-Pakistan relations and a beginning for the settlement of all the other complicated bilateral issues. This treaty, which consisted of one preamble and twelve main articles and the provision for the formation of the Indus Basin Development Fund was universally hailed as a piece of good news. The bilateral desire to make "the most satisfactory utilization" of the Indus water by "fixing and delimiting in a spirit of goodwill and friendship the rights and obligations of each in relation to the other" was of course unexpected. But it somehow happened. The main features of the treaty were as follows:

The waters of the three eastern rivers – Ravi, Beas and Sutlej–would be available for unrestricted use by India after a transition period.

During the transition period of ten years India would continue to give some supplies for eastern rivers, and that there would be bilateral exchange of data regarding the water flow and withdrawal.

India has agreed to make a fixed contribution of Rs.83.3 crores towards the cost of replacement work to be undertaken in Pakistan. It was payable in ten equal annual installments to the World Bank which would credit it to the Indus Basin Development Fund. With the contribution from India and other participating countries like Australia, Canada, Germany, New Zealand, the UK and the USA, the Development Fund amounted to Rs.333.3 crores.

It was no doubt favourable to Pakistan. But it was not beneficial to India since it would give her only a small share of the river waters apart from the heavy burden India was to bear. However, the Prime Minister of India spoke aloud of it as a great success because of the "fact that a very difficult and complex problem, which had troubled both India and Pakistan for many years, has been solved satisfactorily". Nehru was jubilant over the "psychological and emotional benefits". But that for satisfying the psychological emotions he had buried the national interests is a fact no objective analysis would fail to discern. Jana Sangh, the militant nationalist organization, which used to come out strongly against any issue endangering India, had condemned the Canal Treaty Agreement as 'disappointing'[9]. There was heavy criticism against the provision that cast the burden of the payment of a heavy sum on bankrupt India, and the treaty was condemned as one of surrender consisting of 'anti-Indian interest' serving to 'placate Pakistan'[10]. This criticism gained much credibility against the background of the unchanging attitude of Pakistan. The treaty, which Nehru praised as the token of a new intimacy was pooh-poohed as just 'compromise solution' by Ayub Khan! Casting slur on all who were associated with the Canal Water Treaty, Ayub reverted to the Kashmir question, which he described as a time bomb that would blow up at any time. He thought that though the rumblings from the river might become silent the Pakistani aggressors could still make their guns boom in Kashmir. However much India would compromise, it would be ineffective in her relations with Pakistan, which grew arrogant with every conciliatory stand India took. In fact, India got nothing from the Indus Water Treaty, but a psychic dejection resulting from financial loss and a sense of betrayal. Yet it was pitiable that even after having learnt such souring lessons she would not prepare herself to accept the realities and leave the path of foolishness in her future dealings with the enemical neighbour. The mass migration of 1947 created the problem of the repatriation of the evacuee property. It was estimated that nine million Hindus and Sikhs migrated to India while 7,900,000 Muslims crossed over to Pakistan, abandoning their property. According to the figures given by the Government of India the immovable property of the evacuees from Pakistan amounted to Rs. 5,000 million while that was left in India was worth only Rs.1,000 million. But Pakistan contented that the amount due to the migrants from India would be more than what would go to the refugees to India. In the meetings of the Indo-Pak representatives, which took place time and again, India suggested a government-to-government settlement. But Pakistan insisted on the sale and exchange of movable property through individual effort. It was agreed and there was a little progress in the exchange of the movable property. The Nehru-Liaqat Ali agreement of 8 April 1950 provided the refugees from East and West Bengal, Assam and Tripura the right to take with them movable property and a cash worth Rs.150 in case of adult persons and Rs.75 by each migrant child. The implementation of this programme met with a little impasse since the Pakistan Government under its revised currency regulation allowed the India bound migrants to carry only Rs.20 each. However, the audience between the Foreign Secretaries of the two nations in July-August 1959 had cleared the impediments in the payment of the pension of the evacuees[11]. The representatives of the two nations had met a number of times during 1960-62 to implement the agreement regarding the movable property and agreed to expedite the settlement of the major issues and strive earnestly to restore the movable assets of the displaced persons in either country. But the discussion on the transfer of lockers and safe deposits and the transfer of bank accounts ended in smoke[12]. Consequently, the Ministers of Rehabilitation from both the countries, having met at Calcutta in July 1961, came to an agreement and authorized the implementation committee to work out the procedure of the transfer of bank accounts, funds, lockers and safe deposits. Many steps had been taken in this direction. On 28 August 1962 Mr. M C Khanna, India's Minister of Works, Housing and Supply revealed that except "a few lockers and safe deposits" everything belonging to this category had been transferred. According to his reports, India was to transfer accounts worth Rs.10.73 lakhs to Pakistan while the latter's due was about Rs.47.73 lakhs. This was no doubt a desirable step towards bilateral cooperation. But no repatriation or transfer of property could keep its pace with the exodus of refugees in 1964 and 1971 from Pakistan to India. And the attempt to transfer the evacuee property to both the sides proved a failure during the oceanic eruption of infiltrators into Kashmir. In such an atmosphere of trouble and turbulence nothing could prevent an impending Indo-Pakistan conflict.

References

1. Karunakar Gupta, *India in World Politics*, Calcutta, 1969, p. 201.
2. *Ibid*, p. 203.
3. *Dawn*, 2 June 1957.
4. *The Hindu*, 29 August 1957.
5. *Dawn*, 10 August 1957.
6. *Times of India*, 23 September 1959.
7. *Times of India*, 10 October 1959.
8. *Times of India*, 8 April 1960.
9. *Organiser*, 26 September 1960.
10. *Times of India*, 20 September 1960.
11. D C Jha, *Op. Cit.*, p. 309.
12. *Ibid.*

5

Towards Tashkent

The demise of Jawaharlal Nehru on 27 May 1964 put the nation in great sorrow. It was mourned nationwide. The Pakistani citizens and their President Ayub Khan had expressed their sincere sympathy, which was telegraphed to Indian President Dr. Radhakrishnan in 'profound regret'. ZA Bhutto, Pakistan's Foreign Minister, heading the Pakistani delegation that attended Nehru's funeral, expressed his grief in well-chosen words. The otherwise fire-breathing press and all the other political parties of Pakistan cooperated in mourning the death of the Indian Prime Minister. Bhutto was now soft-tongued and assured in well chosen words that Pakistan would not make any jarring statement against India nor would refer to Kashmir affair at the time while a new government was to take over[1]. Ayub Khan, while expressing his sympathy on the death of Nehru, considered it as an occasion for searching of hearts in order to have a fresh look at the Indo-Pakistan relations. "On our part" he said, "we shall respond to any sincere move for the improvement of Indo-Pakistan relation". In a message sent to the new Prime Minister Lal Bahadur Sastri, he described the latter's election as a good augury for Indo-Pak relations, and expressed his readiness to remove the impediments which had bedeviled the bilateral relations for the past seventeen years. Desirous of solving his country's problems with its immediate neighbour, Sastri was very much jubilant over the Pakistani initiative for friendship. Naturally he gave a hearty response to the Pakistani call for friendship and understanding. Along with many friendly statements and positive responses, Sastri in a broadcast on 11 June 1964 said, "for too long have India and Pakistan been at odds with one another" and that "we must reverse the tide". As a token of friendship Sastri landed in Karachi on his return trip to India from Cairo. In the three hour meeting between the leaders of both the nations, they were "firmly of the view that these (Indo-Pak) relations needed to be improved"[2]. During this talk, which Sastri described as "very pleasant and useful" the two leaders were reported to have deliberated issues like Kashmir, the ceasefire violations etc. Even *Pakistan Times* hailed it as a "good beginning"[3].

But the high hopes regarding the bilateral relations soon receded. All pleasantries and gestures of friendship proved mere gimmicks. The pleasantry was of course there. But no step was taken to settle the issues at stake, and Ayub would not stop playing the Kashmir dice. Simultaneously with the green flag he waved at India, he stated that the people of Kashmir would not "wait indefinitely". His Home Minister, Khan Habibullah Khan ruled out all possibilities of Indo-Pak amity if the Kashmir issue remained unsettled[4]. Z A Bhutto referred to India's colonial policy in Kashmir. The malicious and derogatory statements Bhutto made against India in his uncontrolled oratorical frenzy elicited worldwide contempt. A universally noted journal wrote, "Undiplomatically sharp attacks by Pakistan's Foreign Minister Bhutto, ... have done much to vitiate the effectiveness of the conciliatory statements made by President Ayub"[5]. But having seen that his whole future prospects in Pakistani politics was dependent on how he was to capitalize the hate-India sentiment, Bhutto could not avoid harping on the Kashmir issue. His President was more ambitious than him. Ayub was mad after putting on the mantle of Jawaharlal Nehru in international politics. Besides, Pakistan's relationship with Communist China was so close that she was expecting Chinese help in case an Indo-Pakistan war would break out. The Chinese incursion against India in 1962 was a further boost to Pakistan's aggressive tendency.

But India was as adamant as ever, and would not yield to any external threat. Already victorious in battle, she was now headed by a commoner of uncommon wisdom, stature and sagacity. Lal Bahadur Sastri, India's Prime Minister declared outright that his nation was not prepared to surrender before any demand that would bury the national honour[6]. M C Chagla,

India's Education Minister also made no bones about ruling out any basic change in India's stand on the Kashmir affair[7]. Meanwhile the violation of ceasefire continued as before. In the meantime Gulzarilal Nanda, India's Home Minister made the proposals to bring Kashmir under Articles 356 and 357 of the Indian Constitution. Kashmir Legislative Assembly also took steps to facilitate this, providing that Kashmir would be governed by a Governor appointed by the President of India, instead of the administrator designated 'Sadar-i-Riyasat' elected by the Kashmir Legislative Assembly[8]. As was expected Pakistan called it as "annexation" of Kashmir. To Bhutto a war was badly called for. Having prepared the working paper known as the Bhutto Plan, he declared that it was the right time to tackle the Indian problem. Having been at the hustings against the strong candidature of Miss Fatima Jinnah, Ayub Khan also wanted a war to gather the popular plaudits by championing the cause of Pakistan against India.

Pakistan's military adventure against India had begun in January 1965 in the Rann of Kutch, a marshland with 320 miles length and 50 miles width. Pakistan had already an eye over the Kutch area, and had been raising claims on it in the light of the Imperial Gazetteer of India. Time and again Pakistan stated that Kanjarkot, an area well within the Kutch was a Pakistan occupied one since 1947. Though India had raised verbal objections to this she took no timely action to frustrate the Pakistani demand. The Pakistani intrusion therefore continued, leading to an armed clash with the Indian Army. The Pakistan Army attacked Point 84, thirty miles east of Kanjarkot, intruding about six miles into Indian area. And on 23 April, Kutch witnessed the great holocaust with Pakistan launching a massive offensive on a front of 60 miles with an infantry of 25000 strong backed by tanks and heavy artillery. However Indian Army had strongly stood this reckless attack. Indian Prime Minister ruled out the likelihood of a unilateral withdrawal and completely left it to the Army to "decide its own strategy and deploy its man power and equipment in the way it deems best". The hostility was temporarily called off, thanks to the mediation of the British Prime Minister, Harold Wilson at whose instance the bilateral dispute over the Kutch was referred to an international tribunal, which gave 90 per cent of the disputed area to India and the rest to Pakistan. This indeed had resulted in the stepped up audacity of Pakistan when it got a strip of land in Kutch where it had absolutely no territorial right[9]. This could only boost up the morale of an immoral state. As an analyst of International politics very aptly puts it: "From a position of strength Pakistan pushed India into the acceptance of an international award over a matter relating to what it had been proclaiming was its own territory"[10]. The Kutch agreement was signed on 30 June, which provided for the restoration of the status quo that existed prior to 1 January. The proposal for mutual withdrawal of forces, though seemed promising, was however to founder on the reckless intransigence of Pakistan, which had been nourishing aggressive designs in Kutch, and later infiltrated into Kashmir. Peace terms were perfect on accord, but had no effect. And Pakistan could not be anything but more than satisfied over the undue concessions she got in Kutch. Jubilant at this, Pakistan only turned audacious and aggressive. India as usual became the customary looser. India defeating Pakistan during all the latter's incursions, and the Western powers interfering in favour of the aggressor became the standard pattern of all the settlements of Indo-Pakistan issues. The imperialist policies of these occidental powers to fish in troubled waters had in fact little concern for justice and even ordinary principles of human relations. No wonder they turned the best connoisseurs of Pakistan's comic shows staged against India. Soon after the conclusion of the Kutch agreement Z A Bhutto told the Pakistan National Assembly, "if we subscribe to the principle of total war… we have to fight where the problem lies, i.e., in Jammu and Kashmir" and that Pakistan "can never be complete without the people of Jammu and Kashmir forming part of Pakistan"[11]. The Kutch agreement was thus a diplomatic defeat of India because even after the cession of Indian area to Pakistan the latter was not satisfied. It thus became very vivid that Pakistan's aggressive policy would not die out at India's policy of yielding to satisfy the enemy as was reflected in the treaties of Indus Water and Rann of Kutch.

Attempt at any negotiation for a peaceful settlement was further frozen with Pakistan sending thousands of trained infiltrators into Kashmir. This offensive named 'Operation Infiltration', which Pakistan started on 1 August aimed at capturing the entire state of Kashmir by organized raids more methodical than those of 1947. This infiltration was only the first step of what was to develop into a full-scale war deploying more than 50,000 'Gibralter Forces' who were trained at Muree. Bhutto had already made it clear that Pakistanis should support their Kashmiri brothers in their struggle for liberation in the hope that the Kashmiris would welcome the infiltrators as emancipators. This however ended as a mere dream. Because the people of Kashmir, contrary to the expectations of the aggressors, had aided and supported the State Government in its operations against the invaders[12]. In the initial phase of infiltration, Kashmir was seriously threatened. By 9 August 1965 the infiltrators reached the neighbourhood of Srinagar, clashed with Indian security men and made plans to cut off the Srinagar-Leh route. They seriously damaged bridges, petrol and lubricant pumps and pickets of Indian armed forces. Chhamb, Kargil, Poonch and other areas witnessed serious clashes[13]. To quote India's Foreign Minister, Y B Chavan, "they were able to make some advance into our territory in the initial phase", and were able to inflict some casualties on policemen guarding vital points[14]. The UN Secretary General's appeals and serious concerns did not get any Pakistani response. Pakistan even denied its role in this infiltration[15]. This only stiffened the Indian attitude to turn sharp and stern. On 11 August 1965 G L Nanda, India's Home Minister warned of retaliation "if any country takes liberties with our frontiers"[16]. Prime Minister of India, Lal Bahadur Sastri also, ruling out the passive attitude from the Indian side, categorically stated that "force will be met with force" and that "aggression against us will never be allowed to succeed". This was followed by a massive military operation from the Indian side. On 15 August the Indian forces marched ahead and crossing the ceasefire line they trooped into three Pakistani positions northeast of Kargil. The Pakistani village of Avan was shelled, and some positions across the ceasefire line in Tithwal were attacked. The Indian army reached the Haji-Pir pass on 29 August. India had genuine justification for this military retaliation. Because Pakistan had violated the assurance it had given to the UN that it would not interrupt the Indian communication to Leh, the condition on which India evacuated Kargil. Besides, Pakistan's secret plans to grab the state of Jammu and Kashmir the very time the Kutch agreement was being signed was inconsistent with the norms of honesty and decency. To quote

Lal Bahadur Sastri: "The conscience of the world would be shocked to know that even at the time this agreement (on Kutch) was being signed, Pakistan had already drawn up a plan of armed infiltration into Kashmir and was training its personnel in Muree for the operations which were undertaken over a month later, even before the ink was dry on the agreement of June 30". Naturally India could not respond to such a move with a smiling face.

Attitude of both the parties became hardened. There was heavy shelling and prolonged military operations in Chamb-Bimbar area. Pakistani operators shelled the Poonch area and their occupation of Mandi continued unchecked. The escalation of tension between the two nations shook the conscience of the world. The United Nations took its initiative to bring them to the negotiation table. According to the suggestions of its observer in Kashmir, Gen. Nimmo, the UN called upon the warring nations to come to a bilateral agreement. The UK, USA and USSR too had expressed deep concern over the growing tension and urged both the nations to give up military operations. All these however proved ineffective.

All the subterranean methods having proved ineffective, the cobra hissed out openly. Finding the pretence and disguise useless, the dictator of Pakistan launched a major military attack, grandiloquently called 'Operation Grandslam', on 1 September 1965 in the Chhamb sector to capture Jammu and to bottle up the Indian army stationed there. Ayub dreamt of a decisive military victory, which would send tremors to New Delhi and help him triumphantly ride to Srinagar, Kashmir's capital city. He had hoped to succeed where the founder-father of Pakistan had failed. In an oratorical frenzy he unleashed the tigers of fanatical emotion against India. In his 'We are at war' broadcast of 6 September, Ayub declared: "The one hundred million people of Pakistan whose hearts beat with the sound of 'Illah Ill Illah Mohammad Rasul Illah' (There is one God and Mohammad is his prophet) will not rest till the Indian guns are silenced for ever". More over, Ayub was sure of the Chinese support for his nation in a collision with India. His strategy had evidently got the support of Beijing. On 4 September Chinese Foreign Minister, Marshal Chen Yi visited Karachi to hold discussions. The Chinese Premier Chau-En-Lai was keeping himself in touch with the developments. His visit to Karachi that preceded these developments was indeed a prelude to more Sino-Pakistan relations. Naturally Ayub expected of China to open a second front against India. And this would of course have happened, but for the warning from the USA and the USSR not to "fish in troubled waters". Pakistan's march into Chhamb continued unabated and by 5 September their total advance into Indian area there was 17 miles[17]. Having got a strong foothold in Chhamb sector, Pakistan army's Commander in Chief Gen. Mohammad Musa, addressed his soldiers thus: "You have got your teeth into him (the enemy). Bite deeper and deeper until he is destroyed. And destroy him you will"[18]. To India it was indeed a setback; she could not check the Pakistani invasion there. On the other hand Indian army advanced into Azad Kashmir, occupying Pakistani positions in the north of Tithwal. Indian Air Force boarded on Mig-21 was reported to have violated the Pakistani territory in strength. The two nations, as the *New York Times* reported, "for all practical purposes" were at war.

The war thus having begun, the world community began harping as usual on bilateral agreement. The UN Secretary General appealed earnestly "to indicate immediately... intention henceforth to respect the ceasefire agreement". Gen. Nimmo's official protest and urgent request of 4 September to withdraw the Pakistani troops from the Chhamb sector was simultaneous with the US sending a cable, requesting for immediate ceasefire[19]. The Soviet Premier Kosygin too urged a "reciprocal withdrawal" of troops and suggested "negotiations for the peaceful settlement". President Nasser of UAR, Tito of Yugoslavia and Lester Pearson, Prime Minister of Canada offered their good offices for mediation[20]. But these calls fell on deaf ears. True, India was responsive to the call for peace and to respect the voice of the international community. But she would not sacrifice her territorial integrity as she did many times earlier. Sastri, the Prime Minister was more determined and alive to realities than his imaginative and emotional predecessor. Along with reiterating his desire for peace, Sastri said: "What is essential ... today is that Pakistan should undertake forthwith to stop infiltration across the ceasefire line and to withdraw infiltrators and its armed forces from the Indian side of the ceasefire line, and the international frontier between Jammu and Kashmir and West Pakistan". He also wanted it to be ensured that the Secretary General of the UN "will ascertain from Pakistan if it will accept the responsibility for withdrawing not only its armed forces but also the infiltrators and for preventing further infiltration". But Pakistan remained evasive, and the later debate in the Security Council pertaining to the Chhamb occupation proved failure.

However, India could not remain a mute spectator to foreign incursions into her territories, and naturally she prepared herself to stem the tide of Pakistani aggression. Seeing her position in Chhamb hopeless, she planned to strike in some other area where she had an advantageous position[21]. It was planned to strike the enemy wherever possible, and Pakistan soon saw to its dismay that India wrested initiative from its hands by carrying the war close to the Lahore sector. On the morning of 6 September India opened a three-pronged offensive across the West-Pakistan border from Firozpur, Gurdaspur and Wagh-Amritsar area[22]. It was reported that Indian Army was moving towards Lahore Sialkot and Kasur. The Lahore bound army reached the outskirts of the city about fifteen miles from the border[23]. Pakistan was forced to switch from offensive to self-defense, and soon Pakistan tanks and artillery were seen moving back from Chhamb to the Lahore sector. The Pakistan army operation was on the verge of collapse. The war exploded the myth of Pakistan's military invincibility and also the propaganda that the defense of East Pakistan lay in the strongly defended West-Pakistan. While the Pakistani troops were making desperate bid to withstand Indian retaliation, the eastern wing was left absolutely defenseless. All what Bhutto told his people, was that the safety of East Pakistan was guaranteed by the Chinese[24]. On 16 September China served a three-day ultimatum on New Delhi, calling upon it "to immediately dismantle the military installations on the Chinese side of the Sikkim border or face serious consequences", and moved its troops threateningly to the Indian borders. But the firm and unwavering Sastri would not yield to threats and would not retrace his step. He made it no secret that "we are fully vigilant, and if we are attacked, we shall fight for our freedom and integrity. The might of China will not deter us from defending our territorial integrity". With total indifference to the Chinese threats, India inflicted severe reverses on Pakistani forces. And within fifteen days Ayub realized that his dream of unfurling the

Pakistani flag over Srinagar could not be realised. He knew that he would never win.

Having got an edge over the Pakistani soldiers, Indian army was preparing to bite deep into Lahore, and Pakistan began making frantic appeals to President Johnson of America to intervene. A defeated Ayub descended to the level of saying that "this business of taking bits of each other's territory is not the answer". The international community also made its public and private exhortations for ceasefire. Though Pakistan had already been advised by many nations to reach a peaceful settlement with India, in her arrogance she had ignored that call. But with humiliation of defeat, she responded to it quite warmly. India, not averse to any peaceful settlement, agreed to a ceasefire on 23 September and ended the twenty-two day war. However this can't be hailed as a victory for India in the sense that it could not silence the aggressive neighbour. True, India's performance in the war was better than that of its adversary. It had helped, as Major General P S Bhagat opined, "to wash clean the black mark against the army in general and the officers' corps in particular". But that the war was called off while it was to lead to a full-scale victory, which would have helped India settle all her dues with her hostile neighbour was indeed very unfortunate. As it was realized later, by having allowed an easy escape for a habitual aggressor who used to throw to winds the assurances she had given the international community time and again India had indeed committed a great blunder. Pakistan was just bowing to the occasion, and she bowed out quite easily from the self-invited defeat. And what India did was repeating her past mistakes. Naturally though the fighting stopped temporarily, the situation on the border continued to remain tense, as there was no disengagement of the forces. Though the Security Council repeated its call to both the sides to withdraw to the points they held on 5 August 1965, it was coldly ignored.

Soon there came the Soviet initiative. At the insistence of the Soviet Premier both the parties concerned reached Tashkent on 3 January 1966 for sorting out their differences[25]. Though the Tashkent conference started in a promising atmosphere, it could hardly achieve anything in Indo-Pakistan relations. Kosygin said, "the Government of Soviet Union was guided exclusively by the feelings of friendship for the people of Pakistan and India".

But a mere friendship was not enough to settle the Indo-Pal differences. The neutrality of the Soviet Union could not hel settle the enmity, and the basic problems between India an Pakistan that affected their relations remained unsolved. Tru there were pleasantries. The Prime Minister of India said, "th use of force in international relations can be justified only as necessity for repelling aggression. Our mutual assurance to rejec the use of force means, therefore, that each of us has agreed t respect the territorial integrity of the other"[26]. The territoria integrity thus had come up as the main issue. Ayub while replyin to Sastri's offer of a no-war pact said that an agreement rejectin war between the two countries could be effective "only in th event that it follows upon some specific measures for settlin the disputes that divide them". Thus both the parties state their positions tactfully. And in the evening of the first day o the conference a Pakistani spokesman said that if the problen of Jammu and Kashmir, "the root cause of the trouble was no settled, then Indo-Pakistan relation would collapse"[27]. Besides in private and informal talks with Kosygin the Pakistani Presiden conveyed his firm intention to raise the Kashmir issue on al possible occasions[28]. Naturally all meetings of the subsequen days failed to find a satisfactory solution to the Kashmir issue The bilateral attitude at Tashkent was well summed up in th report of the *Hindustan Times* of 10 January 1966. It wrote "Unless a miracle happens the Tashkent Conference should enc tomorrow on an unmistakable note of disagreement betweer Prime Minister Sastri and President Ayub Khan. A detente or any basic issue is considered impossible".

However on the sixth day both the parties reached a dramati agreement. They reaffirmed their obligation under the UN charte to abandon the means of force and to settle their disputes througl peaceful ways. Therefore, without referring to the Kashmi problem (which was left there surely to be settled on some othe plane than the negotiation table!) they entered into an agreemen for the time being. A nine-point declaration was signed which provided for the withdrawal of all armed personnel by both the sides to their 5 August position on a date not later than 25 February 1966. They also pledged to observe the ceasefire and to abide by the principles of noninterference in each other's internal affairs[29]. But there was neither a no-war pact nor an assurance from Pakistan that that it would not sent infiltrators into Kashmir in future. Thus the much-publicized Tashkent agreement was signed, leaving the basic issues untouched. This agreement, which had frustrated both the soldiers and Indian patriots, had however gained much publicity. Sastri described it as a "unique international agreement in diplomacy" while Ayub hailed it as "a new stage in the development of relations between India and Pakistan"[30]. However a critical analysis of things would bring out the exact nature of this much eulogised diplomatic victory and 'unique international agreement'. It was of course a diplomatic victory for the USSR since it averted any possible Chinese interference and helped the Soviet Russia emerge successful where the UN and the USA had failed. To India it was indeed a diplomatic defeat, a disgrace and shame. Having fallen into the Russian trap, her territorial integrity and national interests were jeopardized. As the then Bharatiya Jana Sangh leader A B Vajpayee described, it was "a betrayal of the assurance" given by the Government of India to its people and Parliament. And yet it could not satisfy Pakistan, for barely had the ink on the accord been dry Pakistan started to rearm itself to launch the next offensive against India in December 1971.

References

1. *Pakistan Times*, 31 May 1964.
2. D C Jha, *Op. Cit.*, p. 144.
3. *Pakistan Times*, 14 October 1964.
4. *Ibid.*, 30 May 1964.
5. Christian Kind, "Move on Kashmir", *Swiss Review of World Affairs*, Zurich, October 1964, p. 12.
6. *The Hindu*, 6 June 1964.
7. *Ibid.*, 30 June 1964.
8. *Times of India*, 31 March 1965.
9. V B Kulkarni, *Pakistan: Its Origin and Relations with India*, p. 155.
10. Maharaj K. Chopra, *India: The Search for Power*, Bombay, 1969, pp. 291-292.
11. D C Jha, *Op.Cit.*, p. 228.
12. V B Kulkarni, *Op. Cit.*, p.155.
13. *The Statesman*, 12-15 August 1965.

14. Lok Sabha Debates, Series 3, Vol. 44, 16 August 1965, Col. 128-30, quoted in D C Jha, *Op. Cit.*
15. *Pakistan Times*, 14 August 1965.
16. *The Statesman*, 12 August 1965.
17. *New York Times* (International edition, 7 September 1965.
18. *New York Times* (City edition) 6 September 1965.
19. *The Statesman*, 4 September 1965.
20. *The Hindu*, 4 September 1969.
21. *New York Times* (International Edn.), 7 September 1965.
22. *The Hindu*, 7 September 1965.
23. *New York Times* (International Edn.), 7 September 1965.
24. V B Kulkarni, *Op. Cit.*, p. 156.
25. *The Statesman*, 4 January 1966.
26. S S Bindra, *Indo-Pak Relations*, New Delhi, 1981, p. 54.
27. *The Statesman*, 5 January 1966.
28. *The Hindustan Times*, 5 January 1966.
29. *The Statesman*, 11 January 1966.
30. S S Bindra, *Op. Cit.*, p. 59.

6

The Crescent Breaks Apart

(The War of 1971)

The innumerable meetings on the negotiation table could not avert the possibilities of a collision between India and Pakistan. Kashmir continued to be the hotspot. The problem of East Bengal Muslims who formed the Pakistani minority loaded India with the unbearable burden owing to their exodus to India to escape Pakistan's governmental tyranny. The internal ills of Pakistan, political tyranny as well as economic discrimination, did affect India, its nearest neighbour. The war of 1971 too, like all the earlier wars, was the aftermath of Pakistan's domestic turmoil.

As referred to earlier, ever since the origin of Pakistan its eastern and western wings were not on good terms[1]. To the economic disparity between East Bengal and West Pakistan, and the latter's bureaucratic highhandedness over the former were added many other problems related to culture, language and politics, resulting in an unprecedented conflagration. On almost all issues Pakistan acted like a terrorist state, which used to terrorise its own people in order to silence their protests and get them succumb to many antidemocratic policies and arbitrary administrative measures the Government of Islamabad took. Pakistan was a typical Islamic state or theocracy, which followed the tyrannical policy of wiping out a particular language in order to destroy its related culture and incorporate the subject people into the conqueror's way of life. Indeed Pakistan excelled all the other Islamic states in this aspect. The Bengali speaking sophisticated Muslims with their cultural roots steeped in the traditions of Bengal were always a neglected lot. The tyrants of West Pakistan did not give the East Bengalis an equal status in

Pakistan's public life. There was no psychic accommodation and the Government failed to give justice to the East Bengalis. Indeed from an administration, which had years ago bombed the Id gathering of the Baluchis to teach them a lesson, no people could expect any better deal. The cultural differences between the East Bengal and West Pakistan grew unbridgeable. The Islam prevailing in the East Bengal was more flexible, enlightened and accommodative than the rigid one of West Pakistan. Having got a graceful touch of the Hindu, Buddhist and animistic practices, it was tolerant of other sects and faiths, and the practice of Hindus and Muslims enthusiastically participating in each other's festivals was a common sight in East Bengal. This enlightenment of the East Bengalis inspired them to have a culturally developed system of administration, which the West Pakistanis opposed tooth and nail. Islamabad was hell-bent on destroying this cultural identity of the East Bengalis and sought to bring them down to the level of savagery common to the West Pakistanis. As a maiden step in the direction of demoralizing the Bengalis, the Pakistan Government started moves to force on them Urdu as their lingua-franca. In the Constituent Assembly its Bengali members were denied permission to speak in their mother tongue. But proud of the rich heritage of Bengali language and culture, the East Pakistanis could not reconcile themselves to Urdu becoming their official language. There was protest as far back as the time of Liaqat Ali Khan who opined that "Pakistan is a Muslim state and it must have its lingua-franca, the language of the Muslim nation. It is necessary for a nation to have one language and that language can only be Urdu". The administration of Islamabad tried to make the people believe that the best way to hold together the two geographical pieces of Pakistan was the enforcement of one language and one culture. And the Pakistani Government audaciously started the imposition of Urdu on East Bengal. Already the 1951 census showed 54.6 per cent of the East Pakistanis as Bengali speaking, and only 7.2 per cent as Urdu speaking. But this reality notwithstanding, the Government declared Urdu as the National Language, and followed a ruthless and remorseless imposition of it on the Bengalis[2]. Naturally the Bengalis met this with violent reactions, and Dacca, the seat of higher learning became the hotbed of discontent. The forcible assimilation policy could only drive a wedge between the two wings. The linguistic discrimination was combined with the educational deprivation the East Bengalis suffered. An assessment of the educational records of the early two decades of Pakistan makes it clear that despite the considerable increase in the number of students the number of primary schools in East Pakistan had only fallen owing to the governmental policy of deliberate negligence. This was against the four and a half times increase in the number of such schools in West Pakistan. The governmental policy of dehumanizing and deintellectualising was carried on through all possible means with the result that the East Pakistanis developed the suspicion that their province was becoming a colony of the West Pakistan. The plight of the East Bengalis was well summed up by Sheik Mujibur Rehman in his graphic description, "*swadhin deshe paradhin nagarik*" (dependent citizens of an independent country). As could be expected, this naturally triggered off a national feeling among the East Bengalis who felt constrained to think of the need of an administration of their own that would rid them of the exploitation of West Pakistan.

However, it should not be misunderstood that the East Bengalis were turning anti-Pakistanis. Indeed they did their best to avoid any possible breach with the west through peaceful and constitutional methods. As a measure to redress the grievances of the East Bengalis and to ensure the integrity of Pakistan, Mujibur Rehman enumerated his famous Six-Point Programme at an all-party convention held at Lahore on 12 February 1966. The six points were:

1. The constitution should provide for a federation of Pakistan in the true sense on the basis of the Lahore Resolution and for a Parliamentary form of Government based on the supremacy of a directly elected legislature on the basis of universal adult franchise.
2. The Federal Government shall deal only with two subjects – defence and foreign affairs – with all residuary subjects vested in the federating states.
3. There should be either two separate, freely convertible currencies for the two wings or one currency with two separate Reserve Banks to prevent inter-wing flight of capital.
4. Fiscal policy shall be the responsibility of the federating units, which would be vested with the power of taxation

and revenue collection. The federal government shall be provided with requisite revenue resources for meeting the requirements of defence and foreign affairs.

5. Constitutional provisions shall be made to enable separate accounts to be maintained of the foreign exchange earnings of each of the federating units, under the control of the respective governments of the federating units.

6. The governments of the federating units shall be empowered to maintain militia or paramilitary force in order to contribute towards national security.[3]

Mujibur Rehman's demands, which were entirely in order, received rousing approbation in East Pakistan. The popular appeal of the Six-Point programme was so unnerving to the Ayub administration that as one could expect the military administration at Islamabad went on with its usual tirade against East Bengal. As any sane man could think, if this scheme would have been accepted it would have averted the possible breach of East Bengal with West Pakistan. But this would never dawn to the Pakistani leader. Addressing a gathering at Rajshahi on 16 March 1966, Ayub scoffed at the Six-Point Programme, and misinterpreted it as aiming at the birth of a greater sovereign Bengal, and threatened that the fulfillment of such a "horrid dream" would spell disaster for the country, and turn the East Pakistanis into slaves[4]. Speaking at the Muslim League session at Dacca, he asked its delegates to be prepared to face even a civil war likely to be forced on them, to protect the sovereignty and integrity of the country[5]. During his tempestuous visit to East Bengal, the President of Pakistan warned the people of East Bengal against becoming mad after the Six-Point Programme, and that the denial of his warning would entail severe consequences. But this could not douse the revolutionary fervour generated by Mujibur Rehman and his new programme. Giving scant regard to the fire-breathings of the President, the movement went on gathering unprecedented tempo. Sheik Mujib and Fazzal Hussain who spearheaded the movement rejected all the offers of the West Pakistani clique as prizes for abandoning the movement. The movement had unleashed so great a popular uprising that during the first two months of 1969 many were killed, injured and arrested. Ayub could not carry on any longer. Already the

Islamabad administration had become the synonym for corruption, which flourished against the backdrop of increasing administrative chaos[6]. There was increasing popular turmoil, and Ayub saw himself on a seat of thorns. Having found it difficult to carry on any more and finding no other alternative, he bowed out of office under the pressure of the very same army that had sustained him in power. On 25 March, Ayub announced to his people that General Aga Mohammad Yahya Khan had been requested to take over the responsibilities of the Government. He justified his handing over acknowledging that the whole country had been plunged into "an abyss of senseless agitation by well-tutored and well-backed elements"[7].

Pakistan, finding herself in a precarious state and seized with the fear of an impending dismemberment, called for a sagacious and resourceful statesman. But already ruled out by the world military experts as not fit enough to become a military General, Yahya was not the man for the occasion. "His incurable addiction to carnal pleasures and his limited mental faculties undermined his capacities to deal with the grave situation"[8]. True he seemed to be promising when he declared: "My aim is to transfer power to the elected representatives of the people"[9]. But there were discernible similarities between the regimes of Ayub and Yahya except in that the latter made his policy decisions in consultation with the top brass of the administration just to commit his peers to "collective responsibility for the unforeseen and unpopular results"[10]. It had been sarcastically said that Yahya, "the best of brutal bunch", was acting like an egalitarian in accepting his colleagues' advice. Yahya's aim as could be well understood was to perpetuate the predominance of military rule with the help of democratic approval though he never appreciated the inherent strength of democratic aspirations. Even when he made the announcement for the conduct of 1970 elections, he was confident that none of the political outfits of Pakistan would be able to get sufficient seats in the Assembly to form a majority government. But it proved a national misfortune that he failed to make an exact estimate of the potential aspirations of the East Bengalis and to act according to the verdict of the ballot box. All of a sudden he issued the legal framework order (30 March 1970) clearly laying down the scheme for the composition of national and provincial assemblies, the criteria for becoming their members, their allowances, privileges, etc[11]. In the three hundred member National Assembly of Pakistan Mujibur Rehman's Awami League party secured a sweeping majority. It got 160 seats as against Zulfiqar Ali Bhutto's Pakistan People's Party's 86 seats. Having come out as the leader of the majority party, Mujib was to be selected as the Prime Minister of Pakistan in accordance with the democratic principles, and he was declared the future Prime Minister of Pakistan by Gen. Yahya[12]. A jubilant Mujib, confident of forming the government, declared his intention to implement his Six-Point Programme. But that he would neither form the government nor would implement his scheme was in Pakistan's political destiny, and that Pakistan could not rid itself of the curse of military regime was written on its fate-line.

Power hunger is more intoxicating than erotic pleasures, and it often overrides all considerations of justice and prudence. And the clamour for power was the usual Pakistani scenario, which has been its bane throughout its very short period of political existence. Bhutto was typical of a power monger who would resort to any unjust means provided it would install him in the seat of authority. The assembly election had indeed made him kiss the dust in popularity though not in humility. But he was not prepared to accept the reality of his political plummeting. With only a handful of seats in the Assembly, Bhutto was still audacious to make it open that he would not cooperate with the new political developments in Pakistan unless he was chosen the Prime Minister! He was not prepared to sit in the opposition bench[13]. With no respect for democratic standards, he put forth a new scheme no national minded citizen could think of – two Prime Ministers for one country! Indeed the father of this theory of two Prime Ministers for one country did not mind whether his highly unpatriotic proposal, if endorsed, would lead to the partition of Pakistan. To see his dream fulfilled Bhutto coined a shamelessly convenient scheme. He suggested that while transferring power at the centre, it should be to the two major parties of East and West Pakistan. "Our position", he said "is that the majority party in East Pakistan together with the majority in West Pakistan could democratically represent the country"[14]. Bhutto had thus mired the entire nation in a political impasse, which could have been avoided but for President Yahya Khan's stand, which buried all the scruples and principles of statesmanship.

If Yahya had stood firm using the argument of force against Bhutto's audaciously barbaric political stand, perhaps the situation could have been saved. But he did nothing of the kind because he too, like most of the Punjabis, could not reconcile to the idea of Bengalis becoming supreme in Pakistan's governmental affairs[15]. Besides, though Yahya had earlier masqueraded as the saviour of Pakistan's democratic polity and declared Mujib as the future Prime Minister, he knew that the growing political mess in the country would help him too. Depending on the convenient excuse regarding the futility of holding the Pakistan National Assembly session when P.P.P. and other parties had fallen out with the majority party, he decided to postpone the opening of the Assembly. Yahya Khan's announcement about the indefinite postponement of the National Assembly session, which was broadcast on 1 March 1971, came as a rude shock to the East Bengalis who took it as a breach of faith and a supreme act of treachery. Besides, Yahya made a futile attempt to make the political parties forget their differences and stand together under his military rule by taking up the Pakistani rulers' usual stock-in-trade, the 'Hate-India' propaganda. Thinking that the anti-India propaganda would make the Pakistani political parties stand united against the common enemy, Yahya said, "the general situation of tension created by India has further complicated the whole position"[16].

Mujibur Rehman was however adamant and would not play into the hands of General Yahya nor compromise his programme in letter or spirit. Having realized the futility of negotiations and decent deliberations, the Awami League launched a civil disobedience movement with strikes being observed throughout the length and breadth of East Pakistan. Sensing the impending problems he had to face from the East Bengal, Yahya had already geared up the military engine to face any eventuality. Step by step he took all required measures to tighten the military control over the Pakistan's administrative machinery. He dissolved his civilian cabinet on 21 February and started taking his top army officers including martial administrators into confidence with an eye on securing the full cooperation and the collective involvement of the fighting machine in his future programme. Censorship was clamped down on the press, which was barred from reporting the clandestine movements of the army officers except in context of the official press release[17]. Under the pretext of Indo-Pakistani tension consequent on the 30 January hijacking incident, which was apparently stage-managed by Pakistan itself purposefully, Yahya began to mobilize the defence forces. Armed forces and a large supply of ammunition were ordered to Dacca. The Pakistan Air Force airdropped soldiers in large numbers. Tanks were brought to Dacca from their defensive positions on the Indian border. It was, as every movement conveyed, a preparation for a military retaliation to the Bengali uprising. In fact by the time of Yahya's March announcement of the postponement of the Assembly session the Pakistan army had been prepared to suppress the rows and riots it would spark off.

The Presidential announcement, postponing the Assembly session caused widespread disgust among the East Pakistanis. As it would result in an uncontainable conflagration Yahya had effected some changes in the top brass of the military administration there. He had replaced Vice Admiral S M Ashan with Gen. Tikka Khan. Ashan, renowned for his gentleness and generosity, Yahya knew, would not fit in the butcher's role necessary to execute his scheme in East Bengal. Already this General appeared to have been one of the few officers who had expressed their reservations regarding many of Yahya's dictatorial policies. Tikka was of an entirely different character, and was of hot temperament. He had started his life as an illiterate soldier in Pakistan Army who never graduated to any higher standard of intellect or culture despite the high ranks he rose to in his service. A military man of the lowest caliber, the confidential report about him read "this man is not fit for higher rank". To this expert in manslaughter, terrorising the masses was the best solution to the problems. "Carnage was Tikka Khan's religion and he vigorously practiced the three R's of war – ruthless, relentless and remorseless"[18]. Arson, stabbing, massacre, mass-rape and all the associated barbarities this general of butchery unleashed against the people of East Bengal which can well be counted as a chapter of man's inhumanity to man were of unimaginable magnitude even to the most notorious criminals of history. No wonder, Tikka was to Yahya the right choice!

The protests and agitations in Dacca proved beyond the control of the Eastern Command of the Pakistan Army. About the situation in East Bengal an Indian military expert makes the following observation:

> Had the massed crowed in its fervour and commitment marched on the relatively unprepared Eastern Command Head Quarters of the Pakistan Army and demanded immediate surrender, the Bangladesh might that day have emerged as a new nation. Certainly a price would have been paid in lives – but it would have been cheaper than that which has ultimately been paid.[19]

The Army Head Quarters was indeed caught in a tense mood over its incapability to meet the situation. Tikka had no alternative than to rush the message "Give me enough force and I'll crush them in 48 hours". He urged to 'overkill'. Yahya who knew that the forces mobilized to East Pakistan were not sufficient to deal with the Bengali uprising which would take the wind out of his sails now wanted some more time for the reinforcement of his army for the final showdown.

Now the General turned out to be the jackal of diplomacy. He enacted the most treacherous drama. The report came overnight that the charismatic leadership of Sheik Mujibur Rehman, the growing demand in West Pakistan for the transfer of power to the Mujib group and the swiftly eroding foundations of Bhutto's political influence compelled President Yahya Khan to adopt a conciliatory attitude towards Mujib. The talks between Yahya and the leaders of Awami League held at Dacca seemed promising and mutually accommodative. The attitude of Yahya was so entertaining that it appeared to Mujib and his followers on 23 March that they would be called to take over power. On 25 March Yahya left Dacca.

But it was only on the next day the East Bengalis came to know of the evil designs of Yahya. Tajudin Ahmed who acted as Chief Minister of East Bengal during the incarceration of Mujib, observed that the Dacca discussions were in fact stage-managed as a "strategy of deception". General Yahya gave an impression of negotiating with Sheik Mujibur Rehman while the West Pakistani forces in East Bengal were being reinforced[20]. The negotiation drama created so artful a delay that by 25 March six shiploads of West Pakistani troops were transported to the province. The Army was now fully prepared and there was no more need for any pretence.

Though it was only on 26 March that Yahya declared all political parties in East Bengal banned, in the night of 25th itself the Pakistani Army started its crack down over the people there. Having seen Mujibur Rehman arrested, Yahya arranged for his own get away to West Pakistan, entrusting everything to Tikka Khan. Already crowned with the epithet 'Butcher of the Beluchis', Tikka started to handle the Bengal issue in his own characteristic style! The West Pakistanis could not however wipe out from the bosoms of the Bengalis what they held dear and desirable – autonomy from the butchers of the west, and Mujib's declaration of East Bengal as the independent state of Bengladesh received massive support[21].

But this would not reduce the gravity of the witch-hunt of the Pakistani Army. Many unimpeachable authorities testify to the brutality of operations against the unarmed people. The killers from West Pakistan practiced a massive genocide from 26 March till they were thrown out in December. The army operation aimed at exterminating the minorities and to treat the Muslim elite similarly to convert the entire province into a land of docile slaves. Antony Mascarenhas, Correspondent of the *Sunday Times* of London, reported on how the Hindus in East Bengal were either exterminated or dehumanised. He wrote:

> I saw Hindus hunted from village to village and door to door, shot offhand after a cursory 'short-arm inspection' showed they were uncircumcised.

This barbarity had behind it a religious justification. It was propagated that so long as Hindus or any other infidels live in East Bengal, the Bengali Muslims would never become the true followers of Islam[22]. The military opened a reign of terror against the Muslim intellectuals and those who refused to give up their mother tongue and cultural tradition. The University of Dacca with its lofty tradition of culture and education became the target of attack. Both its boys and girls stubbornly resisted to be dehumanised. The academics of the University had always been strongly opposed to the dictatorial policies of the Pakistani Government. And already in 1969 there were sporadic incidents in which its young women had hurled brickbats at the police from its dormitories to register their protests against the oppressive regime[23]. Now in 1971 the Pakistani soldiers got a long awaited opportunity to 'teach' the students and their elders a lesson that would follow them to their grave. The mendacious hordes in military uniform attacked the university campus with machine guns and systematically leveled its buildings to ground. After hunting down the inmates of the university in hundreds, the frenzied 'jihadists' preyed upon the intellectuals in the city, the doctors, the lawyers, engineers and other educated classes who formed the brain and muscle of the Bengali intelligentsia. East Bengal had already been the victim of a natural calamity. Hit by cyclone in 1970, which claimed around some 500,000 lives, it requested the Islamabad administration for help, to which Yahya had responded stating "my government is not made up of angels"[24]. To this already suffering region the manslaughter of 1971 proved the last straw on the camel's back. Villages and towns saw the dance of death on the corpse of about three million. The number of those left homeless amounted to twenty million. The bipeds in military uniform took thousands of young women and girls forcibly to the military camps to be dishonoured as prostitutes[25]. The Pakistan army went on with its rampage, forcing the Bengalis ruthlessly out of their settlements. As the pressure mounted political cadres and professionals, intellectuals and personnel from army and civil services fled to India. The Pakistan Army lashed out into rural areas bordering with India, unleashing terror, loot, arson and mass rape throughout the length and breadth of East Bengal. Millions who survived unfortunately to see their homes and property either destroyed or looted, started their exodus to India, which embarked on a massive relief operation for the migrants. India received assistance through various international agencies and foreign governments to feed and accommodate these refugees. Even the World Bank served its warning on India that her economic development would be seriously stunted by the cost of supporting the refugees. The report estimated that if the refugee population would rise to nine million as was expected, the cost of the refugees upkeep for India's fiscal year 1971-72, would amount to about $ 700 million. Already by the end of August 1971 it cost India nearly Rs.376 million. All these notwithstanding, India's endeavours to mobilize international opinion against the Pakistani policy of driving refugees to India brought forth hardly any response. The military operation of Pakistan aimed at making East Bengal culturally and politically sterile was to undermine India's political stability, communal harmony, social progress and economic development since she was to accommodate and feed thousands of refugees from East Pakistan and to contain the fifth columnist and the pro-Pakistani fanatic elements[26]. In addition to the mounting military and refugees pressure, Pakistan sent a large number of spies and saboteurs to India to ferret out military secrets, destroy important installations and disrupt transport and communication system. These intruders were also instructed to create communal tension in India to weaken Indian Government's ability to meet the new situation effectively.

But India was not a nation of plentitude so as to share her prosperity with the newcomers. With her own problems, which were of Himalayan proportion India could not pull on any longer feeding the Bangladeshis. And naturally she was compelled to find some way to check the East Bangali incursion. The Government of India started a worldwide campaign to pressurise the comity of nations against Yahya's policy of exterminating the Bengalis. On 2 November, the Prime Minister of India, Mrs. Indira Gandhi stated in London about India's determination not to be "saddled with another country's problem" and that "all refugees must go back". But her mission in the West yielded hardly any result. The non-cooperation movement the Awami League launched in self-defence transformed itself into an armed resistance almost amounting to a war of independence. The East Bengali youth who were left homeless consequent to the Pakistani military outrage, organized to train themselves in the use of arms and started guerilla activities causing untold havoc to the Pakistani forces. When it seemed difficult for Pakistan to stem the tide of the awakening Bangladesh nationalism she thought it wise to place the onus of the outbreak on India so that she may get the help of China or the US whose anti-Indian stand was evident on many previous occasions. Already on 30 January 1971 an India Airlines Fokker Friendship Aircraft was hijacked, and was blown up in full view of television camera at Lahore Airport on 2 February[27]. Since Pakistan failed to book the culprits in line with the UN resolution on aerial hijacking, India banned the over-flights of Pakistan aircraft across its airspace. In addition to the complaints made to the Security Council about the restrictions on the flights across the Indian airspace, Pakistan escalated tension moving her troops to the Indian frontier. Meanwhile the liberation forces inside East Bengal liberated large areas in many districts where they set up local administration. Lead by General Osmani, they pressed forward from the liberated enclaves and territories[28]. However, the Pakistani Army repeated attacks on the liberated areas and organized widespread sabotage in Nadia, Cooch Behar, Dinajpore and Karimganj Districts. On 21 November 1971 they launched a major attack on a liberated area near Boyra. Overrunning the Mukti Bahini (Liberation Force) positions, the Pakistani tanks advanced towards the Indian border where thirteen of them were destroyed by the Indian forces. The Indian Air Force Gnats gunned down three of the four Pakistani Saberjets, which intruded into India's territory. Declaring a state of emergency, General Yahya Khan announced that he would start fighting a war within the next ten days. On 3 December 1971 he ordered pre-emptive air strikes on a number of Indian airfields in imitation of the Israeli 'Blitzkrieg' of 1967 against Egypt[29]. On the same day at 5.47 PM Pakistan launched surprise air strikes on India's forward airfields all along the border near Punjab and Rajasthan. Pakistan made 24 air strikes on India's airfields and installations at Avantipur, Srinagar, Amritsar, Pathankot, Faridkot and Agra. But this imitation of the Israeli 'Blitzkrieg' proved very poor since India was fully prepared to counter the Pakistani treachery. Well informed of the possibility of Pakistani attack, India could properly retaliate in time. Mrs. Gandhi, India's Prime Minister, in her broadcast at twenty minutes past midnight called upon her people to stand united and repel the aggressive designs of the enemy. And by the dawn of 4 December the Indian Air Force fighter-bombers were on their wings, unleashing relentless bombardments at Chander, Risalwala, Kohat, Peshawar, Mianwali, Murid, Walton and Shorkot. The oil storage tank at Keamari, the Karachi port, was bombarded and set aflame.

Addressing his people in a broadcast on 6 December, Gen. Yahya said: "God willing, the holy jihad against the treacherous enemy, India, will continue till the victory is ours". God was but unwilling to help a tyrant whose victory would have dug the grave of the East Bengalis and fastened untold problems on India. Soon to his dismay, General Yahya found his army on two fronts, on the eastern front under General A A K Niazi and on the west under Tikka Khan. Notwithstanding his own incapability and of his Generals, Yahya harboured high hopes owing to his expectation that his close allies America and China would not wait to see Pakistan eating the humble pie. The anti-Indian interest of China had been time tested and its policy of silent acceptance of Yahya's military savagery on the people of East Bengal had further boosted up his animosity. Though during the Indo-Pakistan war of 1965 the US had warned China 'not to fish in troubled waters' its political and diplomatic attitude towards India by now had undergone a total difference. Richard Nixon, now the President of America, tended as far back as 1954 itself "to favour military aid to Pakistan as a counterforce to the continued neutralism of Jawaharlal Nehru's India", and his advisor, Dr. Henry Kissinger's subterranean diplomacy and mysterious movements had done away with all possibilities of fostering the Delhi-Washington intimacy. Shortly after the outbreak of the war the US stopped all economic aid to India and sent her seventh fleet to the Bay of Bengal to bully her. Besides, Pakistan invoked the help of the Arab countries, which sent American bomber aircrafts to strengthen her air arms. About ten F-104 Jordanian aircrafts were in Pakistan as was confirmed by the States Department spokesman, Robert Mc Closkey[30]. Yahya's evil designs expressed themselves in many ways including the scheme to seize Amritsar and nearby areas to be welded into Khalistan and to turn it into a bargaining counter for acquiring Kashmir. Fully alive to the clandestine moves of the enemies, India got herself ready militarily and diplomatically. The Indo-Soviet treaty of 1971 brought for her a strong friend and elevated her status in international politics. This treaty, the Article 9 of which provided that "in the event of either party being subjected to an attack or a threat thereof, the high contracting parties shall immediately enter into mutual consultations in order to remove such threat and to take appropriate effective measures to ensure peace and security of their countries" obviously meant that if China or the USA would assist Pakistan against India the USSR would step in on the latter's side. This military alliance ensured that Pakistan would not be helped by both of her allies.

Having fully reinforced itself with a well prepared military and friendly relation with Moscow and being subjected to pressure from all the Indian Parliamentarians irrespective of party difference, India announced its recognition of Bangladesh on 6 December and started retaliatory action in East Pakistan by establishing military links with the Mukti Bahini to isolate the Pakistani forces in the east and to liberate Bangla Desh from them at the earliest[31]. When the Pakistani military buildup on the eastern and western sectors began to crumble before the advancing Indian Army, Yahya hoped to make good this loss by trying to capture Kashmir by gathering his armed might in the Chhamb sector so that he might, by making a breakthrough into Kashmir, isolate it from the rest of India. Pakistan even erected a temporary lodgement across the Munnawar Tavi, but was pushed back across the river[32]. In Poonch also the Pakistani attack was beaten back. Attempt for a second attack was foiled through carpet-bombing by AN-12 Aircraft and Vampire attacks.

In the western sector Indian military proved its mettle and might. In Punjab, Pakistani forces shelled and attacked Indian border posts from Dera Baba Nanak in the north to Anupgarh in the south. The Pakistani battalions, reinforced by armour and artillery, unleashed similar attacks on Indian positions at Hussainiwala and Fazilka. They also mounted an attack on the Ranian-Shamsher and Fatehpur Burj salients. But all these initial Pakistani efforts were successfully beaten back by the Indian forces. Clearing away the Pakistani forces from the posts they occupied, the Indian Army triggered off its counter attacks. In the Partapur sector India improved her positions along the Shyok Valley and captured thirty-six out of the total eighty Pakistani posts in Kargil[33]. By occupying the Chicken Neck salient near Jammu, the Indian Army could successfully forestall the Pakistani threat to the Indian line of communication to Akhnour. In Rajasthan as well as in Kutch Indian forces were equally victorious. In Kutch, Indian Army captured Nagarparkar, Virawah, Vingoor, and the Chhad Bet Complex. The success the Indian Army had made was so great that by the time of ceasefire in the western sector, Indian forces were holding 5,619.06 square miles of Pakistani territory as against 121.32 square miles of Indian area under Pakistani occupation. Indian Navy had presented a very spectacular performance. Bombarding Karachi and some minor ports on the Makran coast, and sinking Pakistani destroyers and minesweepers, it operated on the high seas effectively.

East Bengal saw the Pakistani reinforcement on a massive scale. It consisted of about thirty-five infantry battalions, four thousand Frontier Corps Troops, twenty-five thousand East Pakistani Civil Armed Forces, thirty-five thousand armed Razakars, five thousand West Pakistani Police Personnel, two squadrons of armour, six artillery regiments, twenty Sabre Jet Aircrafts and a large number of gunboats. It was indeed a tartar to be defeated, and the Indian Army was to undertake a tough operation in East Bengal since its terrain did not permit swift movement of heavy armour. But this disadvantage hardly stood in the way of Indian forces thanks to the support of the Mukti Bahini, which by establishing itself into regular formations of sizable strength, alienated the Pakistani forces from the population. Through elusive methods, and guerilla warfare the Mukti Bahini succeeded in making the invaders "blind and deaf", confessed General A A K Niazi, after the Pakistani surrender. The East Bengali students, under the leadership of Quadir Siddique had very ably backed the Mukti Bahini led by Colonel M A G Osmani. The daring operations by the Indian Air Force and Navy had a great demoralizing effect on the Pakistani soldiers. The air coverage the I A F provided for the Indian Army and the bombardments the Indian Navy unleashed against the Pakistani naval posts had great encouraging effect on the Indian armed forces.

The joint operation of the Indian 'Mitra Bahini' and the Bengladesh 'Mukti Bahini' took the enemy by surprise. In the eastern sector, Shamshernagar including the airfield and Majilispur Suigon fell within no time. In the northwestern sector Thakurgaon was taken while Darsana and Gazipur in the western sector could hardly withstand any longer. On the fifth and sixth of December, Indian Army captured many key communication centres and other positions. By December 7, when the Indian Army stormed into Jessore Contonment, took Lalmonirhat and Sylhet and trooped towards Chandpur, the Pakistani defences were virtually crumbling. The Indian Navy captured six Pakistani merchant ships in the Bay of Bengal. On 8 December when the Indian Army, taking the fortresses of Comilla and Brahmanbaria, barged on to Dacca to round up that town, the Pakistani soldiers made a frantic effort retreating to Barisal and Narayanganj in a bid to escape by the sea route, which was blocked by the Indian Navy[34]. By 13 December, Pakistan was facing a complete defeat. On the same day General Manekshaw, Chief of Indian Army

Staff, asked Major General Rao Farman Ali, military advisor to the Pakistani Governor in Dacca, to surrender so that the Dacca bound Indian Army might not be constrained to reduce the Pakistani garrison with force. General A A K Niazi decided that surrender was preferable to futile resistance, which would only result in heavy loss of lives. Thus on 16 December he signed the instrument of unconditional surrender, the signatory on the Indian side being Lieutenant General Jagjit Singh Aurora of the Indian army. The liberation of Bangladesh was completed, and on 17 December India announced a unilateral ceasefire expecting a "corresponding immediate response from the Government of Pakistan"[35]. Though Yahya Khan realized that East Bengal was irretrievably lost he was not prepared to give up his bluster, and continued boasting before his ignorant people that the "Ghasis of Pakistan" would become silent only after recovering every inch of the Pakistani territory. But his fire breathings soon ceased and his government agreed to stop all fighting. Yahya Khan, after bequeathing the dishonour of defeat to Zulfiqar Ali Bhutto, bowed out of his office on 20 December 1971.

The war that came to an end on 17 December had some moralizing effect on India and her Army. Indian victory was rightly hailed as a triumph of right over wrong, of secularism over bigotry, of moral values over brute force, of the will of the people over the conspiracy of the few. "This victory had ended a monstrosity in geography and started a new chapter in history"[36]. After having defeated Pakistan, India did not want to wreak vengeance on that nation in any way. Pakistan ever since her birth has been a thorn in the Indian flesh. Her inhuman relationship with India did not deserve any sympathetic treatment. All this notwithstanding, India did not want to destroy Pakistan. With her commitment to the long drawn tradition of non-aggression, India was not desirous of annexing her neighbour's territory. India's aim was only to help liberate Bangladesh, and as that was done she did not press for anything more and was ready to come to terms with Pakistan forgetting that it had unnecessarily forced on her the burden of a war. As one of India's former Presidents, R Venkata raman stated some years ago, India took a "better way to transform enmity into friendship and to change history's unhappy course"[37]. India's declaration of ceasefire at the right time, which revealed that war was not to her an end in itself raised her prestige as strict adherer to the principles of peace, and cleared the misunderstanding created by the Pakistani scandals that India is an aggressor state. True, Pakistan broke into two, but India did not seek it. It was indeed an unexpected development born out of her own inhuman and oppressive policies against her fellow citizens for which India could not be blamed. India only helped liberate an innocent people who had been groaning under the tyranny of West Pakistan by her timely intervention. This being the exact state of affairs, any freedom-loving nation or people could only think of India as a doughty defender of freedom, not only of her own, but of her oppressed neighbours as well.

The breakup of the crescent was the will and verdict of history, which could in no way have been averted. Lord Mountbatten, before his tragic death in August 1979, explained that he did everything in his power "to save India as a unity". He said,

> I have often told the tale of how I pursued him (Jinnah) with argument upon argument, but nothing would shake him. He was fanatical in his desire to build Pakistan as a Muslim state. The fact that he could not even build one state, that there had to be two, almost 1000 miles apart did not deter him.

The last Viceroy of India, having no doubt in his mind that such an arrangement was bound to collapse, told Jinnah that the two parts of Pakistan would break up within twenty-five years of its independence[38]. That a state born of fanaticism and bigotry could not stand long is the lesson the history of Pakistan presents. Bengal had thus gone out of Pakistani control, and if the policy of arrogance and suppression is to be continued, there is the likelihood of Sind, Baluchistan and other dissatisfied areas following the Bangladesh example. Blaming India would not wash Pakistan of its blame for the loss of her eastern parts. It was born out of the irresponsibility and recklessness of her dealings with her own people. But Pakistan would not learn any lesson that history taught her.

The Indo-Pakistan hostility came to a temporary halt with the signing of the Simla Agreement. In the summit, which opened on 28 June 1972 in Simla, Mrs. India Gandhi warmly welcomed Mr. Z A Bhutto. Bhutto said that he too was sincere to respond to the wishes of the people of the subcontinent who were fed up with the past strife and conflicts and were eager to see a chapter of friendship and amity opened in Indo-Pakistan relations[39]. On the second day of the summit the talks reached a "crucial stage" with Mrs. Gandhi insisting on an over all settlement which would cover some basic issues along with those arising from the December war. Since such a settlement would involve the Kashmir problem also, Pakistan remained silent on it. In fact Pakistan's stand was very much judicious. She wanted to get back the occupied territories and the prisoners of war before the talks would pass on to the Kashmir dispute. Following this, India drew the attention of Pakistan to the need of solving the outstanding disputes and the establishment of a durable peace, which would be possible only through the settlement of the Kashmir issue. But Bhutto wanted that the Kashmir issue be "frozen and tackled at a more propitious time". On the contrary, he demanded the release of the prisoners of war by India as a preliminary step towards a durable peace, and to give up the trial of a selected number of Pakistani military officers on war crime charges by Bangladash. Pakistan also demanded to get back the occupied territory from India notwithstanding that it had been illegally occupying Azad Kashmir since 1947. As could be expected Pakistan conveniently did not refer to Azad Kashmir when she demanded back the territories which India occupied in 1971. Naturally such a programme was bound only to collapse, and it seemed the summit would fail. But Bhutto said that he was "not going to shut the door". It is also interesting to note that he could not shut the door since such an arrogant and uncompromising stand would have shut up inside India both Pakistan's territories and the prisoners of war. Were he to shut the door, he would have had to return home empty-handed.

But there came a sudden bolt from the blue. The impasse disappeared dramatically and all the hurdles seemed to have disappeared and India and Pakistan signed an agreement on 2 July[40]. What was the immediate reason for this sudden and unexpected change in the attitude of India, which signed the agreement without terms and conditions, still remains an enigma. The Prime Minister of India and the President of Pakistan hailed this signing ceremony as a "new beginning in the relations between India and Pakistan"[41]. It was bilaterally agreed that "the principles and purposes of the U N charter shall govern the relationship between the two countries" and that they would settle "their differences by peaceful means mutually through bilateral negotiations or by any other peaceful means mutually agreed upon between them. It was agreed to respect each other's territorial integrity and sovereignty by observing the policy of non-interference in each other's internal affairs and to abstain from the threat or the use of force. Prevention of hostile propaganda and the resumption of communication were on the accord, and as a means towards attaining durable peace the signatories agreed to withdraw the armed forces "to their side of international border". It was agreed that in Jammu and Kashmir "the line of control resulting from the ceasefire of 17 December 1971, shall be respected by both sides"[42]. Both the parties agreed that any settlement between the two nations could be reached at through bilateral talks and "other peaceful means".

Though the Simla Agreement was signed it could not provide a final solution to the Indo-Pak problem. For, after the signing of the Simla Accord the Pakistani spokesman said, "we remain where we are until a final settlement is reached" which meant that this much publicized agreement was not a final one. More over the Pakistani delegation deliberately abstained from being a party to any kind of a "No War" declaration. Thus was signed the Simla Agreement, leaving all the issues unsettled. It is interesting to notice that when the situation was highly favourable to India, India's victory over the enemy being total, she failed to settle her longstanding issues with the aggressor state. With the support of the USSR having been already won, it was sure that even if India would take a tough stand there would not have been any interference of the other superpowers. Besides, the victorious India had with her 90,000 prisoners of war and a large tract of Pakistani territory. In such a favourable state India could have turned a tough bargainer. She should not have made so large a concession as she did unless there was some compensation, which the accord does not record. Instead of asserting her moral will over the aggressor, she let Pakistan have all the advantage.

There was widespread dissatisfaction in India about the Simla Accord among the various nationalist outfits, intellectuals and patriots. Strongly condemning this agreement, A B Vajpayee, the leader of the Bharatiya Jana Sangh, described it as a "sell out" and called upon all the parties to demonstrate against this "black agreement". According to him Pakistan's agreement to renounce the use of force was totally meaningless since 'renunciation' had been agreed upon by Pakistan several times earlier only to be thrown to the winds shortly thereafter. Besides, he argued that the agreement to settle the disputes by "other peaceful means" was likely to keep the doors open for a third party intervention. He further criticized that the agreement to withdraw the troops to the international border would only imply that India would give up more than 5000 square miles of Pakistani territory while 3000 square miles of India's territory in Kashmir would remain with Pakistan. He charged that there had been "some sort of secret understanding" between Mrs. Indira Gandhi and Zulfiqar Ali Bhutto during their talks at Simla. True, by stating so Mr. Vajpayee was not casting doubt on the patriotism of Mrs. Gandhi. But he called the attention of the nation to the fact that she should have taken her cabinet colleagues also into confidence in regard to the provisions of the agreement which had come as a bolt from the blue after the talks of the days immediately preceding the agreement had been written off as having failed[43]. It is again interesting to note that Mr. James P. Sterba's report on the Simla Agreement in the *New York Times* was headlined "Simla Accord: Behind the progress report there is possibility of a secret agreement"[44]. Years after when Mr. Vajpayee demanded answers in this regard and a full text of Mrs. Gandhi's talks with Mr. Bhutto at Simla he got only an unsatisfactory reply. Replying to his query, the official spokesman of the External Affairs Ministry said on 10 April 1978: "I do not know about it. I am not competent to talk about it. It is not on record anywhere", and he suggested that the parties directly concerned, Mrs. Gandhi and Mr. Bhutto may be approached[45]. Indeed one may be prompted to ponder whether these talks concerning the fate of the two nations were so silly and insignificant as to be kept only in the memories of the parties directly concerned.

In his memoirs titled *A Diplomat's Diary* India's former diplomat Triloki Nath Kaul expresses disappointment with Mrs. Gandhi's performance at the Simla Summit with Z A Bhutto. It is true that "she was hailed as Durga, the Goddess of war by Sri Vajpayee because of her toughness during the war", he says.

However she squandered away its gains in her eagerness to show "magnanimity in victory". T N Kaul further criticizes her "for not getting a final settlement of the Kashmir question at Simla", and writes,

> She tried hard but Bhutto said if he agreed to a final settlement at Simla he would be overthrown and the military would take over power and increase tension with India. When I suggested it at the conference table, Bhutto, addressing Smt. Gandhi, said, 'Madam, I assure you that within two weeks of my return to Pakistan I shall prepare the ground for it (a final settlement of Kashmir Question)".

Thinking that the Simla meet would end in failure, Kaul left Simla a few hours prior to the conference ending at late night of 2 July 1972 and came to Chandigarh to make arrangements for the return of Bhutto and his daughter Benazir. But what happened at Simla was contrary to what Kaul thought. Mrs. Gandhi signed an agreement on the night of 2 July after a one-to-one meeting with Bhutto at "The Retreat" after the parties had packed their luggage for the return. "No one else was present", but Mrs. Gandhi's Secretary and economic advisor who was outside the room and has said that there was verbal understanding for a final settlement of the Kashmir question along with an agreement on the Line of Control. But this final settlement from the part of Bhutto had never come. He could not save himself from the military coup about which he had spoken at Simla.

Kaul makes an interesting revelation of the reason why Mrs. Gandhi failed to get an agreement converting the ceasefire line in Kashmir into the international border in the parleys held at Simla from 28 June to 2 July. It was a gesture of goodwill towards the People of Pakistan that would befriend them in course of time. Indeed this wild goose chase had started from the time of Jawaharlal Nehru, which had yielded no result at all[46]. Better to say, the policy of appeasing Muslims, started from the time of Gandhiji as a means to gain the goodwill of Muslim League and which continued in post-independent India, yielded no result. In fact it only made the Muslim League and its creation, Pakistan, more arrogant, uncompromising and audacious enough to pooh-pooh the foolish generosity of India and its leaders. And this was the chief characteristic of Pakistan in all its dealings with India.

At Simla Bhutto was given two clear alternatives. He was asked whether he wanted to get back first the prisoners of war or the 5000 square miles of territory India captured from Pakistan. Bhutto outfoxed Mrs.Gandhi by asking the territory first. Bhutto's daughter Benazir who accompanied him to Simla explains the evil and clever design behind such a demand. She writes in her autobiography *Daughter of the East* that she was in fact surprised at such a topsy-turvy priority of her father as there was an impatient demand for the release of such a large number of prisoners of war. But Bhutto calmed her and told,

> The POW's will be freed in any case. Prisoners are human problem. The magnitude is increased when there are 93000 of them. It would be inhuman to keep them indefinitely. And it will also be a problem to keep on feeding and housing them. Territory on the other hand is not a human problem. Territory can be assimilated. Prisoners cannot. The Arabs have still not succeeded in regaining territory lost in the 1967 war with Israel. The capturing of land does not cry out for international attention the same way as the prisoners do[47].

But this diplomatic fact of history did not dawn on India's Iron Lady. This was the first great victory of Bhutto. Second, Bhutto like all his predecessors was determined to keep alive in future a vital bone of contention, and he knew that any settlement regarding the Line of Control and the Kashmir Question would only undo this. It was in the interest of Pakistan that the Ceasefire Line should not be converted into an international border. Again Bhutto proved successful in getting the issue of Kashmir inserted into the Simla Agreement as an unsettled one between India and Pakistan so that the latter could project it as the reason for any conflict between the two nations in future[48]. By signing such an agreement Mrs. Gandhi was indirectly, though inadvertently, accepting that the Kashmir issue was something yet to be settled.

Mrs. Gandhi's Secretary and Economic Advisor, P N Dhar gives his version of her tame surrender to Bhutto at Simla. He says that Bhutto used all wily and shameless tactics to save the talks from breaking down. When Bhutto and Indira Gandhi were alone talking Bhutto softened her by saying that he had to prepare his country and its National Assembly to accept the

Line of Control as a permanent border for which he needed two weeks. Dhar who was standing outside the room probably overheard everything. *Mujh par bharosa kijye* (Trust me), Bhutto implored her again and again and won over her. But Dhar says that this was only an oral and not written agreement. Spoken words vanished into thin air and what remained were India's unsolved problems as they did prior to 1972. What the soldiers of India gained militarily the Prime Minister of India fretted away diplomatically!

True, love of peace and magnanimity to the neighbour are good qualities a nation must develop. But it should not have jeopardized national interests. However the Lady of the Simla Agreement did not take this into consideration with the result that it only aggravated the aggressiveness of the enemy. No wonder, after going home in a victorious mood, he took all the credit for striking a winning bargain and threw all his promises to winds. While addressing his nation on his return from India, an elated and audacious Bhutto said, "I had gone to India with two views, first to get our territory back and then to get our Prisoners of War back. I have done the first in five months [a judicious gain] what the Arabs could not get done in five years". He further said that "I will get the POWs back too because India cannot keep them for long because international pressure is turning against India". The moderate diction and the slipper-licking diplomacy Bhutto resorted to while in Indian soil gave way to the reckless and arrogant statements, the moment he landed in Pakistan. There was no moderation in his words. On the other hand, as V P Bhatia observes, he started preparing for a nuclear arsenal to checkmate India forever. The chameleon made contradictory and villainous statements about the Accord. On 3 July 1972, while addressing a cheering and frenzied mob he felt no shame or prick of conscience to air his inborn vile that "the right of self-determination is the Kashmiris' right and no one can take it away from them". Thus the Simla 'understanding' or the Simla Accord could only boost the Pakistani arrogance. It was one of the great tragedies of Indian history and a great national misfortune that Mrs. Gandhi's Pakistani counterpart could easily fool her.

References

1. See Chapter III.
2. S S Bindra, *Op. Cit*, p. 122.
3. Subhash, C. Kasyap, *Bengla Desh: A Study in International Legal Norms and Permissive Conscience*, Bombay, 1972, p. 8.
4. It should be noted that the East Bengalis felt the need of their own land being protected from foreign invasions. During the 1965 war, only the security of the West Pakistan figured in the Pakistani interest, while the East Bengal was left completely defenseless. Hence the Six-Point Programme envisaged the creation of a paramilitary force in East Pakistan.
5. *Pakistan Observer*, 17 March 1966.
6. *Ibid.*, 21 March1966.
7. D K Palit, *The Lightening Campaign: Indo-Pakistan War–1971*, New Delhi, 1972, p. 28.
8. V B Kulkarni, *Pakistan: Its Origin and Relations with India*, p. 159.
9. *Ibid.*
10. *The Dawn*, 28 November 1969.
11. D K Palit, *Op. Cit.*, p. 29.
12. S S Bindra, *Op. Cit.*, p. 126.
13. *The Dawn*, 15 January 1971.
14. *Pakistan Times*, 21 December 1971.
15. *The Dawn*, 16 March 1971.
16. V B Kulkarni, *Pakistan: Its Origin and Relations with India*, p. 160.
17. *Pakistan Observer*, 2 March 1971.
18. D K Palit, *Op. Cit.*, p. 30.
19. V B Kulkarni, *Pakistan: Its Origin and Relations with India*, p. 165.
20. D K Palit, *Op. Cit.*, p. 33.
21. Col. S P Salunke, *Pakistani POWs of War in India*, New Delhi, 1977, p. 2.
22. *The Statesman*, 27 March 1971.
23. Antony Mascarenhas, "Genocide", *Indian Express*, 18 June 1971.
24. V B Kulkarni, *Pakistan: Its Origin and Relations with India*, p. 166.
25. "Good Soldier Yahya Khan", *Time*, 2 August 1971, p. 30.

26. V B Kulkarni observes that according to his neighbour Dr. Mrs. Vandana Walvekar at least 10,000 East Bengali women had become pregnant in Pakistani 'military operation'. Mrs Walvekar was a noted gynaecologist who was one among the doctors sent from India to Bangladesh to help these unfortunate women subjected to the mass rape of 1971 rid of their hated pregnancy.
27. The pro-Pakistani attitude of at least a section of the Muslims had been detrimental to India's internal security and the ideal of secularism. Raising the pro-Pakistani slogans, they often fanned out against the Hindus. Already in 1964, Tamil Nadu Chief Minister, M Bhakthavalsalam felt constrained to warn the Muslim League against its 'treacherous' campaign against the country and called the attention of the State's legislature to the party's habit of shouting the slogan "Pakistan Zindabad". See *The Hindu*, 31 March 1964. The same slogan, it was reported, could be heard in the streets of some northern districts of Kerala during the 1971 war.
28. S P Salunke, *Op. Cit.*, p.1.
29. *Ibid.*, p. 4.
30. V B Kulkarni, *Pakistan: Its Origin and Relations with India*, p. 167.
31. *Ibid.*, p. 168.
32. *The Statesman*, 5 December 1971.
33. S P Salunke, *Op. Cit.*, p. 5.
34. *Ibid.*
35. *Ibid.*, p. 8.
36. *The Tribune*, "Ceasefire in the West" (Editorial), 18 December 1971.
37. *Hindustan Standard,* "The Agony is Over" (Editorial), 17 December 1971.
38. *Indian Express*, 15 March 1992.
39. V B Kulkarni, *Pakistan: Its Origin and Relations with India*, p. 196.
40. *The Statesman*, 29 June 1972.
41. *Indian Express*, 3 July 1972.
42. *The Hindu*, 3 July 1972.
43. Appendix–III.
44. A G Noorani, "Was there a secret Bhutto-Indira Pact?", *Sunday*, April 1978.
45. *New York Times*, 3 July 1972.
46. A G Noorani, *Op. Cit.*

47. India had in fact with her three trumps to force Bhutto agree to end the Kashmir dispute for ever by permanent partition of Kashmir. Partition of Jammu and Kashmir was in fact the purpose of the ceasefire of 1 January 1949 also. To put it right, Pt. Nehru had been trying hard from 1949 to 1960 when the Canal Water Agreement, highly favourable to Pakistan, was signed to make it agree to the partition of Kashmir. Indeed the wily Pakistani rulers kept dangling such a hope before Nehru, which however was not to be given effect to. The American archival documents also show that the USA too favoured such a settlement, but the Pakistani attitude was to grab more. "What we have, we have. What will you give from what you have?" was their attitude. See V P Bhatia, "Diplomatic disaster at Simla", *Organiser*, 3 August 2003.

48. *Ibid.*

49. It is interesting to note that Pakistan always tried to project the Kashmir issue as the reason of the bilateral disagreements. Though it strove to include the Kashmir in the Tashkent Agreement Lal Bahadur Sastri did not agree to it. He had in fact refused to any mention of Kashmir as the cause of Indo-Pakistan tension in Tashkent agreement as Ayub and Bhutto insisted there.

7

The Bleeding Kashmir

Whenever Pakistan was faced with serious internal problems its rulers diverted the attention of the people towards Kashmir issue. They cautiously guarded themselves against any measure that would help solve Kashmir and other differences to bring an enduring peace. Though peace with India would find an important place in the election manifestoes of contestants at Pakistan Assembly elections, the wily politicians that they were, they conveniently forget these assurances given as soon as the elections were over. They would bank on the anti-India feeling to retain their power and peace with India would remain to the ordinary Pakistanis an eternal mirage. The rulers of Pakistan were well aware of the fact that absorption of Kashmir would be detrimental to peace in their land, for it would expose Pakistan to terrorist menace and they would find the Kashmiris more unmanageable than the Pathans, Punjabis and Baluchis. And they thought it better to play Kashmir against India.

As noted previously, Kashmir has already become the diplomatic chessboard of international power politics, besides the political mess it was turned into by both the Indian leaders and Pakistani miscreants. And as time passed on Kashmir became the hunting ground of many more who converted it into a gambling arena of their fortunes, both personal and political. The only exception were the native Kashmiri Pandits whose loyalty to their state was beyond question. It is true that Sheik Mohammad Abdullah had never been influenced by any pro-Pakistani sentiment though he banked on that country externally. He could also not be deemed, a true Indian national in the light of his mysterious behaviour, which were well revealed on many occasions. He knew that any contact with Pakistan or a merger of Kashmir with that country would certainly spell the doom of his political as well as personal future. His life itself would be endangered in a terrorist country where even the most sagacious leaders of early Pakistani generation like Liaqat Ali could not thrive. Though he had a kind of love for the newborn Islamic country he never wanted to be a Pakistani for such a move, he realized, would destroy all his plans for the future. To ensure the protection and promotion of his interests he would do nothing that irritate either India or Pakistan. He did not utter a single word of condemnation against the Pak soldiers for their brutal assault on the Bengalis whose pitiable plight was the same as that of the Kashmiris till they were forced to surrender to the Bangladeshis. As D N Dhar very rightly puts it, "He was trying to be on the fence, not expecting the defeat of the Pak force"[1]. His personal ambitions overrode all national considerations and religious sentiments. An opportunist, he never wanted to be with either India or Pakistan. Though the Sheik's desire to make Kashmir an independent sheikdom continued to haunt his imaginations throughout his life he knew that it would be safer for him to remain with India than with Pakistan where the life of popular leaders were never safe or secure. Therefore, as a wise option he chose to be with India. Kashmir thus proved to him a fertile ground for the realization of his goals. Kashmir in fact became a breeding ground for all anti-nationals and opportunists. How to prolong the Kashmir issue rather than solve it outweighed the considerations of all those who were involved in it. Consequently, Kashmir continued to bleed down the decades that followed.

Sheik Abdullah started negotiations with Indian leadership for a new constitutional set up in Kashmir in order to safeguard his political future[2]. Having emerged victorious from the war of 1971, Mrs. India Gandhi was in a very strong position and therefore Sheik Abdullah had to agree to enter into negotiation with her. The negotiations between Mr. Parthasarathy on behalf of the Indian Government and Mirza Afzal Beg acting for Abdullah dragged on for a long time and finally an agreement was reached on 13 November 1974[3]. According to it the state of Jammu and Kashmir would continue as a state of Indian Union governed by Article 370 of Indian Constitution. The state could exercise some residuary powers, legislate on matters relating to the welfare, culture, social security of the Kashmiris, amend or repeal laws coming under concurrent list which would be sympathetically considered by the President of India. The power to legislate to prevent defiance of the sovereignty and territorial integrity of India or cessation of parts of Indian territory from the Union or insulting the National Flag, National Anthem and the Constitution, was reserved with the Union government. The Indian constitutional provisions already applied to that state would remain as they were but with reasonable modifications and adaptations. The appointments, powers, functions, duties, privileges and immunities of the Governor, the superintendence, direction and control of elections by the Election Commission of India, and adult suffrage and composition of Legislative Assembly required the consent of the President of India. The accord left the question regarding the nomenclature of Governor and Chief Minister without any agreement[4].

That the Kashmir accord could not offer a permanent solution to the problems in the valley was a fact realized by all who were witnesses to the later developments there. Perhaps Mrs. Gandhi too knew that Sheik Abdullah, though undependable, could not be kept away from power in Kashmir in the absence of a reliable substitute. The selection of Sheik was thus fully negative. The Accord could not abrogate the special status Kashmir was accorded under Article 370. Members of Jana Sangh like Atal Behari Vajpayee and socialist M P Jneshwar Misra protested against the Accord since it did not do away with this obnoxious article, which gave Kashmir a status different from other Indian states.

But it brought temporary peace to the place. It is true that 'Mrs. Gandhi was at her best that day' and that there was great jubilation over the Accord in the valley as opined by M J Akbar[5]. "Although Kashmir's special status, enshrined in Article 370 of the Indian Constitution was retained, the state was termed a constituent unit of the Union of India"[6]. The power of the Union Government to legislate against trends to defy the sovereignty of India gave India control in crucial areas. It was ensured that things would not be rolled back to the 1953 status. The designations of Sadar-I-Riyasat and Prime Minister of Kashmir were replaced with Governor and Chief Minister respectively as in the case of other states.

It was stated in some quarters that it was Sheik Abdullah's confirmation of the Instrument of Accession that Maharaja Hari Singh had signed that made him acceptable to the Indian authorities[7]. The development that followed however proved that in supporting him Indian rulers were backing a wrong horse. The Sheik, who became Chief Minister on 25 February 1975 having been chosen for the office by the Congress legislature party, revived the National Conference and became its President. He who had lauded "Jawaharlal's vision and statesmanship, combined with Indiraji's courage and decisiveness" however turned his back to the Congress's invitation to join that party[8]. He refuted everything that happened from August 1953 to February 1975 as a "dark patch in the History of Kashmir". Indeed even the Accord itself was to him an "artificial and exhibitionist show of false progress"[9]. He even talked about an independent Kashmir!

As could be expected Pakistan was highly irritated at the Kashmir Accord. Besides India's nuclear explosion too increased tension between India and Pakistan with the latter becoming crazy to attain nuclear capability as a counterpoise against her neighbour. Though Pakistan had no potential then to develop nuclear capability equal to that of India it stressed the need of an 'Islamic Bomb' as a counter check to the 'Hindu Bomb' and 'Christian Bomb'! The Pakistani warmongers audaciously picked up the embers of communalism to unite the otherwise mutually warring factions in their land. It was Bhutto who for the first time brought out the idea of a nuclear programme for Pakistan. Earlier, addressing Pakistan National Assembly, Bhutto said: "If India builds the bomb, we will eat grass and leaves, even go hungry. But we will get one of our own, we have no alternative"[10]. Soon after taking over as the Pakistan President, Bhutto is reported to have briefed his country's top scientists at Multan in Punjab on the need of developing a nuclear bomb. True, he did not remain in power for so long a period as he desired. But he set the Pak nuclear programme on rails before being deposed by Gen. Zia Ul Haq. Though exhortations for the nuclear programme had little impact on the general Pakistani public and the illiterate masses busying with the daily life the cry for an Islamic Bomb helped the dictators of Pakistan to remain in power by playing on public fears, and helped turn at least a few Pakistanis against India.

Even before the Kashmir Accord was signed Pak politicians had started intensifying their agitation to liberate Kashmir, protesting against the negotiations in progress. The announcement of the Accord was received in Pakistan with the most acrimonious chorus of disapproval from Pak leaders. They disparaged it as a 'sell out'. Zulfikar Ali Bhutto exhorted for a strike throughout Pakistan on 28 February 1975. According to him Kashmir Accord had flouted the terms of the Simla Agreement and the UN requirement for a plebiscite.

War or peace with India was not the main concern of Bhutto. This man who with a minority in Pakistan National Assembly claimed to be the ruler of Pakistan against the brute majority won by Awami League and had even proposed the idea of two prime ministers for Pakistan had never changed. Instead of developing a desirable relation with the neighbouring nations or maintaining a healthy democratic tradition inside his own country Bhutto resorted to all unfair means to remain in power. A power monger to the core as he was, he utilized the governmental machinery fully to ensure popular support in his favour. His last minute efforts like revision of price structure of 1976, which hiked the price of cotton as a gesture of goodwill to cotton cultivators or lowering of the price of fertilizers, increase in the amount of agricultural credit as well as subsidy, sanctioning of loans to major industrial projects, 'liberal import policy' and all the much trumpeted populist measures were parts of his strategy to win the forthcoming election. He passed the 'Peoples Representation Bill' in November 1976 to debar the leaders of National Awami Party. And by January 1977, when the Election Commission declared the final electoral list for National Assembly and four Provincial Assemblies, Bhutto had become confident to win. A jubilant Bhutto declared that elections would be held on 11 March 1977 and the National Assembly would be dissolved on 10 January 1977. But the gathering of new clouds on Pak political horizon cast a big shadow on his overconfidence. No sooner did he dissolve the National Assembly than the opposition parties declared the formation of Pakistan National Alliance to contest the election. At the hustings Bhutto used the help of both military and media. The presence of armed forces in many of the constituencies was heavily criticised. All election speeches of Bhutto were given national coverage by the government media, which callously neglected the opposition leaders. Mounting violence and utmost acrimony between PPP and PNA marred the two months long election campaign, and the Federal Government finally clamped curbs on press freedom. The Pakistan Federal Union of Journalists demanded total freedom for the press in their 'seven-point' demands alleging that "the forthcoming general elections without a free press would be an exercise in futility"[11]. However, the landslide victory of Bhutto did not get popular acceptance in Pakistan. The opposition allegation that Bhutto had manipulated election machinery in his favour badly mutilated his image. Rejecting the validity of the March 7 general elections, the PNA urged its elected nominees to the National Assembly to resign and insisted on fresh elections under the direct supervision of army with a caretaker government in office[12]. And the general agitations that followed irrespective of the military actions of the Federal Government, took the whole situation out of control. The dastardly battle in the name of democratic order finally stranded Pakistan politics in its traditional quagmire. The comic democratic interlude once again came to end when the Chief of Army Staff, Gen. Zia-ul- Haq deposed Bhutto, set aside the civil administration and declared Martial Law in Pakistan. This was followed by the mass arrest of the political leaders who were likely to be threats to the future military rule of Gen. Zia. He described these arrests as part of taking the leaders into 'protective custody' and the military coup as a 'contingency plan' to solve the constitutional impasse snowballing from the acrimony among political parties about the issue of holding free and fair poll. Masquerading himself as saviour of Pakistan's stability, the General said,

> I want to make it absolutely clear that neither I have any political ambition nor does the army want to be taken away from its profession of soldiering ... I was obliged to step in to fill the vacuum created by the political leaders. I have accepted this challenge as a true soldier of Islam. We are absolutely determined to carry out a '90-day preparation fair play' leading up to free and fair general elections"[13].

Later development clearly showed that Gen. Zia's military coup was designed for annihilating his foes at the earliest. Indeed to Zia who was afraid of his own survival if Bhutto would once again assume power the only alternative to save even his life was in the execution of the latter. After a long show of judicial proceedings, which proved a mess of contradictions, lack of clear evidences and the failure of prosecution, Pakistani Supreme Court on 24 March 1979 finally sentenced Bhutto to death on the charge of murdering the father of Ahmed Raza Kasuri. The sentence was carried out at 2 AM on 4 April 1979 in the Rawalpindi Central jail. Thus ended the life of one more Pak Prime Minister who had throughout his life been a murderer of democracy. The Pak politician who never gave credence to democratic aspirations as was proved by the 1971 Bengal issue and later elections, which he manipulated for his personal gains, had to spend his final days under the new tyrant who had stepped into his shoes. Once again it was proved that democracy in Pakistan would ever remain only a brief interlude between long martial regimes.

The Zia period did not witness any tangible and positive development in Pakistan's relations with India. True, one of the last decisions of President Zia's life was to confer Pakistan's most coveted civilian award, *Nishan-I-Pakistan* on India's former Prime Minister, Morarji Desai in honour of his "commitment and services to the promotion of ties between the two countries". This show of goodwill by the then Pak President had raised much smoke and dust among the Indian politicians, particularly the ruling Congress group, which took it as an affront to the then Prime Minister of India, Mr. Rajiv Gandhi. This, the Congressmen had taken against the backdrop of the award of *Bharat Ratna* earlier to Khan Abdul Gaffar Khan by Mrs Indira Gandhi, and took the *Nishan-I-Pakistan* conferred on Morarji Desai as a retaliatory measure. It was again taken as Zia's reward to Morarji, for his having remained uncritical of the hanging of Zulfikar Ali Bhutto in 1979. Looked from one side all these may appear true. But a more careful perusal of facts would bring to limelight some of the realities related to these controversial aspects. Looked from any point, the *Bharat Ratna* conferred on Khan Abdul Gaffar Khan can't be viewed negatively. To a good extent he was the lover of India who always desired to live in an undivided India, which according to him would be a happy heaven for both Hindus and Muslims. But once partition took place he accepted it as a historical reality, and did his best to help India and Pakistan keep friendly relations. His effort was always positive, seeking to bring peaceful and tranquil relations between India and Pakistan. By all means he deserved the

Bharat Ratna conferred on him. Viewed from any angle, the Border Gandhi deserved this highest recognition.

It is an undisputed fact that Indo-Pakistan relation during the short Janata interregnum was to a large extent cordial and there was normalization in mutual relations. But Morarji was not the man to be judged by ordinary standards. Belonging to the old generation of highly principled Indians, this man and his convictions can't be equated with the unscrupulous politicians of modern times and their high-sounding slogans on ethics, which have become mere claptraps of a political party. He firmly believed that it was not fair to interfere in the internal affairs of a neighbouring country. Therefore he held fast to his considered opinion that it was not within his right to comment on an action of the government in office in Pakistan during his time. As the Prime Minister of India, he held it was his duty to accept the decisions of the Chief Executive of Pakistan as that nation's decisions[14]. Therefore, it should not be taken that Morarji approved of Zia's dealing Mr. Zulfikar Ali Bhutto. It cannot however be contradicted that the Janata Party government, which came to power in India after the defeat of Mrs. Indira Gandhi in 1977 general elections managed to remain on good terms with Pakistan. Also the Indian Ministers of the time, like Morarji Desai, Atal Behari Vajpayee or George Fernandes were men of extraordinary perception who could not be easily fooled on matters of foreign relations and national security. It is true that there was much talk about India-Pak amity and India's Foreign Affairs Minister Atal Behari Vajpayee visited Islamabad in 1978 to sign the important accord on Salal Dam, which aimed at safeguarding the interests of both countries on the flow of Chinab waters. But the Government was alive to the threats Pakistan posed behind her friendly gestures.

The term of Gen. Zia-ul Haq in Pakistan coincided with many unexpected changes in India and its neighbourhood like the rise and fall of the Janata Party government, the Soviet invasion of Afghanistan, Mrs. Indira Gandhi's return to power, the alienation of the Sikhs, assassination of Indira Gandhi and the coming of Rajiv Gandhi to the Prime Minister's office.

The Soviet invasion of Afghanistan brought about altogether new attitudes and trends in Asiatic politics. The presence of the Soviet Army at his doorsteps had greatly worried Gen. Zia who soon championed the Pak cause as the bulwark against Communism in his bid to win US friendship. In India Mrs. Indira Gandhi returned to power. Though alarmed at the Afghan development, Mrs. Gandhi took a neutral stand on the matter. Middle East has always been the breeding ground of terrorism, and Afghanistan a land of intolerance and political instability. It is true that the Afghans were so proud and pugnacious that they would not tolerate any imposition of outside rule on them. With no strong authority to control their affairs Afghanistan became a centre of terrorism, planning Jihads, organizing political hijacking, spreading intolerance and exhorting for mass destruction the world over. Islamic terrorism caused serious headache to many of the poor nations of Asia, India being the worst affected. It was not that the Prime Minister of India, Mrs. Gandhi was not shrewd enough to sense the ramifications of Russian interference in the affairs of Afghanistan. But she made her own assessment of the situation against the backdrop of the political realities of the time. USSR has been India's time tested friend who supported her in her hours of need. Definitely Mrs. Gandhi could not forget the Russian veto on Kashmir resolutions in the UN. She could also not be ungrateful to the 1971 military alliance and Russia's strong support. Considering these historical realities she decided to remain neutral. Consequently, she did nothing to persuade Soviet Union to withdraw its forces from Afghanistan and tried to remain on good terms with both Moscow and Kabul. The Soviet Union too was not interested in alienating India. In fact the USSR wanted to improve its relations with India and the Soviet Foreign Minister Andrie Gromyko visited New Delhi to justify the presence of the Soviet troops in Afghanistan. But as already noted India had her reservations about the issue though it did not make any open pronouncement. The Soviet Union also offered a highly generous arms package to India in May 1980, which amounted to 1.63 billion dollars in the form of credit payable over a period of 10 to 15 years[15]. The arms transfer package included MiG-25 'Foxbat' aircraft and T-72 tanks which would boost India's military capability in the light of the US-Pak military relations which was likely to reach an unprecedented crescendo[16].

Coinciding with this was the development in Punjab where the call for Khalistan, which was an undesirable offspring of Mrs. Gandhi's political manipulations, assumed horrific dimensions. Defeated in 1977 elections, Mrs. Gandhi nursed the political vendetta against the new Janata Government, which Loknayak Jayaprakash Narain guided. Her impatience and intolerance to remain without power made her design new strategies however heinous it might be and however much it would lead even to national disintegration. A power hungry Indira now resorted to woo Sikh militancy by developing factionalism in Punjab as a means to gain political influence in that state. Indeed her policy of breeding Sikh terrorism and giving it a religious tinge by describing Jarnail Sing Bhindranwallah as a spiritual leader caused great havoc to Indian nationalism by turning the otherwise strong and the mighty patriotic community of India anti-Indian at least for the time being. In fact the Sikh call for Khalistan, the Pakistani support for it, the estrangement between Mrs. Gandhi and Bhindranwallah shortly after the former became Prime Minister, Mrs. Gandhi's giving the nod to launch 'Operation Bluestar' which was more horrendous than the Jallianwallabag tragedy and the assassination of Mrs. Gandhi in October 1984 which is said to have been the result of a Sikh plot, were the aftereffects of Mrs. Gandhi's political miscalculations, and lack of national and patriotic vision and farsightedness[17].

It is undeniable that Pakistan had been supporting the cause of Khalistan and helping Sikh insurgents with arms and ammunitions in their militant operations against India. Indian Army, in the course of 'Operation Bluestar', seized a large number of weapons evidently smuggled from the bordering areas of Pakistan into Punjab. The Sikh hijacking of two Indian aircrafts to Lahore in the very same year proved the existence of Sikh terrorist hideouts in Pakistan sheltered by the Pak government. General Zia tried to be on good terms with Rajiv Gandhi after the assassination of Mrs. Indira Gandhi. He attended her funeral in New Delhi and announced a three-day official mourning in Pakistan as a token of goodwill towards the departed Indian leader. But Pakistan took no concrete steps to scale down the support and help it extended to the cause of Khalistan and the Sikh terrorists. Both Rajiv Gandhi government at New Delhi and the Punjab state government at Chandigarh time and again claimed to have gained possession of 'concrete proofs' incriminating Pakistan for its role in helping the Sikh insurgents. According to India's former Home Affairs Minister Santosh Mohan Dev these documents seized by the police from the Golden Temple at Amritsar in May 1988 speak volumes on the instructions and large supplies of sophisticated weapons the leaders operating in Pakistan had been sending to terrorists in Punjab[18]. This is further proved by the fact that Pak government turned a blind eye on the Sikh and Pakistani terrorists illegally crossing into Indian territories. The renowned Pakistani writer, Tariq Ali has opined that there were a number of training camps for Sikh terrorists within the close proximity of Peshawar[19].

Zia pretended to champion the cause of Islam as the first step in his move against India. "Extensive efforts were made to Islamize the law and economy. Islamic penalties were introduced, a system of Shari'a courts established, and the Shari'a declared the supreme law of the land"[20]. Second he tried to turn the Pakistani wrath against India as a means of self-protection from it, which would otherwise have endangered him. He styled as champion of the Islamic cause by declaring *Jihad* against India, the nation of infidels! He was not concerned of whether he would succeed or not. But an anti-India policy being an imperative for his survival, Zia too harped on the theme of 'hate-India', which raised him to the status of defender of the faith. And he took up the Kashmir issue to be at dagger heads with India.

Kashmir was on the agenda of Zia-ul-Haq right from the beginning of his dictatorial regime. Evidences abound in regard to his plan of seizing Kashmir. Zia is reported to have briefed his Corps Commanders and the Inter Service Intelligence's top officers in April 1988 after he had ordered Gen. Akthar Abdul Rehman to prepare a plan to liberate Kashmir[21]. Zia's briefing of April 1988 ferreted out and passed on to India's RAW by a mole in October 1988 is as follows[22]:

"Gentlemen, I have spoken on this subject at length before, therefore, I will leave out the details. As you know due to our preoccupation in Afghanistan, in the service of Islam, I have not been able to put these plans before you earlier. Let there be no mistake, however, that our aim remains quite clear and firm – the liberation of Kashmir valley–our Muslim Kashmiri brothers cannot be allowed to stay with India for any length of time, now. In the past we have opted for ham-handed military operations and therefore, failed. So, as I have mentioned, before, we will now keep our military option for the last moment as a *Coup-de-*

grace, if and when necessary. Our Kashmir brethren in the valley, though with us in their hearts and minds are simple-minded folk and do not easily take to the type of warfare to which, say, a Punjabi or an Afghan takes to naturally, against foreign domination. The Kashmiris, however, have a few qualities, which we can exploit. First his shrewdness and intelligence, second his power to persevere under pressure; and the third, if I say so, he is a master of political intrigue. If we provide him means through which he can best utilize these qualities – he will deliver the goods, sheer brute force in any case is not needed in every type of warfare, especially so in the situation obtaining in the Kashmir valley, as I have explained earlier.

Here we must adopt those methods of combat, which the Kashmiri mind can grasp and cop with–in other words, a coordinated use of moral and physical means, other than military operations, which will destroy the will of the enemy, damage his political capacity and expose him to the world as an oppressor. This aim, gentlemen, shall be achieved in the initial phases.

In the first phase, which may, if necessary, last a couple of years we will assist our Kashmiri brethren in getting the hold of power apparatus of the state by political subversion and intrigue. I would like to mention here that as no government can survive in occupied Kashmir unless it has the tacit approval of Delhi, it would be unrealistic to believe that MUF or any such organization can seize power through democratic or other means. In view of this, power must 'apparently' remain with those, whom New Delhi favours. We must, therefore, ensure that certain 'favoured politicians' from the ruling elite be selected who would collaborate with us in subverting all effective organs of the state. In brief, our plan for Kashmir, which would be code-named as "*Op. Topec*", will be as follows:

Phase I

A low level insurgency against the regime, so that it is under siege, but does not collapse as we would not yet want Central Rule imposed by Delhi.

We plant our chosen men in all the key positions; they will subvert the police forces, financial institutions, the communication network and other important organizations.

We whip up anti-Indian feelings amongst the students and peasants, preferably on some religious issues, so that we can enlist their active support for rioting and anti-government demonstrations.

Organise and train subversive elements and arm groups with capabilities, initially, to deal with paramilitary forces located in the valley.

Adopt and develop means to cut off lines of communications between Jammu and Kashmir and within Kashmir and between Kashmir and Ladakh by stealth, without recourse to force. The road over Zojila up to Kargil and the road over Khardungla should receive our special attention.

In collaboration with Sikh extremists create chaos and terror in Jammu to divert attention from the valley at critical juncture and discredit the regime even in the Hindu mind.

Establish virtual control in those parts of Kashmir valley where Indian Army is not located or deployed. The South Kashmir may be one such region.

Phase II

Exert minimum pressure on the Siachen, Kargil and Rajouri-Poonch sectors to force the Indian Army to deploy reserve formations outside main Kashmir valley.

Attack and destroy base depots and HQ, located at Srinagar, Pattan, Kupwara, Baramullah, Bandipur and Chowki wala (Chowki Bal) by covert action at a given time.

Some Afghan Mujahideen, by then settled in Azad Kashmir, will then infiltrate in selected pockets with a view to extending areas of our influence. This will require detailed and indigenous planning. The fiasco of Operation Gibraltar (1965) holds many lessons for us here.

Finally a special force under selected retired officers belonging to *Azad Kashmir* with the hard core consisting of Afghans will be ready to attack and destroy airfields, radio stations, block Banihal Tunnel and Kargil-Leh Highway.

At a certain stage of operations Punjab and adjacent areas of Jammu and Kashmir will be put under maximum pressure internally by our offensive posture.

Phase III

Detailed plans for the liberation of Kashmir valley and the establishment of independent Islamic state in the third phase will follow.

We do not have much time. Maximum pressure should be exerted before the general elections in India and before Indian Army reserves, which are still bogged down in Sri Lanka become available. By the grace of God we have managed to accumulate large stocks of modern arms and ammunition from US consignments intended for Afghan Mujahideen. This will help our Kashmiri brethren achieve their goals. Even if we create a kind of *Azad* Kashmir in some remote parts of occupied Kashmir as a beginning, the next step may not be as difficult as it appears today. On the other hand, it should also be noted that a part of Indian Army, particularly the infantry, would be well trained by now for such situation due to their experience in North Eastern Region and more recently in Sri Lanka. But the situation in Kashmir will be somewhat different; more like the *Intefada* of *Palestine* in towns, and on the pattern of Mujahideen in the countryside to attack hard targets. A period of chaos in the state is essential in the circumstances.

And what of our Chinese friends? They can do no more than ensure that Indian forces deployed against them are not moved out; but this may be required only at the last or the third stage of our operations. Of course, if we are in serious trouble, the Chinese and our other powerful friends shall come to our rescue one way or the other. They will ensure if we do not win, at least, we do not lose.

Finally, I wish to caution you once more that it will be disastrous to believe that we can take on India in a straight contest. We must, therefore, be careful and maintain a low military profile so that the Indians do not find an excuse to pre-empt us, by attacking at a time and at a point of their own choosing, at least before Phase I and Phase II of the operation are over. We must pause and assess the course of operation after each phase, as our strategy and plan may require drastic changes in certain circumstances. I need not emphasis any further that deliberate and objective assessment of the situation must be ensured at each stage; otherwise a stalemate will follow with no good for Pakistan. Pakistan *Paindabad*".

Pakistan's evil designs had already started operating in Kashmir even before Zia briefed his Generals on the *Topec*. Mirza Aslem Beg, Pakistan's former Chief of Army, in an interview to the US journalist S. S. Harison revealed that "right from 1986 onwards thousands of ISI trained Kashmiris were being sent to Afghanistan for battle inoculation and subsequent return to fight in the valley"[23]. Aktar Abdul Rahman, one of the Generals whom Zia had entrusted with the Kashmir operations was optimistic of winning Kashmir by 1991 with the help of the Kashmiris who according to him were sworn to sacrifice life to liberate that state. As opined by the former Chief of Pakistan's Inter Service Intelligence, Brigadier Haroon Rashid, "General Akhtar was so profoundly involved in this that he himself met with these Kashmiris who were prepared to lay down their lives for the liberation of Kashmir from the stronghold of India and its access with Pakistan"[24]. But his fatal end along with Gen. Zia-ul-Haq in the air crash of 17 August 1988 put the plan at a low key.

But the *Topec*, which was a psychic boost to the ideology of terrorism in Kashmir, had its damaging effect on that otherwise peaceful state. Terrorist outfits, which mushroomed in secrecy turned audacious to come out in open when they got the ISI directions, and decided to work for the common agenda to liberate Kashmir under the banner of the newly formed Kashmir Liberation Alliance. The common minimum programme they decided on included the fight for the Kashmiris' right of self-determination, the gaining of independence for Kashmir and also to keep the alliance from being used as a cat's paw by either the government or opposition in Pakistan. There were also other minor outfits in Kashmir like the Jamat-e-Islami, which was not much counted for in Kashmiri politics. Ridden roughshod over even by the National Conference, its members were the worst sufferers of the orgy of violence that erupted in Kashmir following the execution of Bhutto. But this could only add to the zeal and dedication of the workers of this organization which, by 1986 rose to have 10,000 hardcore members, 25,000 ordinary members and more than 50,000 sympathisers. Another organization, Azad Kashmir which was close to Jamat-e-Islami invited the Asian wing of the World Islamic Organization in January 1981 to declare support to the Kashmiris' right of self-determination. Suffice it to say, Islamic fundamentalism was gaining ground day after day. Added to this was the role of alien Mullahs whose support acted as a religious imprimatur to the fundamentalist outfits like Jamat-e-Islami. These Mullahs who had been central Asian migrants, though have been despised and excommunicated by the Kashmiris earlier, gained influential social and spiritual status in Kashmir in later times. Fanatics to the core, they tempered and steeled Islamic fundamentalism in Kashmir beyond all flexibilities. As the renowned freedom fighter Peer Gayas-ud-Din opines,

> This category of priests disseminated fundamentalist philosophy and were the founders of Jamat-e-Islami in Kashmir. They were opposed to Kashmiri nationalism and secular movement and displayed their vehement resistance to radical land reforms, modern education and rights to women. Today this segment of *Mullahs* constitutes bedrock of secessionism and militancy in Kashmir. They express vigourously the demand that Kashmir should be virtual theocratic Muslim state. Jamat-e-Islami is the main lever of Muslim United Front (MUF) and its hardcore constitutes the armed wing – Hizbul Mujahideen[25].

Jamat-e-Islami's official organ, *Azan*, was highly critical of any organization or movement, which would not support the idea of independent Kashmir. Defeating even the Pakistani *Dawn* in fanatical propaganda, this paper with its extraordinary expertise in developing a new blend of communalism and politics excelled all others in unleashing a *hate-India* campaign in Kashmir. *Azan* under the pretext of social reform movement preached the doctrine of Islamic *Jihad* among the followers of Jamat-e-Islami. More aggressive were the activities of Jamat-e-Islami's women wing, Duktheran-I-Millat constituted of the women from the families of foreign Mullahs. Themselves donned in black veils, they forced the Kashmiri Muslim girls to put on veils, which they used for "subversive activities including carrying weapons for their *Mujahideens* engaged in *Jihad*"[26]. Its student outfit, Jamat-I-Tulba was more venomous in its indoctrination of the Muslim students of Kashmir who were orientated in lines with *Jihad*. Having rejected secularism and socialism, Jamat-e-Islami of Kashmir, which outshone its Pakistani counterpart, denounced what it called 'Indian colonialism', 'Brahminical imperialism' and the 'Delhi durbar' as it contemptuously referred to India's Union Government. Having vehemently criticized modern patterns of moral and social behaviour, it worked to revamp and refashion the Kashmiri society in conformity with the '*Shariat*'. It unleashed a virulent campaign against family planning, which it lambasted as un-Islamic, cleverly designed by the Central Government to convert the Muslim majority into a minority in the state. The Jamat-I-Tulba trained students to fight political battle to establish the Muslim world in Kashmir as also the world in general. In the field of education it indoctrinated young Muslim minds on fundamentalist lines and to make them develop an anti-Indian outlook. A passage in the text prescribed for Class III reads:"We are Kashmiris and our country is Kashmir. It is surrounded by India, China and Iran"! Through package of books, pamphlets and leaflets, which were freely distributed they sought to sow the seeds of anti-Indian feelings in young minds. In most cases Mosques were the hub of their activities and the sanctuaries of the terrorists. The Jamat-e-Islami upheld *Jihad* as the legitimate weapon for the Kashmiri Muslims to liberate themselves from India[27]. Jamat-e-Islami of Pakistan and *Azad Kashmir* gathered financial and other support for their activities. Jammu and Kashmir Liberation Front established way back in 1965 had always been in the good books of Pakistan and it rose in the latter's esteem whenever it operated against India. Its president Aman-ullah Khan was warmly welcomed by Pakistan following his deportation from England in 1986 in connection with the kidnapping and assassination of an Indian diplomat in 1984. Their joint plan to liberate Kashmir however foundered on the rock of Pakistan's suspicion about their attempts of establishing an independent Kashmir outside the Pakistani fold. The Pakistanis then went on launching pro-Pakistan outfits like Hizbul Mujahideen, Al-Jihad Force, Al-Umar Mujahideen, Allah Tigers, Muslim Mujahideen, Peoples' League, Islamic Students League, Zia Tigers and a host of such major and minor bodies, all sworn to merge Kashmir with Pakistan. All the Kashmiri terrorist organizations were in one way or the other linked to Pakistan's ISI. One may note how anti-India forces from within and without Kashmir joined in their effort to destroy that state:

> All of them were working as directed under the laid plan. What made their operations easy was the political mess created by

> the politicians of Kashmir who were constantly involved in a power game. Be it Farooq Abdullah, Ghulam Muhammad Shah, or Mufti Muhammad Sayeed. They had created circumstances for an alliance of anti-India forces to fight elections in 1987. It was known as Muslim United Front (MUF). It was a front constituted of mainly Jamat-e-Islami, Islamic Students League, Peoples' Conference, Awami Action Committee, Muslim Conference and Itihad-ul-Muslimeen. Some of the hardcore MUF had already returned from Pakistan on the eve of elections [1987]. They had returned after gaining experience in guerrilla encounters in Afghanistan and were fully trained. Most of them had actually participated in the communal carnage of Feb. 1986 at Anantnag in Kashmir valley in which scores of Hindu temples were damaged and desecrated[28].
>
> The leaders of most of these organisations were notorious terrorists who had organized isolated and mass murders. Crossing the Line of Control and taking refuge in Azad Kashmir to escape Indian police, they founded the most dreaded criminal network under the leadership of Hamid Sheik, Ashfaq Majid, Javad Ahmed Mir and Yasin Malik. This new group, the HAJY as it was known, revived terrorist activities and boosted up the work of JKLF in Kashmir valley. In 1992 JKLF was reorganized with Yasin Malik as its president.

With anti-Indian bodies mushrooming, the condition in the Kashmir valley worsened irreparably. By 1989 bomb blasts became common and between January and July 1989 seventy-two blasts took place which killed five persons and injured fifty-two. Among those one hundred fifty seven suspects arrested in connection with these blasts around eighty were trained in Pakistan or Pak-Occupied Kashmir. Some of them were released on parole on the eve of *Id* only to join the terrorists again. Such government actions only added to the audacity of the criminals. As Jagmohan rightly observes, "One success after another acted as a strong tonic to the eagle" with the result that he gained greater confidence and "soon chose for its pray the roof-garden of the palace of power itself". No wonder, the VIPs connected to India's Union Ministry became the new targets of attack. Kidnapping of Dr. Rubia Sayeed, daughter of the Union Home Minister, Mufti Mohammad Sayeed by JKLF terrorists on 8 December 1989 saddened the whole nation. Many leaders condemned it. But amidst the bewilderment that embarrassed the governmental machineries in the state and the Center, the

Chief of Pakistan based JKLF, Amanullah Khan threatened to kill Rubia, forcing the State to give in to terror tactics[29]. Mr. V P Singh, India's Prime Minister yielded to the emotional appeals of his Home Minister. It was supported by most of the political parties including the BJP, which however pointed out that such surrender would not have happened had it been in the case of one of its own leader's daughter. This is how Premnath Bhat, *Organiser's* Srinagar Correspondent reported the matter:

> People were anxiously waiting to hear from the Union Minister at least once that his daughter was not as important as the country and so he would not like repatriation in exchange for release of five dreaded terrorists who have killed many Rubias and Rehmans in Kashmir. This was the first test of Janata Dal Government in its pledge of safeguarding the integrity of the country. It was after loss of so many lives that these five terrorists were arrested. They were responsible for brutal killings of so many in the valley. Still the entire Indian Cabinet instead of demonstrating manliness and selflessness, made a total surrender before the handful of terrorists. To save one life they agreed to all the demands of KLF leaders unconditionally.
>
> Patriots have embraced gallows smilingly to save the honour of their motherland. But in India a man who could not win a single election in Kashmir for three decades rose to the position of Sardar Patel without any sacrifice and in his first flush let down the entire country by acting the Gen. Niazi way.
>
> The matter would be a little different if this surrender has taken place for rescuing a common man or restoring a poor girl to her parents. But here for personal purposes the entire nation was put to shame and ridicule when the Central Government made an appeal to Pakistan to persuade the Kashmir Liberation Front leaders to release the kidnapped daughter of our Home Minister.
>
> ... During these five tense days [days of Rubia's abduction] thousands of paramilitary troops were rushed to Srinagar. All the top security officers and commandos were flown to Srinagar and it was hoped that the new Government will crack down on the handful of terrorists, smash their hideouts, arrest them and seize their arms. But, alas! The Indian Government succumbed to the demands of the terrorists after it failed to pressurize them with the combined appeals of Babri Masjid committee leaders and all prominent Muslim communal and religious leaders[30].

Whatever might have been argued in favour of or against the government stand, the fact that the "inexperienced government caved into the demands of the newly-born terrorist group of no consequence" boosted up terrorist activities in the valley. Release of the five top terrorists – Hamid Sheik, Sher Khan, Javad Ahmed Zarger, Mohammad Kalwal and Mohammad Altaf Butt was celebrated with great jubilation in the valley. This incident gave an impression even to budding terrorist outfits that the Government of India is only an inert plastic material that could be pressurised into anything they liked and that they were in a position to achieve their goal. As could be expected terrorists began to rule the days to come. What followed was a series of bomb blasts, arson, massacre and serious violation of human rights.

The dawn of 1990 was welcomed by a terrible bomb blast. Mr. Jagmohan, former Governor of Jammu and Kashmir sums up the situation as follows:

> In the disturbances, which took place on January 2, two persons were killed and nine injured. On January 3, the Inspector of Intelligence Bureau, R. P. N. Singh, was shot dead. January 5– the day on which the first batch of the UN officials arrived at Srinagar–was observed as 'self-determination day'. During the curfew, explosions and disturbances occurred in which one person was killed and several others were injured. On January 6, violent clashes occurred and the valley was rocked by four explosions, injuring thirty persons. Another fifty persons were injured in the disturbances on the following day in Srinagar, Baramulla, Sopore and Badgam.

January 8 saw new heights of violence in the valley in which thirteen persons were killed and one hundred injured. In an attempt to intensify the impact of terrorism, a police official was blindfolded, gagged, brutally tortured and then hanged from a tree in Hyderpura[31].

The situation worsened beyond all limits, and as *The Statesman* had already reported, "Kashmir Valley has been effectively left at the mercy of the militants. As it exists now, Kashmir is very nearly lost to the nation". The message of the State and Central Governments to the militants, this paper reported, appeared like "All right, we are leaving. Do what you want"[32]. Indeed nobody including the Central and State authorities knew how to steer clear of the situation. The rest of India did not know that Kashmir was heading towards an irreparable situation. The Central Government offices, installations and other officials proved the main targets of the terrorists' bombs. Pakistan based Kashmir Liberation Alliance had gained complete control over the valley, and what followed was a long chain of murder, massacre, mass-rape and what not[33]. This virtual breakdown of law and order in Kashmir was greatly appreciated by Pakistan. Even the Pakistani press became jubilant over it. *Nation*, the popular Pakistani daily applauded the situation as one in which Kashmiri Muslims' struggle for freedom was at its peak and a historic opportunity to break the shackles of Indian bondage, had arrived.

It was a virtual war, an offensive mounted on India by the Kashmiri terrorists and Pakistani agents in collusion. Kashmir turned out to be the hot bed of Islamic terrorism against India, the Hindus and all the heritages of culture and tradition. By the second half of January 1990 the fanatics had unleashed the forces of *Jehad* or holy war against the Hindus. Mosques emerged as Jehadist camps. Loud-speakers, invariably from all the mosques of the valley blared forth *Allah-o-Akbar, Musalmano Jago, Kafiro Bago, Jehad aa Raha hai* (Allah-oAkbar, arise and awake Muslims, buzz off infidels, Jehad is approaching). The Jehadists roared: *Ganga Jamuna mein aag lagayenge* (we shall destroy the civilization of Ganga Yamuna). It was by all means the clash between Hindu and Muslim civilizations[34]. Naturally the whole wrath turned against Kashmir's indigenous people, the Pandits apart from the other Indians like some sections of the National Conference or Congress workers and a few Communists whom the mendacious Muslim hordes looked down upon as Indian agents.

However those who suffered the most were the Kashmiri Pandits whose families lived in isolated remotes of Kashmiri villages and some areas of Srinagar and other towns. An educated community, the Pandits have ever since their arrival in Kashmir long ago been engaged in enlightening and educating the Kashmiris, and their dedicated efforts had turned the Valley into the seat of the Goddess of learning and fine arts, the *Saradapeeth* as it was called down the centuries. These people who had settled on the banks of the river Sarasvati referred to in the Vedas and Ithihasas, prior to their coming to Kashmir, had made colossal contribution in the fields of religion, philosophy, Sanskrit literature, medicine, history, aesthetics, etc during their five thousand years of stay in the state. As models of nonviolence, they have never handled lethal weapons or spoken harsh words. Devoted to the study of Vedas and Sastras in all their aspects, the essence of these studies has been coursing in their bloodstream from generation to generation. In times of peace as well as turbulence the protective force of a long line of sages and saints who flourished in the Valley from time to time had guided them. They were a pure academic and highly spiritual people not in the habit of offending others and even opponents. But it was this community, which turned out to be the prime target of the terrorists' attack. So long as Hindu life and civilization continue to exist in Kashmir, the ISI backed militants believed, that state would remain with India. The annihilation and expulsion of this Brahmin group was given top priority among the terrorist programmes than anything else. The bloodthirsty vengeance of the Kashmiri terrorists and the atrocities perpetrated on them made this most peace loving community flee from their hearths and homes. Slaughter of these innocent people became a routine affair.

Sri Premnath Bhat, an Advocate, Notary Public, Freelance Journalist, and leading Kashmiri Pandit leader, was shot dead by scooter-riding terrorists about a hundred yards from his house in Anantnag on 27 December 1989 while he was returning from the court. *Organiser*'s Srinagar Correspondent, Bhat was noted for his scathing criticism on the growing terrorism in Kashmir. In a personal letter to the Editor of *Organiser* a few days before his murder, he had conveyed his apprehensions about the security of pro-India elements in Kashmir. Earlier after the February 1986 riots in Anantnag, he had planned to shift to Jammu but given up the idea for its adverse reaction on other Hindu families staying on in the valley. He wrote not only for *Organiser* but Muslim papers too. The sharp shafts of criticism he sent against establishment and terrorist bodies brought his name into the hit list of militants. Two of the latest stories he wrote in the *Organiser* were 'No one dare speak for India in Kashmir' dated 12 November and 'Kashmir ripe for Army rule' dated 17 December 1989. Premnath's last news dispatch for *Organiser* before being shot dead was 'Kashmir Liberation Front's Spectacular success against India – Untold Story of Rubaiya Sayeed abduction' carried by the weekly on 7 January 1990[35].

Government reports on the dastardly murder of the Hindus are innumerable. A few of them are given below.

The terrorists abducted one Brij Nath Kaul and his wife Ratna and his sister Sunitha on 26 May 1990. After having stripped the women naked and molested them in front of a large number of people, the terrorists took them to an isolated place and gang raped them. Brij Nath was clubbed to death while the women, tied to a jeep, were dragged with high speed and killed[36].

On 19 March 1990 the militants barged into the house of N. K. Ganjoo, a Junior Engineer in the Post and Telegraph department. It was at *Chotta bazaar*, Srinagar. "Ganjoo hid himself in a tin rice drum but was found out. The terrorists did not wait a second; they pumped several rounds of bullets into the drum, as his horrified wife and family watched. Then in a psychic twist, they forced his wife and his daughter to taste the blood soaked rice"[37].

On 6 June 1990 at *Trehgam*, Kupwara one Girija Tickoo, wife of Girdhari Lal Tickoo of Bandipura working as Laboratory Assistant in Government Girls High School, Trehgam, was abducted and gang raped for many days. She was shred into pieces on a bar and saw mill[38].

Terrorists abducted one Asha Kaul from her native village of *Achabal*, gang raped and tortured her in an abandoned Hindu house. Her abandoned dead body was later recovered decomposed[39].

The vandalism of the terrorists was not confined to the Hindus alone. The blood thirst and schizophrenia made them blind to distinguish between their own brethrens and others with the result that they smashed the widely propagandized ideal and myth of Islamic brotherhood. So many are the cases of the terrorist abduction of Muslim girls.

The story of 17-year old Rafiqa Banu is only one among hundreds of such incidents. The militants abducted her on 13 June 1992 and raped her for many days before they threw her dead body into river Jehlum at Baramulla[40].

On 1 January 1993 at Kupwara terrorists had shot dead three Muslim women along with the head of the family, Mohd. Ramzan Payer and his son Parvez[41].

On 26 November 1993 the militants barged into a house at Rangwar, Kupwara and indiscriminately fired and killed two Muslim women and an infant and three others of the family[42].

Hundreds of both Hindu and Muslim men, women and children became the victims of terrorist orgy and sadist pleasure. Reports distinguish between the methods of killing Hindus and Muslims. In case of the former the militants resorted to "killing by hangings, strangulation, beheading, slitting of throats, skinning alive, blowing the bodies by tying dynamites, nailing and gunning down the innocent victims"[43]. True, the Muslims of Kashmir too were subjected to terrorist torture, but it was the Hindus, especially the Pandits who suffered more than anybody else.

Threatened by the Muslim majority brandishing *Kalashnikovs* all around, the horror stricken minority took to mass exodus from the Valley at the earliest. The fanatic militants wanted to ensure that the Pandits leave the Valley. They pasted posters on the walls and gates of their houses and other places like the temple walls warning the Pandits to flee from Kashmir or get killed. They issued an ultimatum, through the newspaper, *Alsafa* on 4 April 1990, asking them to leave Kashmir within two days or meet the end[44]. "Pale, haggard and desperate, they crossed the Pirpanchal and reached Jammu" and sought asylum in *Dharam Shalas*, temples and in private rooms along with their kith and kin. With this exodus assuming large proportions the Government arranged for them refugees camps where they lived in tattered tents and unhygienic circumstances. Many of them had crossed over to various places in India, especially Delhi. The number of the migrant Pandit families registered in different places of India by December 1988 amounted to 29,074 in Jammu, 19,338 in Delhi and 2,743 in other parts of the country, and the number of migrant camps to 15 in Jammu with 4,676 families and 14 in Delhi, accommodating 240 families. In addition, there were many who lived in private houses.

No sooner had the Brahmin households been left by their inmates than they became the target of loot and arson by antisocial elements. "More than 30000 houses belonging to Kashmiri Pandits, hundreds of their business establishments, educational institutions, cultural and religious institutions have been destroyed or burnt with the objective of decimating all traces of 5000 years old history and culture of this non-Muslim minority in Kashmir"[45].

According to Mr. Gulam Mohammad Sofi, Editor of *Srinagar Daily Times* the number of the Brahmin houses burnt up to November, 1997 was 32000[46]. The Muslim militants went on ravaging the temples in the remote areas of Kashmir with a ferocity which reminded many of the orgy of violence Sewell describes in context of the battle of Thalikkotta. *Indian Express* gave the following account:

> The Muslim militants have destroyed at least 40 temples and 150 houses during the past five days ... Most of the incidents have been reported from rural Kashmir, especially Anantnag district in the south and Baramulla and Kupwara districts in the north. In Srinagar city a temple and seven houses at Baramulla, a crematorium shed at Karan Nagar, Migrant houses at Jawahar Nagar, Natipora and some other localities were burnt. In villages like Wadipora at Kupwara, Chinigund, Verinag Peba and Dooru in Anantnag, Shergund in Baramulla, Kokernag and Chaki Narain Das, entire settlements of minority houses, schools, *Dharam Shalas* and *Asrams* were reduced to ashes"[47].

D N Dhar observes, Islamic fundamentalists looted and burnt to cinders the houses of the Pandits though every Muslim had received his education from a Kashmiri Pandit teacher. It was a golden chance for the militants who took possession of valuable items left by the Pandits who escaped with their precious life. There were articles of furniture, furnishings, clothing's, utensils, electronic gadgets, washing and sewing machines, telephones, motorcycles, gas cylinders, cooking ranges, jewelry of gold, silver and other precious gems, musical instruments, rare paintings, manuscripts and a lot other. Books formed the special targets. The terrorist outfits conducted the loot in an organized manner. "The booty was collected in a nearby mosque and the recipients thereof were divided–part of it going for Islamic Jehad, part of it to the mosque and part of it to the looters"[48]. The Islamic fundamentalism thus grew beyond all control in the soil of Kashmir so that nothing beyond the Islamic tenets was tolerated. Even enlightened Islamic intellectuals would not be spared by the terrorists, leave alone the Kashmiri Brahmin Pandits.

But more pathetic and pitiable than the plight of the Kashmiri Pandits were the attitude of the State and Central Governments and the hypocrisies of certain organizations which masqueraded as protectors of Human Rights in Kashmir. Indeed the National

Front Government, which was in power for long and that too at a stretch turned only a blind eye to the sad state of affairs. Before the politics of collusion between the State and Centre, both of which wanted to see themselves in the safe saddles of power, the cry of the Kashmir's Brahmin minority continued to resound in the wilderness of negligence. There was none to attend to the question of protecting them. Committees and findings were so many. Interestingly as Jagmohan rightly points out there were even commissions of ex-High Court Judges [49]. But they could offer no relief to those who had undergone great sufferings at the hands of the terrorists.

This can only be disparaged as "nothing short of cruel joke on the victims of a great human tragedy". It would be relevant to quote Jagmohan's comment that "India does not require outside enemies; we are our own worst enemies", a statement the truth of which was born out by the bias hidden in the 'report' by a committee called 'Initiative on Kashmir'. This report brought out some callous travesty of facts, which virtually rationalized and justified terrorism in a way even the worst enemies of India would not have done. The report instead of unveiling the sad plight of the Hindu minority in Kashmir only covered up the horrible story of terrorist violence. "In the name of human rights the report butchered all basic human rights – the right to secure justice; the right to be heard before being condemned; the right not to have reputation built over the years of hard and honest work to be sullied by false and motivated accusations and personal grudges and prejudices of a few individuals"[50]. There was the People's Union of Civil Liberties' with many of its members having allowed themselves to be blindfolded by some clever ones who had clandestinely colluded with anti-national elements. Naturally the aggressor became the aggrieved in their reports, which helped the terrorists ease their conscience and made them feel that they were the more sinned ones. It is highly deplorable that these were the services the human right bodies rendered to humanity. Like wise were findings of delegations like those led by eminent jurists like V M Tharkunde and his friends who "had gone to Srinagar with a pre-set mind, eager to buy militant's line lock, stock and barrel, pick up fault with Jagmohan and the security forces" for the defensive operations in Kashmir[51]. Indeed the State Government of Kashmir from time to time failed miserably in scaling down terrorism. This is testified to by the appeal the Kashmiri Pandit Sabha and other organizations made to Governor, Gen. K V Krishna Rao (Retd). It said:

> The ineffectiveness of the state Government has not been able to check loot, arson and killing of innocent people. Instead of the Government, it is the militants who are the de fact, rulers in the Valley today. The ruling political forces are solely concerned with their own survival avoiding the wrath of the secessionists ... It is a sad commentary on the present administration that not even a single assailant of the minority ... has been either identified or apprehended by the police"[52].

More tenable than anything is the statement of the Pandits in their "Appeal to the People of India" wherein they relate how the state Government remained phantomlike in the Valley and how they continued to live in that violence-torn place until the arrival of Jagmohan on the scene as the new Governor who too had been under various constraints to book the assailants owing to interference and attacks from many corners with vested interests. Indeed the anti-nationalist forces and power mongers leveled unlimited accusations and vilifications against the new Governor's steps to protect the attacked by initiating measures to curb terrorism. Those who were silent about the terrorist attack on the minority in Kashmir became overnight the defenders of human rights when the Indian security personnel, as a step to counter terrorism, fought down the terrorists. Indeed the fate of this Hindu minority in Kashmir was left to the mercy of the ISI backed militants. And one is naturally prompted to doubt whether they were human right activists or theoretical supporters of the bipeds in human form, advocating cannibalism in polished diction. It would not be out of place to conclude with the following musings of Jagmohan over the misfortunes of this minority group of India:

> In a soft, superficial, permissive and, in many ways, cruel India which has the tragic distinction of creating over one lakh refugees from its own flesh and blood and then casting them aside like masterless cattle to fend for themselves on the busy and heartless avenues of the soulless cities, the chances for Kashmiri Pandits to survive as a distinct community are next to nothing. Split, scattered and deserted practically by all, though for different reasons, they stand today all alone, looking hopelessly at a leaking rudderless boat at their feet and an extremely rough

and tumultuous sea to face before they can reach a safe shore across to plant their feet firmly on an assured future[53].

Their recent appeal to the Pakistani administration to declare the Saradapeeth as their pilgrim centre is of much contextual significance. They applied to the Pakistan President that they be allowed to visit Saradapeeth once every year just as in the case of the Sikhs. But it may not easily be construed that an administration, which continued to whip up the Kashmir issue and pressed all the terrorist machineries into the programme of massacring the Pandits would concede this request. After all the Pandits are not a pugnacious group to fight for their rights. The recent call of the Hurriyat to hold talks with Pandits is of course a welcome one. Asserting that it was keen on the return of Pandits to the valley, the Hurriyat Conference on 24 April 2005 said it would invite representatives of the displaced community shortly to discuss the issue. "Kashmir is incomplete without Kashmiri Pandits and present Kashmiri leadership is trying to fill this gap", Mr. Syed Salim Geelani, President of J and K Freedom Party told the press. "As Kashmiri Muslims miss their Pandit brethren in the valley on every occasion, so do Pandits feel nostalgic about their motherland", he said. But responding to the demand for separate homeland by the few Pandit organizations, he said, "homeland should be in the hearts and minds of Muslims in Valley for their Pandit brethren". Does this mean that if the Pandits would not be able to find a place in the good books of the Muslims in the Valley they would continue to remain ill-fated or that their safe future in Kashmir is dependent on how much place they find in the minds and hearts of the Muslims there? And if such a finding of place in the Muslim minds would cost them too much including their cultural identity, values of life, their Gods and religion it would be the expression of Muslim intolerance and fanaticism rather than brotherhood. Does the Hurriyat expect the return of Pandits-turned-Muslims to the Valley? Indeed the question continues to remain unanswered. Who would take them towards a safe future, the vultures' outfits which wiped them out of the Valley or the pseudo secularists and human right activists or the power hungry politicians of India who, for coming to power, are used to disown their brethren?

In addition to the Kashmir terrorist outfits, the Kashmir desk of ISI and many militant bodies at the global level, there was the Jihad council manned by the Pakistan ISI with its camp at Muzaffarabad in Pakistan Occupied Kashmir. Comprised of all the Pakistani and pro-Pakistani militant organizations, this council acted as the prime agent projecting before the Pakistan Government the need to provide them with the required arms and ammunition. That this organization had secret links with some officers of the Kashmir Government who carried out Pak's game plan, had been exposed by the arrest of Gulam Mohammad Sheik, Administrative Officer in Srinagar's Jehlum Valley Medical College and Mufti Mehraj-ud-Din Farooqi who was formerly an Additional Advocate General of Jammu and Kashmir on 2 February 1992. This coincided with many other secret revelations on cross-border terrorism by both Indian and international organizations. Thus says Salman Khurshid,

> "Pakistan not only made its land available for providing arms training and motivation along *Islamic* fundamentalist line, to Kashmir youth, under the direct supervision and control of its Army and Intelligence agencies, but also has been liberally arming them with sophisticated weapons and financing the ongoing militancy in Jammu and Kashmir since 1988"[54].

In addition to the reports of many from both Pakistani and Indian press, there were statements from world leaders too on the Pak involvement in Kashmir. Even US officials too admitted the matter. While touring India in March 1999, President Clinton categorically stated, "there are elements in Pakistani Government that have supported those who are engaged in violence in Kashmir" and condemned the way Pak Government supported attacks against civilians across the Line of Control[55]. It is again interesting to note that President Clinton later suggested to Pakistan Premier Nawaz Sharif to withdraw from Kargil despite that Indian Army mauled Pakistan's North Infantry there. Besides, Pakistan has been forever part of global militant network, which has given a theoretical framework to international terrorism and it involved groups which worked within areas comprising North Africa, West Asia, the Caucasus and Central Asia as their theatre of operations. And one may wonder how a poverty stricken nation as Pakistan could manage to undertake all these terrorist activities on such a large scale. Funds to meet the expenses involved were raised from the sale of narcotics, smuggling and currency counterfeiting which posed great threat to world peace and cultured life! The 'Golden Crescent' – Pakistan, Afghanistan and Iran emerged as the foremost source of heroin smuggling into the world's major metros like New York and Paris. The Pakistanis carried on this illicit but highly lucrative trade at governmental, organizational and individual levels[56]. Both the means as well as the end of Pakistani politics thus proved to be the subversion of establishments and sabotaging of world peace.

The period of Gen. Zia thus was one of confrontation and acrimonious relations with India though he posed as its good friend. True, he presented himself as an agent of harmony and friendship with India. The two-day visit of his Foreign Secretary, Sattar to Delhi in June 1988 to deliberate on all bilateral issues pending and the visit of an Indian delegation to Islamabad to improve postal services between the two countries produced positive results. He personally hosted some students of Delhi's St. Stephen's College between June 28 and July 5 as a token of acknowledging his Indian educational connections[57]. And conferring of Nishan-e-Pakistan on Morarji Desai just four days before his death in the aircrash on 17 August was the finale of the Zia gimmick. The developments in Pakistan's internal affairs, especially Zia's alienation from Junejo whose elevation to Muslim League's presidential chair which earned him a political base in Pakistan proved to the former a shot in his arm. Differences emerged between the two on questions of holding the general elections, restoration of democracy and foreign policy. Again, Zia wanted a fast faced evacuation of the Soviet troops from Afghanistan while Junejo favoured the policy of gradualness in the matter. The differences snowballed into a crisis by the end of May 1988 with the result that Mohammed Khan Junejo was dismissed on 29 May as Prime Minister and the National Assembly was dissolved on 31 May, promising general election within a period of 90 days. All these domestic developments pressurized Gen. Zia so hard that he could not for the time being pursue his evil designs on India.

The death of Gen.Zia in the aircrash, it was suspected, was the result of a conspiracy, which remains still a mystery. Speculations were in the air that Pakistani Shiites who were highly critical of Zia's Sunni Wahabi led Islamization programme, were behind it as also the members of the Pakistani air force and intelligence group who colluded with the Pakistan Peoples Party. The involvements of some from the ISI itself who feared Zia's draconian action in connection with the Ojhari camp disaster and of the USA, which might have prevailed upon the anti-Zia elements inside Pakistan to see some change in Pakistani leadership, were also suspected. All these speculations however vanished before the well-certified 'technical' and 'mechanical' reasons of the aircrash. The enigma thus involved in Zia's death added one more link to the long chain of the murders, political assassinations and mysterious deaths, which continued to cloud Pakistani politics right from its birth.

The death of Zia brought about some sudden shifts in the power structure with Mirza Aslem Beg becoming the Chief of Army Staff and Gulam Ishaq Khan being raised to the office of the President. Though they subscribed to Zia's policy they knew that prolongation of military rule would only aggravate the situation, which had caused the death of their dear military dictator. Hence they thought in terms of a general election as promised by Gen. Zia. And Pakistan went to general elections on 17 November 1988.

The popularity of Benazir Bhutto led Pakistan Peoples Party had by now considerably increased owing to the peoples' anxiety to return to a democratic setup. Naturally the party posed a threat to the successors of Zia and they by all means at their command designed strategies to defeat the PPP. Their brainchild Islamic Jamhuri Ittehad (IJI) or the Islamic Democratic Alliance was thus born out of the ISI forged new friendship among the members of the Muslim League, those hailing from the various Islampasand parties and Zia fans. The new party led by the Punjabi industrialist, Mian Nawaz Sharif who was a staunch supporter of Zia regime, though it emerged only second at the hustings, could checkmate Benazir whose PPP topped as the single largest party winning 92 out of the 207 contested seats. Both being without a pronounced majority resorted to horse-trading and canvassing to form government. They started wooing the National Assembly members of Jamaate-e-Islami, the Awami Party and Mohajir Quami Movement. Nawaz Sharif and his IJI failed to gain the support of the required number though Ishaq Khan in collusion with the army deliberately delayed calling Benazir to form the government. Ultimately pressures from various corners including that from USA left Ishaq Khan and his coterie with no other alternative than inviting Benazir to take over.

But the Zia lobby could not be so easily bullied. Indeed the masters of intriguing that they were, Aslam Beg and Ishaq Khan brought out new strategies to trap Benazir. With their knowledge of Bhutto family's hostile attitude towards the army and other groups, which had supported the Zia regime, they moved cautiously lest an unbridled Benazir should turn against them. After all, it had been the tradition of the Pakistani politics to go to any extent to wreak vengeance on political opponents, as had been the cases of Liaqat Ali, Bhutto and even Zia. Hence they set up some preconditions for Benazir taking over as Prime Minister. The strings thus attached included that she would in no way diminish the dominant role of the armed forces in Pakistan's politics or take any action against its members who were hostile to the Bhuttos and PPP. It was agreed to retain the 8th amendment of the Pakistani constitution, which endowed the President with special rights to dismiss an elected Prime Minister whenever the former deemed it necessary for national stability and security and appoint the Chiefs of Armed Forces without the Prime Ministerial consent. Also she would not tamper with the defence and foreign policies systematized by Gen. Zia. It was thus ensured that Benazir too could not help recognize the military domination over the country's administration and that she won't be permitted by the *junta* to purge the national politics of the hurdles which had very well become an internal part of Pak administrative structure.

Yet these shameless impositions did not prove problematic to Ms. Benazir who was anxious to hold the reins of power. Power hunger overrode all other considerations including sense of justice, integrity and independence. One could certainly not expect anything more than this from the daughter of Zulfiqar Ali Bhutto who mooted the idea of two Prime Ministers for Pakistan so that he could be one! And once again it was clear that Pakistani democracy would remain a mockery and that no democratic effort would be able to ignore the dominance of the military element. The agreement thus having been satisfactory to all concerned including USA whose ambassador Robert Oakley was contend that the conditions of the agreement would not deter his nation's interests, Benazir finally swore in as Prime Minister on 2 December 1988, followed by Ishaq Khan taking over as elected President on 12 December with all the powers Zia enjoyed. Thus was sealed off the fate of a democracy in the best interests of a group of power hungry politicians, military *junta* and alien forces[58].

Indian democracy too was something more or less the same as in Pakistan except in its military factor. Indian military establishment unlike that of Pakistan was highly disciplined. Its officials, experts in many a faculty of knowledge as they were in martial arts, were noted for decency, dignity, enlightenment and respect for democratic values. Many of them were well known even for their spiritual bent of mind which always made them take it as their duty to safeguard their nation and its democracy, a duty they would however do only if the democratic set up of the nation would call upon them to. They were the true icons of Indian democracy, independence, integrity and national honour. It would be an unpardonable sin to compare even an ordinary military official belonging to the great tradition of Gen. K M Cariappa or the like lofty ones with Pakistan's notorious masters of butchery like Thikka Khan or Zia ul Haq. Indian Generals were the highly disciplined officers of lofty tradition, and had feathered the cap of Indian democracy in the best way they could. But this was not enough to maintain the vitality of a democratic republic, which calls for a sublime and enlightened political leadership, an element India lacked at times. In fact Benazir's Indian counterpart unfortunately lacked shrewdness, farsightedness, political insight or a deep sense of history and wisdom. Rajiv Gandhi, though a descendent of the Nehru family, did not command the heights his mother or grandfather had. An engineering Graduate who only knew how to fly an aircraft would not fit in to the position of one who was to lead a great nation like India especially at a time when she stood at the crossroads beset with many problems, both in domestic and foreign affairs. A personable and handsome young man, Rajiv was frank and sincere in his approach to the problems that confronted the nation. But sincerity alone would not do. Inexperienced in political activities, administrative capability, diplomacy and strategy, he was only the product of a sympathy wave that dumped him on to the shores of political wasteland.

As was well known it was the sympathy his mother's assassination generated that put him on the saddle of power. Naturally his lack of experience, and incompetence proved to be prime factors that made him a misfit to hold the position of the Prime Minister of India as was proved by the Sri Lankan, Assam, Mizo or Indo-Pak issues. He could never be a match even to Benazir, the Pak Premier.

Perhaps every body except the young Prime Ministers knew that attempts at Indo-Pakistan amity would prove only a soap opera when set against the backdrop of Kashmir tragedy. Engineered by the ISI, the military top brass of Pakistan and both Pakistani and Kashmiri terrorist outfits, all attempts at settling Indo-Pak differences failed.

Indeed even before Benazir became the Pakistan Prime Minister, Rajiv Gandhi had started diplomatic overtures with her. Once it was obvious that she would become Pak Prime Minister he assured her of India's friendship, goodwill and total cooperation through Aftab Seth who was India's Consul-General in Karachi. The SAARC summit of 1998 December proved a platform for both leaders to communicate with each other. Rajiv Gandhi had already sent Ronen Sen of the Foreign Service to Pakistan before the SAARC summit to prepare the ground for their contact. His interaction with Benazir during 1989 aroused great expectations that the bilateral relations would show marked improvement. His speech at SAARC summit reflected this expectation:

> I am particularly happy to be here when the people of Pakistan have elected you, Madam Prime Minister, to lead your great country to progress and prosperity, rooted in democracy. I bring greetings to the people of Pakistan from their sisters and brothers in India. We rejoice in the prospect for friendship and cooperation between India and Pakistan... here in Pakistan democratic elections have led to the installation of new government under your distinguished leadership, giving rise to hope everywhere in the subcontinent of a new dawn of friendship and cooperation between us[59].

Rajiv Gandhi felt that there was "definitely a mood on both sides to try and get things back on the track to normalize" the relations between the two countries since he believed that the PPP's policy was more positive than those of the earlier governments. He definitely thought that Banazir would clean up the Pakistan politics like himself who desired to purge Indian polity of its evils[60]. Consequently there were Defence Secretary level talks at Delhi, the visit of India's Commerce Minister, Dinesh Singh to Islamabad where he had audiences with President Gulam Ishaq Khan and Pak Finance Minister, Mehbubul Haq on the need to improve mutual relations. There were agreements to the effect that each other's nuclear installations and facilities won't be attacked, there would be cultural cooperation, and that the double tax on incomes from international civil aviation transactions would be done away with. The Foreign Secretary level talks held in Islamabad between 21 and 24 May 1989 and the talks on Siachin held on 14 to 17 June zeroed in on matters pertaining to patrolling the border to scale down cross border terrorism. Friendship was thus everywhere in the air and there were high hopes on both sides that the young Prime Ministers would achieve something definitely positive.

But things went otherwise, it being quite impossible for Benazir to be free herself of the hold of the Pak military click, its Intelligence Service, etc. Mired in the manipulations of Ishaq Khan who was unhappy about the initiatives she took, the move to better relations with India met an abrupt end. Consequently, Benazir reverted back to the Kashmir issue and old and discordant Pak policies in the main areas of bilateral relations. For her too there was no other option than resorting to the stereotyped 'hate India' campaign to please the Ishaq group in order to remain in power. The period of Rajiv thus passed with no tangible change in India-Pakistan relations. And in the general elections of November-December 1989 his government gave way to the newly formed Janata Dal coalition government led by V P Singh.

Indeed the problems affecting both the nations were of so great dimensions that their gravity could be made out only when analysed against the backdrop of the worsening relations between the superpowers. In fact the 'White Man' continued still 'burdening' himself to enrich his economic interests at the expense of weaker, backward, poverty-stricken nations dominated by religious fundamentalism as in Pakistan, Afghanistan and some countries of the South East. The historic mission of sowing whirlwind in the third world has by this time passed from British hands to those of USA, the self-styled upholder of liberty and Human

Rights whose violation of liberty and human rights of the powerless and the poor could be the source material for endless volumes on man's inhumanity to man. The white man thus turned out to be a menace to the peace loving people whose life became soaked in sorrow by the greed and arrogance of the West.

With the Soviet Union having withered, the East and Asia-Pacific region have turned out to be a happy hunting ground for USA. Again the progress achieved by some of the Eastern nations like China whose military and economic growth and its sustained expansion of its Asian markets was enviable and India with her highly successful democratic experiment, her self-reliant, modest and sound agro-based economy turned Asia attractive to US interests in various ways. But as China proved rough and tough to the pursuit of US interests donned in humanitarian and philanthropic attire the Western giant turned to more convenient and safe pastures like Pakistan, Afghanistan, India and the unstable and anarchic West Asia[61].

Convenient excuses were found. And these powerless nations, consequent to their backwardness and weakness combined with their slavish psych fell easy victims to Western dictates, even praising their most foolish findings as descending from the Himalayan peak of a White man's brain[62].

The US seemed determined to subordinate the independent national economies to its growing capitalist economy by sheer might. Former US President Mr. Clinton called the spade a spade. Addressing the UN General Assembly he said: "Let me start by being clear about where the United States stands. United States occupies a unique position in world affairs today" and as a matter of fact "intends to remain engaged and lead" the world[63]. The former Deputy Secretary of State, Strobe Talbot put the matter straight: "American diplomacy and military operations are predicated on the premise that the way foreign leaders will behave within their borders has direct bearing on the way they will behave towards other countries including towards America"[64]. This meant that even the internal policies of independent nation states should be brought in line with the foreign policy demands of USA from them. This statement and the approach involved in it, as J N Dixit observes, "raises profound questions about nation states, which are not completely homogenous and which are still in the process of consolidating their pluralistic national identities"[65]. In fact this is nothing other than the repetition of the colonialist attitude of the 18th and the 19th centuries and made it clear that what USA wanted was that world nations should design their political and economic policies in the interests of the former.

America's foreign policy in South Asia and the Middle East being designed in accordance with such a colonialist attitude, it would be necessary to treat the Kashmir issue, the Indo-Pak strained relations, Afghan terrorism and US designs in the Middle East as interrelated issues. In fact it was the US, which encouraged Islamic terrorism in the East, especially in Afghanistan, as a ploy against the USSR whose emergence as a superpower proved anathema to US capitalist interests in the Asiatic region. Even after the collapse of the Soviet Union and in the post-Cold War period US went on with its programme of dealing with the issue of terrorism. US, as the other nations did, knew well that these areas in general and Pakistan in particular were the breeding grounds and beehives of terrorism. Yet it raised no brow against Pakistani sponsored terrorism, even when it bombed Libya and Iran under the pretext of abetting terrorism. It was well known that Pakistan, the top-ranking trafficker of both drug and terrorism, was at the background of Islamic terrorism at the global level. Despite clear evidences to show that Afghan based *Talibans* were strongly rooted in Pakistan and Pak-occupied Kashmir and the repeated call from the side of the Indian leaders to America to declare Pakistan a terrorist state, US attitude to Pakistan was soft and supporting since it would act as the American agent to see terrorism going on unabated in Kashmir and surrounding regions. Indeed it was the American design to see the terrorist virus quarantined within the Afghanistan, Pakistan and Kashmir area so that it may not spread to other regions where its economic interests lay. The US knew that if the *Lashkar-e-Toiba*'s plan to overthrow the American protected Saudi monarchy and replace it with a *Jihadist* one would succeed, it would defeat the interests of the Western powers', especially US' interests in the oil resources of West Asia. This being the case, America was always afraid of an Indo-Pak war in which the Indian army would triumph and uproot the terrorist camps from within the Kashmir valley and the Pak Occupied Kashmir. Because once the terrorists are flushed out of these regions the only safe pasture for them would be the Middle East where American interests were deeply entrenched. This is why the Americans always advised India to keep restraint in times of Indo-Pak military collisions and prevailed upon her not to cross the Line of Control, and urged Pakistan to withdraw from the LOC lest the Indian Army under strategic needs should feel constrained to barge into the POK and clear the area of terrorist enclaves. The US strategy was designed to keep her oil interests in the Middle East safe. American policy, as the veteran writer N S Rajaram has pointed out, aimed at gaining time at the cost of Indian space and Indian lives. "The present policy of America and the world gaining time in exchange for India's space and lives, cannot go for ever. The time gained is not inexhaustible. More seriously, if continued, the present policy would allow the world to fight terrorism to the last Indian. This is what the Indian leaders should guard against"[66]. It is again interesting to note that even when the US was well aware of the terrorist nature of Pakistan it would still support this Islamic state's policies against India. The US military and economic aid to Pakistan was stopped in October 1990 in accordance with the Pressler Amendment. And "one may therefore justifiably question as to why does Pakistan still not figure among terrorist nations in the reckoning of the US State Department in spite of the availability of considerable amount of evidence against Islamabad"[67]. This pro-Pakistan attitude of America has been vivid in almost all its approaches to Kashmir issue. The statement of Ms. Robin Raphel on 13 December 1996 suggesting "maximum autonomy to Kashmir" was indeed very much saddening. Her call to settle the Kashmir issue which would remain only unsolved notwithstanding all electoral activities and formation of a state government there, only boosted up insurgency and Pakistani support to the so called 'freedom fight' of the Kashmiris[68]. The statement of the former US Secretary of State Mr. Warren Christopher that he had asked Assistant Secretary of State Robin Raphel to give "highest priority" to "nuclear confrontation or potential confrontation" between India and Pakistan clearly reveals that the US was the instigator of all violence involved in Kashmiri terrorism[69]. This role that USA was playing in Indo-Pak relations was well brought out by India's former External Affairs Minister Mr. Dinesh Singh when he said, "They [the Americans] are supporting Pakistan because Pakistan is an

Islamic state and they have such interest in West Asia and the Gulf and they think Pakistan could be useful to them and their trade in other Islamic Countries"[70]. Besides, a war torn India with its economic developments spoiled would not cater to America's expectation of making India a lucrative market for its capital in the centuries ahead. But so long as the leaders of both India and Pakistan would not understand the real motives of USA any possibility or probability of finding a solution to Indo-Pak differences would only remain a dream.

Kashmir remained seriously disturbed throughout the times of both Rajiv Gandhi and Mr. V P Singh. Behind the veil of rapprochement Pakistan continued her clandestine support to the Jihadists in Kashmir, and Benazir too pursued the same policy to continue to remain in power. By the days of V P Singh terrorism had snowballed beyond all limits. He who assumed office in December 1989 and his Foreign Minister Mr. I K Gujral were deeply interested in improving Indo-Pak relations and proved to be the staunch advocates of a very warm neighbourly approach to the Kashmir issue. But the developments in Kashmir only doused their flaming friendly zeal with Pakistan[71]. As is well known President Ishaq Khan and Gen. Beg were supporters of terrorism in Kashmir. They established secret cells to consolidate different factions working for the liberation of Kashmir. It was reported that Pakistan-occupied Kashmir Government had increased the grant to Jammu and Kashmir Liberation Front from Rs. 2 crore to Rs. 10 crores, all with the blessings of the Pakistan Government, which wanted its elected Prime Minister too to fall in with their designs[72]. And in her desperate attempt to please the Pak military junta Benazir started an anti-India campaign by openly advocating 'self-determination' for Kashmiris, which the Government of India, she alleged, was suppressing with an iron hand[73]. In her attempt to outdo her political opponents who breathed fire on the question of Kashmir she reverted to a new brand of inflammatory rhetoric. She inaugurated a solidarity week on Kashmir lasting from 2 to 9 February 1990, simultaneous with the IJI calling for a nationwide strike to support Kashmiri secession and terrorism on 5 February, which the Pak Government declared a national holiday. Indian High Commission in Pakistan received news that there would be mass crossing of Pakistanis into Jammu and Kashmir territory between 2 and 15 February with a view to facilitate entry of terrorists into the region under cover of civilian crossings. Despite the warnings from the Indian authorities as well as the foreign agencies including the office of US ambassador Robert Oakely about the possible risk involved in such an audacious attempt, the Pak Government and its opposition did not desist from whipping up mass hysteria. And the Jihadists numbering two to three thousand crossed to the Indian side across the LOC from Chakothi in POK. Some attempts at crossing were made in the northeast of Sialkot too. The bid however was foiled by the decisive action of Indian border security personnel who killed six persons and left several wounded, giving the clear message that India would not be a mute spectator to such border violations. There was of course the usual Pak sponsored propaganda about the Indian forces' brutal attack on unarmed civilians and about human rights violations. That the aggressor always pretended as the aggrieved was well known to all who were familiar with Indo-Pakistan affair and hence Pak complaint did not evoke any international sympathy. This was followed by the Pak bid to muster international support to revive its claim to Kashmir by sending Pak envoys to countries from Australia to North America and the programme of supplying weapons and material support to the secessionist outfits in Kashmir. This coincided with Banazir's visit to POK on 13 March and her provocative speech at Muzzafarabad describing Kashmir terrorism as 'holy *Jehad*', and swearing to drive out Indian administrators from that state. She also mooted plans to launch a Prime Ministerial fund to help Kashmiris, and issued an official notification in this regard on 1 April 1990. This emboldened Pakistani outfits like *Jamat-e-Islami* to declare that more training camps would be set up to recruit "Freedom fighters for Kashmir". This gave a boost to terrorist activities in Kashmir and *Jehad* became the rule of the day.

Pakistan gained in confidence by the spontaneous outbreaks in Kashmir and the thought that its new nuclear capabilities were more than a match to India's conventional weapons[74]. But top military officers in India held that India's conventional and nuclear potential would suffice to beat back any Pak aggression[75]. The Government of India turned assertive with Prime Minister Mr. V P Singh announcing on 10 April 1990 of the strong and decisive retaliation to any Pak attack. Indian High Commissioner to Pakistan Mr. J N Dixit talking to Pakistani Foreign Secretary Tanvir Ahmad Khan and U S ambassador Oakley, cautioned that, "if Pakistani pyrotechnics continued, it should be prepared to face an extremely firm military response not only across the Line of Control but all along the Indo-Pakistan border"[76]. Meanwhile India moved three divisions of its Army from Eastern sector to the western to be stationed at Punjab, Kashmir and some unspecified area on the international border. Indian Army mobilized its artillery to the border and Air Force pressed its radar installations into wartime situation. Pakistan also readied its forces and moved it towards the international border. Tension increased and Indian Prime Minister V P Singh, referring to strong evidences about the Pakistani troop movements along the Line of Control, exhorted his countrymen to be more pugnacious and patriotic with a strong resolution to fight the enemy. Strongly reacting to Benazir Bhutto's call to fight a thousand year war against India, Mr. Singh pooh-poohed Pakistan's capability of withstanding a thousand hours war with India and called upon Indians to be "psychologically prepared" to fight to destroy the enemy[77]. His attitude to Pakistan became stiffer than the stand he took in Rubia Syed's abduction case. Besides, with the Bharatiya Janata Party, one of the powerful partners in his coalition government insisting on adoption of a tough stand V P took to a more aggressive line. Indian Government's decision to allocate more funds to defence expenditure and its Defence Ministry's annual report focusing on the threats from Pakistan were further steps. The growing political precariousness and the intense insurgency in Kashmir made the Government of India tighten up security measures and reinforce its troops along the Line of Control. She was also cautioned by many of her expert diplomats on the matter. A surprise or lightening attack cannot be ruled out, said Mr. AP Venkiteswaran, a former Foreign Secretary who was one of the best informed experts on international relations[78]. India was thus by all means fully prepared to meet an immediate Pakistani attack at any time. Accusing India of mobilizing troops enormously, Pakistan started to move its forces towards Indian border by the end of April 1990[79].

The war scare resulting from the acrimonious exchanges and military movements throughout 1990 caused much concern to the US, which as already mentioned was fully alive to the possible threat to its economic interests in South East Asia and Middle East. It was against this backdrop that US Deputy National Security Advisor Robert Gates and Richard Hass, a member of the US National Security Council made a dramatic visit to New Delhi and Islamabad with the capitalist panacea of 'restraint'[80]. Raising the smoke screen of nuclear threat US President George H W Bush in company of Mikhail Gorbachev of USSR, even felt the need to issue a joint statement urging restraint over Kashmir issue. The US media too played their role in unleashing fear about the nuclear phantom. There were "flights of imagination" says JN Dixit "resulting in books like *Critical Mass* which asserted that India and Pakistan were on the brink of a nuclear war which necessitated Gates to dash to the subcontinent and that it was his consummate skill and US intervention which prevented a nuclear conflagration". According to him there was no truth at all in these speculations. The US' claim that it was they who warded of an imminent Indo-Pakistan show down was off the mark. Yet, simultaneous with Gates mission in operation the Pakistani cry for India's blood went on as usual. Nawaz Sharif, Punjab Chief Minister while addressing mass meetings in POK went on saying that any Indian infringement on the Pakistani border would be met with "each Kashmiri" eliminating "a thousand Hindus". The Jamat-e-Islami's international meet in May to declare support to Kashmiri terrorists attended by Islamic parties the world over shored up legitimacy of the so called "freedom movement of the people of Jammu and Kashmir"[81].

Where the US' call to keep restraint failed the Kashmir movement succeeded! Pakistan's support to what it called the "freedom movement of the people of Jammu and Kashmir" began to boomerang. The 'third option' of a Kashmir independent of both India and Pakistan put forth by Amanullah Khan and other Kashmiri organizations began gaining support, which Benazir could not digest. If Kashmir would become a separate independent entity Pakistan would be left with nothing to fight India. Therefore retracing her steps, she stated at a press conference on 24 May that the desirability of an independent Kashmir is not envisaged in the 1947 enactment that created independent India and Pakistan. She conveniently forgot that the Indian Independence Act of 1947 retained with each Princely state the right to join either of the two new dominions and that it was in accordance with the provisions this Act that Maharaja Hari Singh had signed the Instrument of Kashmir's accession to India, the very same Act which Pakistan had violated when its forces invaded Kashmir within no time of its enactment. Flouting the Prime Ministerial authority the JKLF in Rawalpindi declared the formation of independent Kashmir on 18 June. To Benazir's further embarrassment violent attacks on her government came from among Sindhis, Mohajirs and Punjabis in Sind, and her own existence in Pakistani politics was endangered by the lobbying and factional feud between herself and Ishaq Khan. Yet she would not give up her anti-India tirade and continued to cry for "self determination" to the people of Kashmir which she linked up with the problems of the Muslim minority in India. Consequently all later deliberations on Indo-Pak relations could only end in fiasco. There were suggestions from Indian side to revive many a confidence building measure. The Foreign Secretary level talks that followed were shipwrecked on the rock of Pakistan's intransigent stand on Kashmir and her insistence on adherence to the UN resolutions on that state which was strongly objected to by Indian Foreign Secretary Muchkund Dubey who stoutly defended India's stand on the issue as usual. Pakistan failed to honour its own commitments made in 1972 Simla agreement. When asked about the 1972 Pakistani commitment made by Zulfiqar Ali Bhutto to the former Indian Prime Minister Mrs. Indira Gandhi, Benazir only answered in an evasive manner quite unbecoming of a Prime Minister. During his talks with Benazir, Dubey drew her attention to the assurance her father had given Mrs. Gandhi that the Line of Control in Jammu and Kashmir would be made the plank on which the Kashmir issue would be solved for good. Mr. J N Dixit thus writes about her interesting reactions to it:

> She made two points in response: First, that though she was at Simla, she was a young student then, so she did not recall any proposals or assurances of the type having been given by her father. She said that her father had not mentioned anything about his last private conversation with Mrs. Gandhi before the agreement was signed. She then went on to say that nearly two decades had elapsed since the Simla discussions and, therefore, she did not know how relevant the discussions, or even some aspects of the Simla agreement, were in the changed circumstances in Jammu and Kashmir as well as in the

subcontinent. She said that India should agree with Pakistan to examine the origins of the Kashmir issue and the right of self-determination of Muslims. This particular exchange between Dubey and Benazir led India to the definite conclusion that Pakistan no longer wished to adhere to Simla agreement or the commitments, whatever lip service it may occasionally pay to certain clauses of the agreement as a matter of formality or convenience[82].

Soon her views and opinions proved no longer valid in Pakistani politics. Alleged of mismanagement, corruption, incapability to tackle internal issues and inefficient defence and foreign policies, President Ishaq Khan with the support of Gen. Aslam Beg dismissed her and dissolved the National Assembly on 16 August. And in the general elections that followed Mrs. Bhutto's PPP gave way to the formation of the Government by Nawaz Sharif's IJI. India's political scenario too underwent a change for the worse. The squabble and personal ambitions of leaders within the Janata Dal as well as BJP's strong reservations and objections to V P Singh policy of appeasing Muslim communalism as expressed in his dealing with the Babri Masjid issue, led to the fall of his government in India. The political defection helped the Indian National Congress to fish in troubled waters, and Mr. Chandrasekhar became the Prime Minister of India with the support of Rajiv Gandhi. Throughout the times that followed there were ministerial and foreign secretary level talks. Initiatives of Mr. Chandrasekhar, Mr. Narasimha Rao, Nawaz Sharif or Mrs. Benazir again, did not bring about any tangible progress in India-Pakistan relations. Because during all these times Pakistan have been experiencing political turbulence with the military junta bullying, controlling and sabotaging democratically elected governments and representatives. Consequently, as was usual, Pakistan continued to be the breeding ground of anarchy, instability and terrorism, which increased to a level even the Pakistani Government could not control. Consequently, Kashmir issue and Islamabad's support to terrorism continued. As the delegation of Members of Indian Parliament which met the UN Secretary General Boutros Boutros Ghali on 5 November 1993, pointed out "Islamabad's support to terrorists and operation of training camps would convince anyone that Pakistan is not interested in a sincere dialogue" with India[83]. The situation in Pakistan is such that the fundamentalist leaders, some members of the

Army top brass and terrorist organizations defeat even the best moves made by successive Presidents and Prime Ministers. "Two generations of Indians and Pakistanis", Benazir Bhutto once said, "have been held hostage to the Kashmir issue. It is time, both governments developed an innovative and enlightened approach to resolve the problem". Ignoring her early calls for *Jehad*, she said, "We do not see the Kashmir issue in terms of *Jehad*. The two countries need not go to war". Speaking to press persons at Jaipur in early April 2005 she hailed the many Confidence Building Measures being undertaken by India and Pakistan, and stressed the need of a people-to-people contact to generate goodwill. But she, like several other elected leaders of Pakistan, knew that such an approach could bear fruit only if there was a strong democratic government in Pakistan completely free from army domination, a democracy wherein popular will rules supreme, wherein the military establishment would be the protector of democracy rather than its saboteur. She spoke about the desirability of a stable democracy restored in Pakistan so that India-Pak relations could be on sound and strong friendship. Advocating a pluralistic society and polity in Pakistan she said that political parties with different agenda could work together in her country, taking a lesson from India. But the increasing terrorist activities precipitated by Pakistan's ISI and Pakistan and Kashmir based outfits, shocking incidents of Hazratbal Mosque in April 1993, the Charar-I-sharif incident, the ISI planned attacks at Bombay Stock Exchange and other Indian institutions, later bloodbath in the Akshardham temple and the militant attack on Indian Parliament building, to mention only a few, had an adverse impact on bilateral relations. Though of late there are signs of some improvement in Indo-Pakistan relations, and of mounting hopes of an early accord on all discordant issues between the two sister-countries, the terrorist activities aided and abetted by Pakistan continue to bleed Kashmir and none can predict when peace and tranquility would return to the disturbed valley.

References

1. D N Dhar, *Dynamics of Political Change in Kashmir*, New Delhi, 2001, p. 185.
2. *Ibid.*, p. 184.
3. See Appendix– IV: Kashmir Accord.

4. D N Dhar, *Op. Cit.*, p. 185.
5. M J Akbar, *Kashmir: Behind the Vale*, New Delhi, 2003, pp. 188-189.
6. Victoria Schofield, *Kashmir in Conflict*, New Delhi, 2004, p. 123.
7. Verma P S, *Jammu and Kashmir at the Political Crossroads*, New Delhi, 1994, p. 57.
8. Jagmohan, *My Frozen Turbulence in Kashmir*, New Delhi, 1991, p. 106.
9. Sheik Abdullah's presidential address at a session of the National Conference at Jammu on 24 April 1975.
10. Anthony Hyman, Muhammed Ghayur and Naresh Kaushik, *Pakistan: Zia and After*, New Delhi, 1989, p. 61.
11. R Majumdar, *Pakistan: Jinnah to the Present Day*, New Delhi, 1988, Vol. II, p. 485.
12. *Ibid.*, p. 486.
13. *Ibid.*, p. 491.
14. There are so many cases of irony wherein the nations have exerted their bullying tactics over the neighbours by interfering in their internal affairs. The case of world powers and even of Indian Muslims trying to interfere in the internal affairs of Turkey after the World War I has already been discussed at length. While the British Government wanted to dismember the Turkish Sultanate, the Indian Muslims wanted to reinstate the Caliph. However, as Turkish republicanism grew strongly under the leadership of Kemal Attaturk Turkey could opt for independence according to its own choice. Morarji was also of independent and right thinking nature. Despite his great love for his motherland he would not keep away from airing his opinions about India's wrong foreign policies. For instance the issue of the Liberation Tigers of Tamil Elam and the Indian Government's early policy of supporting the LTTE contrary to its later sending of the Indian Peace Keeping Force to Sri Lanka caused great ideological confusion to many Indian leaders. But Morarji kept no reservations on the issue and openly attacked the Indian Government's policy of supporting the Sri Lankan Tamil Tigers. The Tamil problem was to the Lankans what the Punjab's Khalistan issue was to the Indians and that Indians should look at the neighbours' problems through their own experiences, he opined. He was not a man of double-dealings, using different yardsticks on similar issues.
15. Sumit Ganguly, *Conflict Unending: India-Pakistan Tensions Since 1947*, New Delhi, 2002, p. 82.
16. Peter J.S. Duncon, *The Soviet Union and India* (New York: Council of Foreign Relations, 1989) p. 47.

17. The assassination of India's former Prime Minister, Mrs. Indira Gandhi and the Supreme Court judgment thereafter became highly controversial subjects. True, Kehar Singh one of the main accused was found guilty by the apex court of India and was hanged to death. But this did not close the chapter as such and doubt and suspicion involved in the case made the Government of India order a re-inquiry. Interestingly, India's well-known jurist, Ram Jethmalani who was also the counsel for the accused had so many reservations about the case and at times expressed his doubts regarding the involvement of a foreign lobby other than the Sikhs. This lobby, he seemed to have doubted, was an Italian one which might have had been behind the series of deaths (or murders?) that took place in the Nehru family. He also raised doubts about the visit of Peter Utsinov, the photographer, during the days preceding Indira Gandhi's assassination. He had again referred to a 'foreigner' who roamed about and around the Indian Parliament. Did he mean that deaths would continue to haunt the members of the Nehru family unless and until a foreigner would be India's leader? The legal issues involved in the case and the consequent judgment also leave many a doubt about the mysterious nature of the case. This is how *Indian Express* commented on the judgment, in its editorial of 24 October 1988 headlined 'Consult others':

If since the assassination of Mahatma Gandhi a crime has deserved the death penalty it is the assassination of Mrs Indira Gandhi. To kill the Prime Minister and a defenceless lady at that, is to ask for hanging. Her assassination is certainly among "the rarest of rare cases" in which execution is warranted.

But in all cases the evidence on which persons are to be executed must be such that even those who sympathise with the criminals would find it conclusive. This is specially so in the present case, precisely because of its importance. Were the slightest suspicion to remain about the guilt of the accused, it would be held as an eternal reproach to our country, and would be ground for further enmity.

The evidence about Kehar Singh, who along with Satwant Singh is now condemned to be hanged, leaves one in the air. The birthday of a child is celebrated. Kehar Singh is invited. Beant Singh, the assassin who was shot dead by the guards of the Indo-Tibetan Border Force, and his wife also go along. Provocative *Bhajans* "in the context of Operation Bluestar" are sung. There is no evidence that Kehar Singh deliberately took Beant Singh and his wife to the party to expose them to the Bhajans. "There may not be any such evidence", says the Supreme Court. "But it may not be non-sequitur when one takes an uninvited guest to such a function in the circumstances of the case". Proof enough to hang a man?

Kehar Singh used to visit Beant Singh's house, the families of the two being friends. On one such visit the two of them spent "15 to 18 minutes" on the roof. They do not narrate to Beant's wife what they have talked. "It plainly indicates that Kehar Singh and Beant Singh were combined and conspiring together", says the Supreme Court, that there was "exchange of secret information" between them, that "the said conversation ... could be only to further the prosecution of the conspiracy", that "these talks go a long way in establishing Kehar Singh being a party to the conspiracy". Does a conversation that no one has ever claimed to have heard, go such a long way?

When, about one and a half hours after she is killed, Kehar Singh hears of Mrs Gandhi's assassination he is said by an officer colleague to have remarked, "whosoever would take confrontation with the *Panth*, he would meet the same fate". This, the Supreme Court says, establishes that "he was cognizant of all the details of the coming tragedy and waiting to receive the news on that fateful day". "Unless Kehar Singh had prior knowledge", it says, "he could not have reacted with those words". "This remark shows his guilty mind" says the Supreme Court, "with that of Beant Singh". Hardly. Could it not show a simple mind that has a naïve view of what the scriptures and myths contain? Could it not show an agitated mind? How does it establish foreknowledge of details?

The witness on whose testimony almost the entire case against Kehar Singh rests is Bimal Khalsa, the widow of Beant Singh. The prosecution, having produced her, itself declared her hostile. That apart, her statement was recorded by the police two months after the event. This is understandable says the Supreme Court as she had to be given time to "compose herself". But through out those two months she was regularly interrogated at the velodrome, the sports-stadium-turned-interrogation-centre in Delhi, and even the police have not alleged that she was reticent during these visits. In any event, nowhere does she say that Kehar instigated Beant. In fact, on her own saying Beant Singh decided on his own volition to become a "martyr".

Much is made of Beant Singh taking *amrit* at the *gurudwaras*. The testimony about the matter is contradictory. The court itself says that the ceremony is one in which a Sikh takes a vow to live a pure life. And yet it proceeds on the assumption that not only did Beant Singh take the *amrit* to fortify his resolve to assassinate Mrs Gandhi but also that he did so at the instigation of Kehar Singh. The taking of *amrit* on such occasions is a public function.

The authorities produced no witness from among the priests or others. The sole testimony remained that of Bimal Khalsa and where her evidence was vague, the court fills in the blanks. "It is true", says the court, "that there is no substantive evidence from the testimony of Bimal Khalsa that Beant Singh took *amrit* on October 14, 1984 at the instance of Kehar Singh". But it goes on to affirm that nonetheless Kehar Singh must have been present and also that he, in fact, played "a significant part" in the taking of *amrit* by Beant Singh.

Such is the "evidence". The judgment bristles with other infirmities also. For instance, the accused is to be supplied with copies of all material that may have a bearing on his defence and which the prosecution can possibly furnish. The Thakkar Commission was constituted to examine Mrs Gandhi's assassination. In spite of repeated requests Kehar Singh was not allowed to examine the report of the Commission. Hence the apprehension expressed by the counsel for Kehar Singh that it may contain material contrary to the assertions of the prosecution hangs as a pall over the judgment of this day.

And since the judgment was delivered, official sources have themselves revealed an entirely new fact: namely, that an Atinder Pal Singh has been arrested in connection with the assassination. Has his interrogation confirmed the prosecution's assertions about Kehar Singh or further diluted them? No one but the Government knows.

In brief: the assassins and conspirators deserve to hang; but the "evidence" adduced against Kehar Singh is far from being beyond reasonable doubt. A heavy responsibility thus devolves on the President. A mercy petition filed by Kehar Singh's son is before him. Given the nature of the case he should not go solely by the advice of the Government. He must apply his own mind to the judgment of the Supreme Court, and he must seek the counsel of wise men outside the Government – former judges and others, that is persons who have weighed evidence over a lifetime, who are known for their sturdy independence. Apart from considering the "evidence" on which the Supreme Court has pronounced is sufficient to hang a man, the President must ensure that these counsellors examine the report of the Thakkar Commission so as to be certain that it does not contain anything, which casts even further doubt on the "evidence" against Kehar Singh.

And that precisely because the assassination is the rarest of rare cases. It isn't just that the life of a man hangs on what he decides. The case is a test: our society must show by its conduct that in this case, that specially in this case, that even in this case our society has gone to the farthest extent to ensure that justice, and justice alone is done.

18. Anthony Hyman, Muhammed Ghayur and Naresh Kaushik, *Op. Cit*, p. 61.
19. *Ibid.*
20. Huntington, Samuel. P, *The Clash of Civilizations and the Remaking of World Order*, New Delhi, 1996, p. 116. Zia's policy of Islamisation of Pakistan was indeed a multi-purpose one. First, by styling himself as the champion of Islamic cause he could free himself from the wrath of the Muslim orthodoxy and pristine community, which were always potential sources of danger to the Pakistani rulers. Second, under an Islamic system a woman would not become head of the state. This was a convenient excuse for Zia to keep himself in power and block Benazir Bhutto from becoming the ruler. It is interesting to note that Zia brought about altogether new religious regulations, which had not been even social precedents in Islam. He would enact laws, which are more Islamic than *Quran*! This is how a renowned Islamic scholar comments on it: *Shatim-e-Rasul*, or insulter of the Prophet Muhammad is such a device in Pakistan. There is no command in the Koran that legitimizes the killing of one who insults the prophet. This is strictly a device of the Pakistani authorities at the instigation of the Mullahs. Whenever the Mullahs are challenged to identify the particular Koranic verse advocating the murder of *Shatim-e-Rasul* (swearer of the Prophet), they cannot do so and resort to lies instead. When questioned on the issue, one Mullah declared in the *Daily Jang* (London, August 5th 1994) that it is mentioned in verses in "The Apartment": 57, 61-62. It would appear that this particular Mullah has never read the Koran because "The Apartment" has only 18 verses! See Anwar Shaik, *Islam*, Cardiff, 1994, p. 5.
21. D N Dhar, *Op. Cit.*, p. 1999.
22. *Indian Defence Review*, April-June 1999, Vol.14 (2), pp.23-26.
23. Selig S. Harrison, 'South Asia and United States, a Chance for Fresh Start', *Current History Magazine,* March, 1992.
24. Dhar,. *Op. Cit.*, p. 202.
25. Anil Maheshwari, *Crescent Over Kashmir,* New Delhi, 1993, p. 107.
26. D. N. Dhar, *Op. Cit.*, p. 204.
27. Jagmohan, *My Frozen Turbulence in Kashmir*, New Delhi, 1991, p. 180.
28. D N Dhar, *Op. Cit.*, p. 206.

29. Jagmohan, *Op. Cit.*, p. 334.
30. Premnath Bhat, 'KLF's Spectacular Success against India – Untold Story of Rubia Syeed abduction', *Organiser*, 7 January 1990.
31. Jagmohan, *Op. Cit.*, p. 335.
32. *The Statesman*, 6 November 1989.
33. *Patriot*, 24 October 1989, Calcutta.
34. Dhar, *Op. Cit.*, P. 208.
35. *Organiser*, 7 January 1990.
36. *Profile of Terrorist Violence – in Jammu and Kashmir*, Ministry of Home Affairs, New Delhi, January 1996, p. 43.
37. *Ibid.*, p. 3.
38. *Ibid.*,
39. *Ibid.*, p. 4.
40. *Ibid.*, p. 6.
41. *Ibid.*, p. 8.
42. *Ibid.*, p. 12.
43. Warikoo, K, 'Islamist Mercenaries and Terrorism in Kashmir', *Himalayan and Central Asian Studies*, New Delhi, April-June, 1988, p. 36.
44. D N Dhar, *Op. Cit.*, p. 212.
45. Warikoo, K, *Op. Cit.*, p. 57
46. *Profile of Terrorist Violence*, Government of India, New Delhi, 1999, p. 250.
47. *Indian Express*, New Delhi, 15 December 1992.
48. D N Dhar, *Op. Cit.*, p. 213.
49. Jagmohan, *Op. Cit.*, p. 492.
50. *Ibid.*, pp. 473-474.
51. The statement of the Kashmiri Migrant Forum, 1 May 1990.
52. The memorandum dated 16 January 1990.
53. Jagmohan, *Op. Cit.*, p. 501.
54. Salman Khurshid, *Beyond Terrorism*, New Delhi, 1995, pp. 74–75.
55. *Hindustan Times*, 23 March 2000.
56. *Hindustan Times*, 23 March 2000.
57. J N Dixit, *Anatomy of a Flawed Inheritance*, Delhi, 1995, p. 105.
58. *Ibid.*, pp. 110-111.
59. *Ibid*, p. 113.

60. Ever since Mr. Rajiv Gandhi took over as the Prime Minister of India he strove his level best to cut a clean figure in Indian polity. He even said that his policies would be to cleanse the Indian systems so as to make them different from what India had thus far. But he could only remain tongue-tied before the question, "Does it mean that Madam [Mrs. Indira Gandhi] was unclean?" Because it was his mother Mrs. Indira Gandhi who was the Prime Minister of India consecutively for a long span of time that preceded Rajiv's take over. He never again baffled with 'cleaning'. It all ended up with the political cartoonists pooh-poohing him as "Mr. Clean"!

61. Unlike Indians, Chinese have been a group committed to the idea of cultural nationalism. The kingdom where the Son of Heaven ruled down the centuries was not ready to bid farewell to its ancient culture. Taoism, Confucianism, Buddhism, its medical system of Acupuncture and all the wealth of tradition continued to be the living systems of China's national life even during the days of European penetration and afterwards under the Communist rule. The antagonism towards the European religion, which began in the days of the Opium Wars and had its acrimonious expression in the Thaiping and Boxer rebellions, the Chinese harboured even in the Communist regime. The religious conversion movement, which the European nations have been going on with, as a means to alienate the native people from their national cultures in the New World, was made a punishable offence in the Communist China. Eliminating all the alienating influences and assimilating all what were good in Communist ideology into the national life, the colossal state of China marched down the decades of progress and prosperity. Naturally China proved impenetrable to the western ideologies and vested interested. A nation with own reputed tradition of culture and humanism was ready to develop an economy also of its own and was never bothered of any Western economic embargo or was after any economic concession. She lived on her own, patriotic, proud and pugnacious to any outside interference. See M P Ajithkumar, 'In Search of History's Soul', *Aseemaa*, Mangalore, November, 2003, pp. 23-25. But Indians prove the right reverse. We may notice for instance how the learned Muslim scholar Mr. Anwar Shaik finds fault with India's national community, the Hindus for their lack of national vision:

The Hindus are not lesser sinners than the Muslims in partitioning their Motherland because they failed to match the Muslim hatred with their love of Bharat Mata. If they were the least patriotic, they would have resisted this most diabolical act with the force of arms. History demonstrates clearly that motherland is the goddess that always demands a sincere offering of sweat and blood from her proud devotees, but the Hindus failed miserably on this count. They did not fire one shot to save the integrity of Bharat Mata. Gandhi bragged that India would be partitioned over his dead body, but when the time for sacrifice came, he showed a dishonourable conduct. Instead of dissuading his colleagues as he had pledged to Abul Kalam Azad, he withdrew his opposition to partition before the Congress Working Committee. Far more shabby was the role of Nehru, who was intoxicated with the dream of personal power, though at a devilishly high cost to the Mother India. Gandhi gained his "National Sainthood" and Nehru achieved his ambition of Prime Ministership.

The fact that the Hindus have been reluctant to fight for the honour of Bharat Mata for the last one thousand years clearly demonstrates that lack of national patriotism is the real Hindu malaise. Unless they renounce the anti-vedic principles such as Ahimsa and caste system, they will never make a bold and united nation fit to serve the cause of Bharat Mata, which is the only way ahead.

However, I do not preach narrow nationalism, which in its extreme form can rank as a subhuman cult. The Indian Muslims may class themselves as the children of foreign invaders to nurse their inferiority complex but the truth is that 95 per cent of them have the same Indian blood in their veins as all other Indians such as Hindus, Sikhs or Christians. The remaining 5 per cent have certainly become Indians by the long domicile in this country. Have they got anywhere else to go? Never mind other Islamic countries, even Pakistan, which was created for all Muslims of the subcontinent, shall not take them in. It is high time that they sober up to the reality, and being Indians, start living as Indians, their participation in singing the Vande Matram shall be a step in the right direction. See Anwar Shaik, 'Lack of Nationalism', *Voice of Jammu and Kashmir*, Jammu, June-July, 1996, No. 14.

62. Having been the superpower, the USA styled as possessing a super brain too many of whose findings however ran in contrast even to the ordinary awareness and logic. One may remember the controversies regarding the US claim about its astronaut landing in moon where its flag fluttered in breeze! It is also not very long before that this super brain conceived the idea of Star War, which later proved to be a punctured balloon. The idea to torch the entire non-Americans and to populate post-annihilation planes with Americans alone, was indeed wonderful, an idea that can dawn only to a brutish idiot! But that the God would not

provide horns too to the prancing horse is a natural law, which saved the rest of the world from this polished demon. Might is right and the mighty human being determines what are Human Rights too. Predicated on this premise was the US intervention in the Gulf politics where its audacity had even gone up to the extent of the Voice of America featuring a session on the study of Saddam Huzain's psyche to convince the world that it was the Iraq ruler's psychic abnormality that brought about the war – a safe and convenient finding which seemed to have helped it escape from the onus of having destroyed and devastated others' countries. The most recent of the trial balloons the US floated also faced a meteoric stooping. By the process of its most modern scientific finding, the Cloning, it was claimed that man could now assume the role more or less of the manipulator of creation! The idea like that of the Star War is good. A human being structured out of many qualitative ingredients like Einsteinian intellect, Cleopatran nose and Shakespearean imagination is good to think about. But what US brand of life, soul or energy would fit into this rather unnaturally made bio-organism? That the genetic realities are matters beyond the limits of human being is something these intellectual upstarts forget in their much-vaunted heights of science. No wonder, the doll thus created though suffixed with a Y to make the Dolly could not breath for long. One may not err if to remind the world of the Confucian saying that the most intolerable things in the world are the vanity of an upstart and an amusing smile of well fed fool. But there are people more foolish than the fools in the third world that they still deliberate on the subjects the Westerners left over long ago.

63. Jai Singh, Hari, *Kashmir a Tale of Shame*, New Delhi, 1996, p. 180.
64. Strobe Talbot's talk at the Aspen Institute, 24 August 1999.
65. J N Dixit, "Pressure on India", *Hindustan Times*, 20 December 1999.
66. N S Rajaram, 'Exercise Restraint, for Whose Sake?', *The Hindu*, 16 November 1996.
67. P B Sinha, 'The US and Terrorism' *Indian Express*, Kochi,14 March 1992.
68. Jagmohan's Open Letter to Ms. Robin Raphel, *Times of India*, 11 January 1997.
69. *Indian Express*, Kochi, 7 November 1993.
70. Tavleen Singh, 'Not just indiscreet, but incompetent too', *Indian Express*, Cochin, 14 November 1993.

71. S Viswam and Salamat Ali, 'Vale of tears', *Far Eastern Economic Review*, 8 February, 1990, pp. 19-20.
72. *Organiser*, 26 August 1990.
73. Madhu Jain, "Raising the Stakes', *India Today*, 28 February 1990, pp. 27-29.
74. *Facets of a Proxy War*, Government of India, New Delhi, 1993; See also Dilip Bobb and Raj Chengappa, 'War Games', *India Today*, 28 February, 1990, pp. 22-27.
75. Dilip Bobb and Raj Chengappa, 'If Pushed Beyond a Point by Pakistan, We Will Retaliate', *India Today*, 30 April 1990, pp. 76–77.
76. J N Dixit, *Anatomy of a Flawed Inheritance*, p. 131.
77. *Times of India*, 11 April 1990.
78. *Organiser*, 17 June 1990.
79. *Times of India*, 24 April 1990.
80. James Adams, 'Pakistan Nuclear War Threat', *Sunday Times* (London), 27 May 1990.
81. J N Dixit, *Anatomy of a Flawed Inheritance*, p. 132.
82. *Ibid.*, p. 135.
83. *Indian Express*, Kochi, 7 November 1993.

8
Kargil and After

In India even war was philosophized. Lord Sri Krishna observed on the plains of 'Kurukshetra' that to put down arms in the most decisive hour of war is "unaryan like, disgraceful and contrary to the attainment of heaven". To abandon arms amidst battle is to invite self-destruction. Besides, once forced into war by the enemy it is the duty of the affected warrior to ensure that the battle is carried on to the finish so that there would never again be another provocation from the same enemy. According to the patriot-saint Sri Aurobindo the *Bhagavat Gita* can be interpreted as addressed to a soldier who should dutifully fight to protect himself and those who are at the mercy of the strong and the violent, and uphold truth and justice [1]. War is only a means and its end is greater than the means. True, Sri Krishna could manage to energize Arjuna to make India's ancient battle against untruth a triumph. Unfortunately in the centuries that followed India seldom had such icons of nationalism as in old days though many had quoted them. All the later Kurukshetras, save a few, turned out to be blasphemous.

To ensure prominence among the nations of the world a country has to be very powerful. Strength and potential decide the status of a nation and the approach of others towards it. Enduring relations among countries rest not on permanent friendship but on promotion of their permanent interests, and to uphold one's interests a country has necessarily to be strong so that others may not attempt at dominating it, and arrest its progress and development.

Perhaps this underscored India's attempt at becoming a nuclear power, which would give her a status of equality with other bigger nations. One may recall the response of India's former Home Minister, L K Advani to the question about the US response to a BJP ruled India. That depends not on whether India is to be ruled by the BJP or not; it is dependent on whether India is strong or not, he replied. Indeed India's success in becoming a nuclear power made her proud and self-confident, and raised her prestige among the comity of nations. That no nation including the superpowers could claim superiority over India in nuclear capability has been of great significance. Truly speaking, her infinite economic potential combined with the newly realized position of a nuclear power made her so strong that her importance in world affairs could not be overlooked any more.

The idea of making India a nuclear power had dawned to India's first Prime Minister Jawahar Lal Nehru way back in the 1940s. Responding to the issue of nations attaining nuclear capability, he said that in view of the modern trends in international politics and developments of highly advanced scientific warfare as revealed by the Hiroshima-Nagasaki incident, "each country has to devise and use the latest scientific devices for its protection". His dream of a progressive India made him establish the Atomic Energy Commission in 1948. The many unprecedented landmarks and giant leaps India made in the field of atomic research including the building of atomic reactor, Apsara and the commissioning of Cyrus Reactor made Nehru's dream a reality. A jubilant Nehru was confident that India was "approaching a stage when it is possible for us – to make atomic weapons". His expectation to propel India on this line reached almost half the way in 1964 when India completed facilities at Trombay to reprocess Cyrus spent fuel, making it the fifth country with capability to produce plutonium. The deaths of Jawaharlal and his successor, Lal Bahadur Sastri, and the untimely demise of Homi Jahangir Bhaba in a plain crash checked the progress of India's nuclear efforts. But India had already demonstrated her nuclear weapons capability. Mrs. Indira Gandhi's detonation of the nuclear device in 1974 at Pokran was a striking scientific and technological landmark that raised the national self-esteem of the Indians and sent the strong message to the world nations that India would soon be among the nuclear powers[2]. The world powers' expression of displeasure at India's nuclear advancement including the economic and nuclear non-cooperation notwithstanding, India went ahead on its determined track[3]. But there was no delivery system to make the nuclear device act as deterrence. And to make the nuclear option a reality India pooled all the efforts of her scientific community in the missile-developing programme. Everything proved promising when India's Defence Minister Mr. Venkataraman saw through the Cabinet the proposal of an amount of Rs. 388 crores for missile development and handed over the government sanction letter to the nation's philosopher-scientist Dr. A P J Abdul Kalam. India formally launched the Integrated Guided Missile Development Programme (IGMDP) on 27 July 1983. Thus, says Dr. Kalam: "The proposed projects were christened in accordance with the spirit of India's self-reliance. Thus, the surface-to-surface weapon system became *Prithvi* ("the Earth"), and the Tactical Core Vehicle was called *Trisul* (the trident of Lord Siva). The surface-to-air area defence system was named as *Akash* ("sky") and the anti-tank missile project *Nag* ("Cobra"). I gave the name *Agni* ("Fire") to my long cherished dream of REX [Re-entry Experiment Launch Vehicle]"[4]. The smoke spitting *Trisul*, the "ballistic flight meant for testing the in-flight performance of the solid propellant rocket motor", took off from the test range at Sriharikota on 16 September 1985, declaring to the world that India has air-dashed into the heights only the superpowers so far enjoyed[5]. By 1988 *Prithvi* too neared completion. A surface-to-surface missile with capacity to deliver a 1000 Kg conventional warhead to a distance of 150 Km (It was later developed with capacity to carry the same warhead to a distance of 250 Km) with built-in provisions for modification from long range surface to air missile system, *Prithvi*, launched on 25 February 1988, was epoch making in the history of Indian rocketry[6]. The launch of *Prithvi*, which sent shock waves across the unfriendly neighbouring nations, evoked a response of anger resulting in a seven-nation technology embargo from the Western world. Indeed "the emergence of India as a self-reliant country in the field of guided missiles" as Dr. Kalam says, "upset all the developed nations of the world". And by the next year *Agni* too was ready to be perfectly launched. On 22 May 1989 this missile, the product of five years of continuous effort of Indian scientists at multiple work centres, took off amidst great jubilation of India's statesmen, scientists and patriots. Mr. Rajiv Gandhi, the then Prime Minister described it as "a major achievement in our continuing efforts to safeguard our independence and security by self-reliant means". "The technology demonstration through *Agni*", he said "is a reflection of our commitment to the indigenous development of advanced technologies for the nation's defence". This too, as could be expected, aroused the opposition of the envious world. The Western press including the *Wall Street Journal* made tempestuous uproar and one of the US Senators went to the extent of alleging that India's leading scientist had stolen the *Agni* technology from his country in 1962 forgetting the fact that America did not have such a system 25 years ago. But the Indian scientific community was not taken by the storm they raised. Strongly responding to these untenable antics, Dr. Kalam, wrote:

> In today's world, technological backwardness leads to subjugation. Can we allow our freedom to be compromised on this account? It is our bounden duty to guarantee the security and integrity of our nation against this threat. Should we not uphold the mandate bequeathed to us by our forefathers who fought for the liberation of our country from imperialism? Only when we are technologically self-reliant will we be able to fulfill their dreams[7].

1991, the year of Gulf war saw tube-launched Nag flights. And by 1994 all these missile systems were so fully revised as to meet any threat of aggression from the enemies. The second step in nuclear device detonation was postponed on account of one or other reason or convenient excuses though Dr. Abdul Kalam clearly indicated that the nuclear programme was well under way already in 1989. Mr. Atal Behari Vajpayee during his second term as India's Prime Minister was determined to carry further the nuclear policy of India. It was consistent with "India's nuclear policies related to both peaceful uses and weaponisation from Nehru's time"[8]. His decision to go in for the Pokhran II was fully in accordance with the traditionally accepted nuclear policy of India. And in the wake of Pakistan increasing its arms capability day after day, especially after the beginning of Sino-Pakistan nuclear axis in 1980s and the test of *Ghauri* missile in April 1998, India felt the urgency Pokhran II test. *Ghauri* was Pakistan's acrimonious response to India's *Prithvi*, which meant only 'the Earth'. But Pakistan, which always hysterically found fault with any development in India, took it against the historical

'Prithvi Raj-Ghauri' backdrop. With Pakistan's Ghauri syndrome having expressed itself in developing anti-India missiles, an important phase in Pakistan's nuclear programme initiated in 1972 to deter India and nutralise its conventional military superiority, Vajpayee ordered the nuclear tests in 1998, following which five devices were tested, conclusively proving "India's capability across the yield spectrum from tactical to thermonuclear"[9].

But it was a national misfortune that the Indian politicians never reached the heights and intellectual level that the scientists and military officials of India attained in their respective fields. It was not surprising that there were politically motivated feeble opposition from various parties against the country's nuclear achievements. It also elicited bitter attacks from the so-called superpowers, which so far monopolized the nuclear devices. Indeed their international status as the only few nuclear powers stood shattered. In fact in a world wherein every country could seek its development, what is the relevance of the expression "superpower"? But the idea of India or any nation developing the requisite levels of nuclear weapons and missile capacities to upset the advantages of nuclear possessions by the developed countries could be tolerated by the Superpowers. Hence they raised a hue and cry against the country's nuclear development programme, despite the repeated assurances on the part of Indian governments that they were wedded to the policy of peace in international relations. India has fought only defensive wars against her enemies who attacked her since independence and confirmed that India attaining nuclear capability would in no way affect world peace. Besides, India through her balanced handling of the nuclear devices could prove herself a highly responsible nuclear power and that fearing India's nuclear programme is preposterous. These being the realities, India need not have felt guilty about the Pokhran-II nuclear tests. Unfortunately small people who unreasonably felt apologetic about the achievements of the nation's scientists whose service had brought their nation to the vanguard of world powers ruled the nation. The noble tradition the lions of Indian politics and national ideology like Deen Dayal Upadhyaya and Syama Prasad Mukherjee once spearheaded had been debased by a group of bleating lambs! The people at the helm never realized that

India's nuclear policy was something that was to be drawn up by India only and not on the advice or direction of others. It was disgraceful that the Prime Minister of India wrote to the US President explaining the reasons that prompted India to detonate the nuclear device, like Indo-China boarder dispute and Indo-Pakistan trouble. It was within India's sovereign rights that she tested the solely Indian made nuclear device on her own soil and there was no need for her to be apologetic as to give an explanation to any foreign nation however much powerful it might be. Vajpayee's acknowledgement that India's bipartisan consensus against the Comprehensive Test Ban Treaty or Non Proliferation Treaty "can be changed only if the US makes importance concessions" was in fact shameful. More over CTBT and NPT ceased to have any further relevance when the nuclear proliferation has already become an irrevocable reality. US and Russia already possessed nuclear weapons. In the opinion of the US intelligence agencies China had transferred the complete weapons design to Pakistan in 1983. Closely following the Indian experiment, Pakistan, which was already in possession of uranium for two nuclear weapons, detonated its nuclear devices. There were also reports about the clandestine help West Germany gave Pakistan already in 1974 in establishing a factory manufacturing the nuclear materials, and the German expert help for founding a factory in Multan for uranium enrichment. Yet US did not have any reservation about these nor did it impose any new sanction against the German nuclear help to Pakistan or Sino-Pak nuclear collusion. It is also interesting that the CTBT, which tries to bully the nuclear threshold countries gives special rights and privileges to the P-5 states through the *side agreements*, *Classified Documents* and *Memoranda of Understanding*. The NPT also demands that more nations should approve a protocol giving nuclear watchdogs the right to conduct more intrusive inspection which is more or less equal to the right the US claimed on the eve of its starting the Iraq war under the pretext of punishing that nation for its alleged possession of chemical weapons. This only makes it clear that any powerful nation armed with such discriminatory rights is likely to misuse them for its unjust and unlawful infringement upon the rights of other nationalities. It should be noticed that when the Foreign Ministers from around the world attempted on 2 May 2005 to breath life into this 35-year old nuclear disarmament treaty that came into force in 1970 its credibility stood seriously challenged. The majority of nations complained that the nuclear powers, mainly United States and Russia, have moved very slowly in abiding by the NPT, which calls for them to move towards dismantling their arsenals. Only the US, Russia, Britain, France and China according to this treaty are permitted to have nuclear arms while others are pressurized to give up atomic warheads for good. This would only grate on the patriotic feelings of other nationalities that they have expressed their attitude of non-cooperation with the 2005 NPT meet. Just prior to this meet, Iran threatened to resume producing nuclear fuel. And "North Korea, which said it has nuclear weapons and withdrew from the NPT, on the eve of the conference apparently launched a short range missile into the Sea of Japan, adding to tensions"[10]. It has decided not to participate in the meet. Besides, nuclear proliferation is now a universal phenomenon, which is almost nearing saturation. Russia and the US have most of the world's estimated 30,000 nuclear weapons. Each is believed to have 7,000 to 8,000 operational warheads. India and Pakistan are estimated to have 40 operational warheads each, and Israel is said to have some 200. Added to these is the entry of Iran, North Korea and many such likely ones. Even the Bush administration is saying that the thirteen-point charter adopted at the 2000 Review Conference which called upon all the states to sign the NPT and CTBT is only a historical document that has no operational value today![11] NPT and CTBT thus have turned practically into the jokes of the new century with certain powers using them as cat's paws against their adversaries to safeguard their economic interests as expressed in the US nuclear policy towards Iran or North Korea. And it turns into a highly discriminating treaty with South Asia, mainly India as its main target, and that India should not have given it any face value even or did not cave into it was not against any ethical precept or humanitarian standard.

But whether India and Pakistan were nuclear powers or that India-Pakistan border turned out to be the US described nuclear flash zone, were of no concern to Pak-sponsored *mujahideens* in Kashmir and Pakistan soldiers violating India's territorial integrity. Amidst all the friendship carnival Pakistani infringement on Indian borders went on with the usual intensity as ever. The bugle sounds associated with window-dressed diplomacy of the newly opened Indo-Pak bus service gave way to the fret and fumes of guns and grenades along the Line of Control in Kashmir. True, the Government of India's stand during the time of Vajpayee that opening of more lines of communications with Pakistan would normalize and stabilize the neighbourly relations deserves all justifications. This sudden change in the policy of Bharatiya Janata Party whose leader L K Advani has been urging the world nations umpteen times to declare Pakistan as a terrorist nation appeared one of the Paradoxes which made that Party unpopular among Indian nationalists and finally get down from the saddles of power. In February 1999 India's Prime Minister Atal Behari Vajpayee had inaugurated the Indo-Pak Bus service at Amritsar in Punjab and Lahore in Pakistan. This was followed by the Prime Ministers of both nations signing the Lahore agreement which called upon the two sides to "take immediate steps for reducing the risk of accidental or unauthorized use of nuclear weapons and discuss concepts and doctrines with a view to elaborating measures for confidence building in the nuclear and conventional fields, aimed at prevention of conflict". Indian establishments and officials were actually intoxicated with much hope in the show at Lahore, believing that Pakistan Prime Minister Nawaz Sharif was deeply interested in opening a new chapter of friendship in Indo-Pak relations. Forgetting all the past lessons India learned from her relations with Pakistan, Indian officials mistook these friendly gestures as signs of sincere cooperation and were hopeful of settling the bilateral disputes. They therefore thought that time had come for a desirable Indo-Pak amity[12]. The policy of secularism that sidetracked from the Hindutva agenda and the foreign policy that extended peace and friendship to the aggressor bore no fruit. Instead under the cover of friendship and cooperation India was once again subjected to the Pakistani military aggression with the result that between April and June 1999 Indian soldiers were forced to take up arms along the Line of Control in Kashmir to defend the frontiers of their nation. The conflict was the outcome of the Pak attempt to infiltrate its regular troops and Kashmiri insurgents across the 150 Km stretch of the Line of Control at Batalik, Drass and Kargil in the spring of 1999. It was a preplanned incursion organized by the Pakistan Government, Military and ISI backed insurgents acting in collusion, and as the development in the Kargil sector revealed, the result of a long drawn secret military plan and programme. The intrusion by hundreds of Pakistani soldiers and Jehadists resulted in many weeks of open fight leaving 500 Indian soldiers dead and another 1100 maimed. The Pak military with the acquiescence of Nawaz Sharif planned the operation in Kashmir to revive the Kashmir issue in the international forums and to reinvigorate the ongoing insurgency[13].

Indian Army and other intelligence officials were caught napping at the Pakistani military incursion across the most inhospitable Kargil terrain. "Indian Army" writes Rahul Bedi, the correspondent of *Janes Defence Weekly*, "further compounded the grievous error by its inability to assess either the seriousness or the extent of the intrusion along 120 to 140 Km of the Line of Control almost three weeks after it was discovered in early May in the Kargil sector"[14]. Besides Kargil is most harsh and inhospitable region with its heavy snowfall in the winter season and hence exceedingly strenuous for the army to patrol. "Snaking its way through a snowy, mountainous wasteland up to nearly eighteen thousand feet, criss-crossed by ridges and deep valleys, this area is the second coldest place after Siberia and is under fifteen to twenty feet of snow between October and June". The temperature of the place averages about 20 degree Celsius, plummeting to minus sixty degree Celsius in winter with winter-chill of grave intensity[15]. Naturally this place had not been traditionally subjected to militant infiltration from the border. Again, in these areas Indian army too kept only infrequent patrols and especially during the snowfall the army used to leave the place to reoccupy it after the snow would melt by June. This absence of Indian forces helped Pakistani infiltrators to occupy this terrain during the winter of 1999.

As usual on 5 May 1999 Indian Army's 121st brigade sent out a patrol to reconnoitre the Kaksar area along the Line of Control in Kashmir to survey whether the snow had melted sufficiently as to enable the army to reoccupy the mountain they abandoned in the winter. But ambushed by the Pak militants, and its members killed, the patrol never came back. This is reported to have taken place on 8 May. Consequently, the reconnaissance was speeded up and the officials of the 121st Brigade reached an estimation of about 100 intruders in and around Kargil. But later developments proved that this was only the tip of an iceberg and that the Indian Army's assessment of the situation had fallen wide off the mark. The lack of sufficient intelligence reports was combined with the Army's negligence of such reports about the Pakistani infiltration. According to the intelligence officials, Pakistani deployment along the Line of Control consisted only of a handful of soldiers since she was confident that India would not infringe upon its borders by crossing the Line of Control. Also while considering the geography and war infrastructure in the area Pakistan had an added advantage upon India. A landing strip in Gultari in Pak administered Kashmir for an emergency takeoff and the roads connecting Gultari, and other adjoining military townships to points near the LoC were of great help to Pakistan in case an untoward situation arises. Besides, the Army had utterly neglected whatever little information it got about the Pak infiltration in Kargil. In fact there was still enough intelligence information for 3 Infantry Division responsible for the LoC. "But its senior commanders failed to anticipate the Pakistani invasion, and to gauge its intensity almost three weeks after it was discovered", says Bedi[16]. It was reported that the local people of Yaldor village in Batalik region close to the LoC had informed 3 Infantry Division already in August 1998 about the suspicious visit of about sixteen Pakistanis who ferreted out news about the Indian military deployment there. There was also intelligence about the Pak construction of an all-weather road from Gultari since 1997 and the troops mobilization of the Northern Light Infantry at Sakradu. It was also well known that the December 1998 issue of *Al Dawa*, a Lashkar-e-Taiba monthly from Lahore, reported that militant groups had pushed their way into Kashmir valley through Drass region. Some Pakistani papers also frequently claimed that Pakistan army and mercenaries had been making successful incursions into Indian Kashmir. Already in March 1999 the 3 Punjab Battalion had fired at some armed men dressed in black in the Batalik area before they seemed to have "slipped away to their hideouts and bunkers well inside the Indian territory unknown to the Indian Army". All the evidences available later confirmed that Pak intrusion into Indian area had begun in February and gone on throughout the coming months. But notwithstanding all these and the Pak ambushing of an Indian patrol along the LoC on 8 May Lt. General Krishnan Pal, commander of XV corps, which was in charge of the sector, had refuted the existence of "battle indicators of war or even limited skirmishes" or any "concentration of troops on the Pak side". These and several other wrong and irresponsible statements our army men had made only reveal that they were blissfully ignorant of the deadly developments already in the offing.

Consequently the fact of Pak incursion came to be known to the Indian Army only too late. In the initial estimate of the 121st brigade there were about a hundred Pak intruders hiding among the peaks of Kargil, who could be easily dislodged without further reinforcements. But the full gravity of the situation became known only later, when the brigade's estimation was raised to an approximate 800 militants. As India's National Security Advisor Brajesh Mishra admitted, India had really been "surprised" by the Pak intruders in Kargil, and to its greater surprise, Indian military authorities shortly came to know that Pak soldiers had breached the LoC in Mushkoh Valley, Kaksar and Batalik and that they had occupied about 70 positions along the LoC including a number of strategic salients by the road from Kargil to Leh so that these militants well equipped with snowmobiles, artillery and adequate stocks of supply were in a position to cut off the northern area of Kashmir from its rest[17]. According to subsequent reports the number of the Pakistani intruders amounted almost to two brigades or around four thousand to five thousand soldiers of Pakistan's Northern Light Infantry (NLI) along with the locally recruited Chitral and Gilgit Scouts and many other Islamic mercenaries[18]. Even in such a situation of Himalayan gravity General Pal said: "If they come off (the heights) in the summer they will be slaughtered. And if they don't leave in the winter they will freeze to death". The complacency thus created among the Army men made Lt. General H M Khanna, the Northern Army Commander and overall in charge of the operation to inaccurately brief India's Defence Minister, George Fernandes that the latter declared that the infiltrators would be flushed out within forty-eight hours.

But the situation had become too worse to be tackled in so easy a manner as India's Defence Minister believed. Indeed the lack of information about the strength of the infiltrators, their armaments and their potential combined with the dangerous complacency among the rank and file of Indian Army men and the lack of hindsight among the Indian political leadership into India's past experiences with Pakistan made the initial operations against the intruders a failure. And the Indian troops who pushed their way up to 16000 feet or more heights without any adequate ground cover fell an easy prey to Pakistani snipers and gunners with their favourable command of the heights. It was very clear that the Pak intruders were well entrenched and that their eviction called for strong measures and calculated moves[19]. However, the governmental machinery moved slowly and it was only by 25 May that the Indian decision-making machinery began to undertake a comprehensive analysis of the Kargil development. The high power Cabinet Committee on Security decided to press as many as three brigades into operation in the region. It was also decided to call the Indian Air Force to strike the entrenched Pakistanis in view of that Indian Army was required to be acclimatized prior to its being deployed in the high altitude snow mounts. Consequently, the Indian Air Force unleashed its first air strike against the peaks on 26 May followed by the second round to dislodge the intruders from Batalik, Turtuk and Drass[20]. The 'Operation Vijay' as it was called followed in which the IAF made as many as 550 sorties employing Mirage-200. MiG-21, MiG-23 and MiG-27 airplanes, two of which it lost[21]. The loss of the two aircrafts caused great damage to the reputation of the IAF and morale of its cadres, with the result that it had to begin operations from safer positions.

Indeed it was the Indian Government's immature understanding of the political differences between both India and Pakistan and the plot involved in the US' nuclear diplomacy and guidelines asking India to keep restraint on crossing the LoC and carrying the war into the enemy territory that made India pay a heavy price in beating back the aggressor. India's military history had taught her the practical lesson that if fighting the enemy headlong proves difficult, strike him at convenient places where casualties could be minimised and one could cut deep into the enemy country. But in Kargil operation she didn't follow this path. Truly it was this method India's former Prime Minister Lal Bahadur Sastri employed during the Indo-Pak war of his time when finding it difficult to catch the enemy in Kashmir he ordered the army to cross the Punjab border, carry fire and sword into the enemy territory and take Lahore by storm. Had this successful experiment been repeated in Kargil India would not have had to suffer such loss of men and material as she did. Interestingly many military experts have questioned India's 'restraint' in not crossing the LoC during the Kargil war, arguing that military considerations should have overridden diplomatic and political compulsions in such situations.

This time international background too was favourable to India and her military action would not have met with any super-power intervention to help Pakistan. USA was clearly convinced of Pakistan's aggressive policy in Kargil, and in the course of Nawaz Sharif's visit to China, Chinese leader's had advised him to keep restraint and live on good terms with India. It may also be interesting to note that China appeared to be desirous of developing friendship with India especially against the backdrop of the new developments in international politics wherein she wanted a formidable ally against growing US influence in Asiatic affairs. It is interesting to note that it was as if China was gradually accepting India's new political party in power which the Asian giant looked to as the true representative of India's cultural nationalism, a prelude to the Chinese Premier's later statement that along with the government-to-government relation between Beijing and New Delhi a CPC-BJP relationship would also be desirable. In such a situation nothing unfavourable would have happened in case Indian troops had crossed the LoC. Unfortunately Indian government's baseless fear of fighting escalating into a nuclear war prevented the Army from crossing the LoC, which was a blunder that cost India heavily in terms of men, money and materials. According to Lt. Gen. Moti Dar, a former vice chief of India's army staff, no nation whose borders have been violated would opt to restrict its operations to its own areas even at considerable human cost instead of opting to fight for what is militarily advantageous, as a means to please the international community. He decried the hollowness of the virtues involved in the 'restraint' the government of India showed. Indeed India should not have respected the LoC, which Pakistan did not respect especially when it was sure such a weak-kneed policy would only result in Pakistanis massacring Indian soldiers. Besides there was no need of fearing the Pak nuclear weapon even if India would have to cross the LoC because no one including the Pakistan leadership would be mad enough to use the nuclear weapon just because the LoC was being crossed. No nation would turn so irrational as to unleash a suicidal nuclear war except in critical and desperate situations that threaten their very existence. Gen. Dar observes:

> ...we are obsessed with a perception that the Pakistan leadership is prone to acting irrationally. In international affairs brinkmanship exists and in the case of Pakistan it has almost succeeded. Recently, when we unfolded our nuclear doctrine, a large number of Pakistani leaders and intellectuals have logically asserted that it would be futile and costly to get into a nuclear arms race with India and that minimum deterrence is all that they should aim at. This does not show that the Pakistani leadership is irrational[22].

Besides, it is also foolish to think that a group of politicians who live under full military protection in fear of inevitable assassination attempts would be prepared to face death in an ultimate nuclear fission, which would leave nothing on earth. They won't go in for a nuclear suicide.

True, there were recent reports about the Pakistan militia's plan to use the nuclear missiles, which the army had readied and that it was abandoned under US pressure. In the newly published *Pakistan Between Mosque and Military* its author Husain Haqquani while dealing extensively with the 4 July 1999 meeting between the then US President Bill Clinton and Pakistani Prime Minister, Nawaz Sharif, refers to this Pakistani nuclear plan. Pakistani press *Dawn*, which brought out this curious report on 20 June 2005 quoted Bruce Reidel, a special assistant and a senior director of North East and South Asian affairs at the National Security Council and who was present at the meeting, saying that Sharif "wanted desperately" to find a solution that would allow Pakistan to withdraw from Kargil "with some cover"[23]. Riedel is quoted as having said that, "without something to point to, Sharif warned ominously that the fundamentalists in Pakistan would move against him" and that he would never again be in a situation to meet Clinton. "Clinton asked Sharif if he knew how advanced the threat of nuclear war really was? Did Sharif know that his military men were preparing nuclear-tipped missiles? Sharif seemed taken aback and said only that India was probably doing the same". Clinton now reminded Sharif "how close the US and Soviet Union had come to a nuclear conflict in 1962 over Cuba. Did Sharif realize that if one bomb was dropped ... Sharif completed his sentence (saying) 'it would be a catastrophe", Riedel is quoted as saying. And at the insistence of the US President and his readiness to interfere to save Pakistan from the mess it has slap-dashed into Sharif is reported to have prevailed upon the Pakistan army to abandon its nuclear offensive plan, which it drew up without the consent of Pak Government. Whether the report of the hardliner press *Dawn* could be relied or not one thing that stands undeniable is that Pakistan was afraid of the catastrophe a nuclear war would entail and was prepared to abandon the plan when cautioned of the irreversible danger involved.

This being the reality, Indian Army should have crossed the Line of Control especially when the big nations were advising Pakistan for immediately withdrawing from places it occupied across the LoC. Such a move from the side of Indian Army "could have given India ample chance to clear the occupied territory of all the terrorist training camps". But it was a mistake that India did not do so under the US pressure[24]. Had Indian Army crossed the LoC it would have been a good treatment to the Pakistan malady and the Indo-Pak problem could have been settled for good. But unfortunately India did nothing with the result that though Operation Vijay ultimately proved a success, she had lost many of her army men and too much of material. According to a report in *Straits Times* the war had cost India $ 6.8 million a day[25]. Indian official sources put the number of killed as 487 and that of maimed 1000[26]. But it is easily presumable that the exact figure would be far more than what was given in official records.

The Indian Air Force having unleashed relentless strikes against the Kargil peaks, the army hurried to dislodge the intruders from the hideouts they occupied. Overcoming even the health problems that faced the Kashmir counter insurgency forces deployed in Kargil and the much favourable position the Pakistani troops enjoyed in the terrain along the LoC, Indian Army with its undaunted resoluteness succeeded in assaulting bunkers and redoubts located at considerable heights and recaptured about 21 Pak occupied positions.

Simultaneous with the strong military actions, India started diplomatic moves to win over international opinion in its favour. This move in fact did not face any adversity since the nations that supported Pakistani cause were few. Indeed USA stood first in accusing Pakistan of the Kargil misadventure with the result that she took little interest in helping Pakistan take the issue to the UN Security Council as it did in early times. "Pakistanis are plainly to blame for having started the fighting", wrote *Washington Post*. It continued: "If it was not the elected Government of the country that was responsible, then perhaps worse it may have been a sort of a Pakistani military fundamentalist axis that the government is not in a position to know fully about, let alone to subordinate"[27]. US Assistant Secretary of State for South Asian Affaires, Karl Inderfurth said in an interview that the Pak militants had better leave Kargil for the restoration of peace in the area. "Clearly, the Indians are not going to cede this territory that the militants have taken… They have to depart and they will depart, either voluntarily or because the Indians take them out"[28]. He cautioned both India and Pakistan that events may spin out of control and urged them to see normalcy restored on the border. The US reluctance to interfere was further revealed from the statement of the State Department Spokesman, James Rubin who clarified:

> We strongly support talks between India and Pakistan to resolve this latest dispute and believe that these talks should take place as soon as possible. Ending the fighting in Kargil area can only be accomplished through direct engagement by India and Pakistan. We remain in touch with Indian and Pakistani Governments to express our strong concern, to urge them to show the restraint to prevent the fighting from spreading and to urge both the countries to work together to reduce tensions… We certainly would want them to talk to each other to work out an arrangement to stand down from the conflict. We certainly would want them to talk to not take steps to expand the conflict beyond the current Kargil area[29].

It was good that the early US stand on Kargil issue was neutral. But there was no need of an Indo-Pak talk as suggested by the US. What was required was the withdrawal of Pakistani infiltrators from the Indian areas they occupied especially when Indian had sworn itself to the policy of not crossing the LoC. Replying to whether US would send an envoy Mr. Rubin said that the US position "regarding Kashmir is well known. At this time there are no plans to send a US envoy to the region"[30]. But taking the US' stand on Kashmir of the past half a century one might naturally think that the US would interfere only when it would seem necessary to save Pakistan from a final and disastrous blow by India, a doubt which proved right later when USA urged India not to cross the LoC. However that the US was not ready to favour Pakistan's intrusion into Kargil in the initial stage doused latter's criminal enthusiasm to some extent. And India's willingness to have diplomatic overtures with Islamabad also had some effects. While preparing to leave for China, India's Minister for External Affaires, Mr. Jaswant Singh offered to meet his Pakistani counterpart, Mr. Sartaj Aziz, in New Delhi[31]. Atal Behari Vajpayee reiterated that his government would not rest till every intruder is dislodged. However he expressed his readiness to talk with Pakistan on condition that any such deliberation would strictly be confined to the Pak role in the worsening situation in Kargil[32]. But the talk proved fruitless and turned out to be a comic show when Sartaj Aziz, along with having stated that Pakistan had no control over the intruders, sought for a 'partial de-escalation' in Kargil and an end to Indian artillery firings and air strikes. But Singh sticking to his grounds pressed Pakistan to withdraw its troops immediately.

Meanwhile the Indian Army pressed on with its relentless operations in Drass and Batalik sectors, which overlooked the chief route of supply for the Indian military engaging Pak soldiers in Siachen Glacier since 1984. The possibility of Pakistan Army cutting off this route frightened the Indian Army which planned an early capture of these ridges so that any realignment of the LoC in this area could be effectively prevented. Point by point Indian Army successfully managed to evict Pak intruders from the eastern flank by 21 June and turned towards the formidable Khalubar summit, 5,287 m high, which it took on 7 July after clearing 43 enemy bunkers. Lt. Manoj Kumar Pandey, who had recourse even to single combat to kill the enemy, headed an epic fight in his move for Khalubar and, inspired his soldiers. He succumbed to his injuries only after seeing the last of his enemies annihilated. By the same day the entire Jubar complex too came under Indian control resulting in the complete collapse of Pak defences in adjoining ridges too and Pakistan was left with no other alternative than announce its withdrawal by 11 July from the areas it still held on the Indian side of the LoC[33]. Simultaneously was carried out the army operation to liberate

Tiger Hill complex wherein were located India Gate, Helmet and Rocky Knob. The attacks that started on 3 July lasted up to second week of the month. The midnight operation Indian Army unleashed on 4 July brought India Gate and Helmet under control, completely isolating Pakistanis on Tiger Hills. By 11 July when Rocky Knob and Rhino Horn too fell, Indian Army had won the battle for Tiger Hills, decisively defeating Pakistan's Kargil misadventure[34].

While the battle was raging unabated and the Indian forces continued to emerge victorious Pakistan found herself in a military and diplomatic quagmire and was on the look out for some face-saving tricks. True, US was in no haste to interfere due to many factors like the low priority it had given to south Asian affaires, and her Kosovo engagement. But that the US could not distance herself from an issue that affected the region, which suited her economic interests in many ways was shortly revealed when after a show of scolding Pakistan, urging it to withdraw soldiers from Kargil it made a timely interference. Simultaneous with the US having sent Gen. Anthony Zinni, the Commander-in-Chief of US Central Command to prevail on Nawaz Sharif to call back his troops, Golden Lanpher, the US Deputy Assistant Secretary of State for South Asia touched down at Delhi to appraise the Indian administration of Zinni's message to Pakistan. However the US diplomat did not forget to counsel India to keep 'restraint' this time also! 'Restraint' from the Indian side, as already noted, was necessary to the US, which was always afraid of the possibility of the Indian Army crossing the Line of Control and flushing out the terrorists who may find new pastures in areas where it might endanger American interests. However to Pakistan's dismay Zinni did not entertain Sharif's demand to link the Kargil issue with the general and broader Kashmir problem and the conflict still went on with intensity. But as the war was escalating and the Pak soldiers were facing defeat after defeat, and as the world powers showed little interest in supporting Pakistan Sharif was anxious to bail himself out of the problem. Therefore in early July as a face saving means he visited Washington where President Bill Clinton, though not prepared to hold India responsible for having set off the Kargil imbroglio, however helped Pakistan to bring the war to an early end and thereby saved it from further defeat and disgrace. Pakistan sent its special envoy Niaz Naik to deliberate with the Principal Secretary to the Prime Minister and National Security Advisor, Brajesh Mishra on the steps to be taken for the withdrawal of Pakistani forces from Kargil[35]. But even at this moment a double-faced Sharif was not ready to accept publicly that the Pak soldiers were directly involved in Kargil operations and as eyewash on 12 July he urged the Mujahideens to withdraw from the mountain redoubts. This cheap strategy to convince the world that Pakistan army had no direct involvement in Kargil invasion however had no effect on the international community, and by 14 July Pak infiltrators started evacuating the positions they occupied ceding them to the advancing Indian army, and towards the end of the month the conflict almost came to an end[36].

But that Pakistan's audacious military intrusion stood frozen in Kargil was no matter that would correct its dealing with India in future. Though it was generally said that the post-Kargil scenario was marked with Peace it was also noted for the mutual retaliatory allegations. Kashmir still remained an important issue in the bilateral disputes and it was clear to the international community that there was every possibility of the outbreak of a war of conventional weapons even as the fear regarding the outbreak of a nuclear war was in the air. In fact, Pakistan's anti-India attitude took a turn for the worse when the post-Kargil times witnessed the replacement of the Nawaz Sharif regime with the military government of Gen. Pervez Musharraf. As could be expected, Musharraf, the much-publicized hero and architect of Kargil operations could not be on good terms with India. Like his predecessors he too held that pursuit of 'Hate India' campaign would be the best step for his survival in his new position as the President of Pakistan.

Musharraf's military coup, which invited a chorus of disapproval from the democratic nations of the world including the USA, isolated Pakistan from the world community. Expressing reservations about the military coup, USA imposed additional sanctions on Pakistan's military regime. Bill Clinton who had visited India in July 2001 and spent some days in Delhi made only a stopover visit to Islamabad.

The US indifference towards Pakistan, the Indian government believed, would be a good augury for an improvement in the situation in Kashmir, which had deteriorated consequent to

Pakistan sponsored terrorism. But the decision of Vajpayee government to declare a unilateral ceasefire there during the holy month of Ramadan in 2000 and its later extension for the succeeding seven months only led to increasing terrorism and mushrooming of terrorist outfits in the Valley. As a result the Government of India had to terminate the ceasefire on 23 May 2001. Delhi, in order to improve bilateral relations with Pakistan, extended an invitation to Pakistan's chief executive, Gen. Musharraf to visit India. Musharraf who was soon to declare himself President of Pakistan accepted it and the meet slated for June 14-16, took place at Agra. However, this did not produce anything as expected. Musharraf and his foreign policy makers wanted to bring Kashmir into focus and demanded that the All Party Hurriyat Conference be made a party to the bilateral talks. Vajpayee and his government's coalition friends on the other hand insisted on Pakistan withdrawing support to Kashmiri terrorism, stop narcotic trafficking and give up its claims on Sir Creek and the Wular Barrage and stood stoutly against Musharraf's no-compromise stand on Kashmir question. Indian unwillingness to withdraw forces from the Siachen Glacier too upset the plans of Pakistan and naturally the summit ended a failure. After all, what could be expected of Musharraf who openly though sarcastically had said while at Agra that he had better purchase his ancestral property and live safely in his native land than return to Pakistan settling all disputes with India? Once the disputes with India was settled, he knew, he would have to face more serious domestic problems of Pakistan which the General would not be able to solve. Therefore, he too like his predecessors felt it convenient to continue playing the Kashmir card. But to Musharraf his India visit proved a personal success. His aggressive postures in his meetings with Indian editors sent his popularity graph soaring in Pakistan where the major parties like Pakistan Peoples Party and Pakistan Muslim League were opposed to his military dictatorship[37]. And the Pakistani delegation left for Islamabad blaming the hardliners in the Bharatiya Janata Party for the failure of the summit.

The attack on US' World Trade Center and Pentagon allegedly by the Bin Laden and his Al Qaeda terrorists on 11 September 2001 brought some changes in the American attitude to Asiatic affairs, and Pakistan proved to be its fortunate beneficiary. She gained greater importance against the backdrop of the US' decision to fight Taliban and Afghan terrorism. Prof. Mervyn Dymally thus observes:

> Before September 11, Pakistan was on its way to joining Afghanistan in becoming a failed state. The country's military ruler, Gen. Pervez Musharraf, was an ardent supporter of the Taliban regime, while the military intelligence complex he controlled was responsible for weapons proliferation throughout the Middle East and Asia, along with the export of extremists across the Muslim world[38].

But the new developments changed the US attitude towards Pakistan. In the US estimation Pakistan loomed important in case it would decide to attack Afghanistan since any air strike on Afghanistan from an aircraft carrier or from the US airbase in Diego Garcia in the Indian Ocean required flying over Pakistani territory, which called for the cooperation and support of Pakistan. The pro-terrorist country that Pakistan was soon became an anti-terrorist overnight! Indeed it was as if Pakistan had been waiting for an opportunity to help the US. Though many people from inside Pakistan including the key members of ISI, and other Islamite political parties supporting the Al Qaeda were against their nation siding with the US in the fight against Afghanistan, Musharraf's personal pledge to support America's Afghan war stood unchanged. Considering the precarious situations he and his nation were mired in, the Pakistan President thought it better to be with the US. The military dictator who sabotaged the elected government of Pakistan could not still cut a democratic figure despite all his nimble antics to don the civilian mantle. Besides, he thought that India emerging as a powerful nation under Vajpayee government and improving its relations with the US might steal a march over Pakistan in winning the friendship of the superpower if he would not cooperate with the American war against the Taliban. And in such a circumstance Musharraf decided to be with US lest the latter should target even Pakistan for its support to Taliban. There was also every possibility of Pakistan becoming vilified for its supporting and sponsoring terrorism in Kashmir, which had so far received America's silent approval[39]. Having found itself trapped between the devil and deep sea, Pakistan masqueraded as the strong US ally in fighting the terrorists and at the same time lending secret help to Osama Bin Laden's network in his *jehad* against America. It may be surprising to know that America's most important ally in the subcontinent was sabotaging its war efforts! Evidence was not in wanting to prove that Pakistan was passing on crucial intelligence to its Taliban allies in Afghanistan. More than 7000 Pakistani 'tribesmen' equipped with automatic weapons, rocket launchers, and shoulder fired missiles had made their way to Afghanistan to fight alongside the Taliban. This was an exact repetition of what Pakistan did in Kargil in 1999 in its attempt to wrest Kashmir by force. This led to the ground troops from the US and the Northern Alliance to face thousands of heavily armed 'tribesmen', trained and equipped by Pakistan, carrying mostly US made weapons[40].

During the Afghan war US, like its Afghan war ally, has followed its usual double-dealing in its relations with India though the Bush administration tried its best to assuage India's suspicions about its renewal of the military and economic tie-up with Pakistan. While the US Secretary of State Gen. Collin Powell highlighted Kashmir as central to the relations between India and Pakistan, later Donald Rumsfeld assured India that US policy towards Pakistan would not be allowed to overlook the best interests of India[41]. However the US attitude towards India remained unchanged. Even after Taliban was weakened considerably and the US war efforts ended, India's problems remained as they were, especially with regard to the Kashmir question. In fact, growing terrorism in Kashmir and other areas constituted the post-Agra message from Pakistan whose acts of hate and violence continued and in the Doda district of Jammu some Hindu villagers were kidnapped and slaughtered. This horrific incident came on the top of a series of other outrages like the attack on Amarnath pilgrims, firing along the LoC, bombing and attacking Indian citizens and security forces. The ISI was reportedly involved in this terrorist violence, and the arrest of several alleged ISI agents from different parts of India clearly demonstrated the dimensions of internal insecurity in the country[42]. This was followed by the suicide bombing of the Jammu and Kashmir Assembly in October. The terrorist attack on India's Parliament house in December 2001, of horrendous magnitude indicated Pakistan's decision to carry her anti-India fight right up to the headquarters of India's political system. Indeed "by targeting Parliament, the Jehadi forces, cobbled up by the ISI and Pakistan's army have challenged India to either survive or succumb"[43]. It is also to be noticed that Pakistan's military spokesperson, Major-General Rashid Qureshi warned, "India will pay heavily if they engage in any misadventure". Had it not been for the security personnel who did the commendable job of killing all the five terrorists and frustrating their evil designs, the worst could have happened. This misadventure on Indian Parliament building, which resembled the September 11 terrorist attack on the US World Trade Center, was according to available evidence masterminded by the ISI, Al-Qaeda, and Pakistani based terrorist outfit Lashkar-e-Toiba. Mohammed Afroz who was arrested in November 2001 for his links with SIMI had told Mumbai police during intensive interrogation that Parliament was one of the five targets identified by Al-Qaeda on September 11 and that the Al Qaeda set up an eight men squad that was to tie up with the LeT operating from Pakistan[44]. Musharraf's open pronouncement regarding Pakistan's real stand on Kashmir, also towed the usual Pakistani line. Though in his speech on 12 January 2001 he posed to be a reformer exuding hopes of changing course and distancing Pakistan from terrorism his shrill address to a joint session of POK Assembly and Council on 5 February betrayed the anti-Indianism, which guided Islamabad's state policy. The General was back on his policy of lending "moral, political and diplomatic" support to the Kashmiri "freedom struggle"[45]. Consequently terrorist violence increased by leaps and bounds taking the life of many innocent people including that of Daniel Pearl, the *Wall Street Journal*'s South Asia correspondent whose dastardly murder with his throat being slit was televised through a video camera. 14 May 2002 witnessed another suicide attack near Jammu, an abominable outrage with the despicable purpose of provoking India. It was primarily focused on a camp of the Indian Army and the families of the army personnel there. All these incidents pointed to some new developments in South Asian terrorism. They suggested the emergence of a new threat to India from terrorist groups like Lashkar-e-Toiba or the Jaish-e-Mohammad, the two anti-India groups which Musharraf had banned in January 2002. Operating under changed names, they definitely wanted to let Musharraf know that they could strike at will on either side of the line of control. It was an irony that the terrorist outfits the

Pakistani Generals groomed, often broke out of their control in unleashing terrorism and boomeranged upon them. It was this fact that was brought out from Musharraf's later statement that, "Kargil was a decision taken by the Mujahideens and we got involved because of the action taken by the Indian troops"[46]. This was of course a face saving statement to convince the world of his innocence in this matter. But to one reading between the lines it reveals the collusion between the Pakistan government and terrorists. Since he could not bridle the terrorists or free himself from the unholy nexus with them the only alternative left was to support them. Though he made the high sounding promise that if New Delhi took one step Islamabad would be willing to take two towards normalizing the relations between the two countries he kept reservations about checking the Pak terrorist infiltration into India stating that nobody in the world could guarantee that infiltration could be stopped completely. "You cannot keep a military on high alert for a long period and you would not like people to turn their guns against you and undermine your own government", he said[47]. But India could not remain a silent spectator to Pakistan's dirty soap opera. Already on 13 September 2002, while addressing the 57th session of the United Nations General Assembly in New York, Atal Behari Vajpayee, India's Prime Minister, expressed his nation's determination to end terrorism with all the means at its command[48]. However all these warnings were of no avail. India's policy of peace and restraint only boosted up the arrogance of the enemy and the Pak sponsored violence in Kashmir as well as other places in India continued with unprecedented intensity. And the reign of the Bharatiya Janata Party too ended without having found a final solution to the Pakistan malady and its byproduct, the terrorist violence in Kashmir.

But Pakistan continued to masquerade as peacemaker on the one side while on the other went on sponsoring terrorist activities in Kashmir. One may recollect that the very day Gen. Musharraf expressed his desire to have lasting peace with India there were terrorist attacks on Indian establishment in Kashmir. To the press query about his meeting with India's External Affairs Minister, Mr. Natwar Singh, Musharraf expressed his longing to see India-Pakistan peace process move on a smooth channel. Both, he said, "need to move on CBMs and the dialogue process in tandem with each other". But the very same day the press reported on the sluggish progress of the Indo-Pakistan talks on the Siachen. The first discussion since 1999 on this area of conflict "remained deadlocked over the 'authentication' of maps showing the existing positions of Indian soldiers on the heights of the Saltoro range and Pakistani soldiers at its base". While the Indian side took the stand that an agreement on Siachen would take place only if both sides agreed to authenticate maps, which marked out the Indian positions on the Actual Ground Position Line (AGPL) Pakistan wanted to resolve it on the basis of the Simla Agreement of 1972, implying that India had 'violated' the Simla accord by occupying the Saltoro in 1984[49]. Simultaneous was the terrorist strike on the Central Reserve Police Force camp in the Rajbagh area of Srinagar killing nine personnel. Thus, from the very beginning the talk on Siachen appeared unlikely to bear any fruit. The Foreign Ministers level talks on Kashmir was again bound to collapse with Pakistan Foreign Minister, Khurshid Mahmud Kasuri making controversial statement on Kashmir which according to India's External Affairs Ministry was "not in consonance with the spirit" with which it has conducted the dialogue so far[50]. There was again attempt from the Pakistani side to complicate the Kashmir Issue further. Pervez Musharraf's urge for British mediation in the Kashmir question was not in line with the Simla agreement. "I would love Britain to play a role as an intermediary in resolving the Kashmir dispute" and that the "British help behind the scenes will keep up the pressure", he said[51]. Besides, the increasing America-Pakistan arms deal was bound to derail all attempts at solving the Kashmir dispute since it made Pakistan arrogant. India, raising concerns over the proposed US arms supply to Pakistan told the United States in December 2004 that the nature of the arms sought to be supplied had little relevance to the war against terrorism. Attacking the move for US arms supply to Pakistan, Indian defence officials said, "the Indo-Pak peace process has started gaining momentum and the ceasefire has been holding since November last year and induction of sophisticated weapons at this stage will start an arms race and disturb the dialogue"[52].

Again there started the Bus-Diplomacy, which the Indian authorities thought would lead to better bilateral relations. By

December 2004 Islamabad had agreed to start a bus service between Amritsar and Lahore. According to Pakistani Punjab's Chief Minister, Parvez Elahi Pakistan Government agreed in principle for this bus service and he said, "it was your [India's] turn to complete the rest of formalities". There were moves to have MoUs signed between the agricultural universities of Faislabad and Ludhiana to undertake research in agriculture, horticulture and agro-processing. Punjab Chief Minister Amarinder Singh mooted several schemes including the waiving of entertainment tax on Punjabi films made in Punjab especially in view of Elahi's statement, "We have an age old common cultural heritage and civilization and, therefore, it is our foremost duty to respect the sentiments of the Sikh community"[53].

The year 2005, a landmark in India-Pakistan relations, proved eventful with the starting of Srinagar-Muzaffarabad bus service and the India visit of Pakistan President Gen. Pervez Musharraf, which happened almost simultaneously. The launch of the bus service from 7 April 2005, as agreed between India and Pakistan during the visit of India's External Affairs Minister to Pakistan in February 2005, was acclaimed by Pakistan as a "significant development and a confidence building measure". "The decision to launch the bus service is a very good gesture which will revive links among the Kashmiris on both sides of the LoC", Pakistan's Foreign Ministry said in a press briefing[54]. Both the nations as well as Kashmiris on either side of the Line of Control were jubilant over the bus service as they saw in it an unprecedented opportunity to solidify the bilateral relations and the people-to-people contact between Indians and Pakistanis. The Kashmiris celebrated the occasion ignoring all the terrorist threats since it would help them meet their long lost kith and kin from both the sides of the LoC. Hopes ran high when the bus moved from Srinagar carrying the passengers despite the previous day's terrorist attack on the hotel they were lodged in. It was a moment of emotional bursting for the passengers, mostly of the pre-partition days. India's Prime Minister Dr. Manmohan Singh used the occasion to thank all those who made the new move a success. This, he said, "would not have been possible but for the cooperation of the Government of Pakistan and especially President Pervez Musharraf". Mr. Singh hoped that this would lead to the settlement of many unsolved issues between the two nations, and he expressed his readiness to "hold the hand of Pakistan so that we could usher in peace and development for our people, especially in the state of Jammu and Kashmir"[55]. He also took advantage of the occasion to announce several schemes for the all-round development of Kashmir including plans for employment generation, electrification of villages and incentives for industries. He declared the starting of the Urban Employment Scheme with Rs. 12 crore being set apart for it. Jammu and Kashmir Chief Minister, Mufti Mohammad Sayeed described it as "the road to peace in Jammu and Kashmir" which could not be cowed down by the militants' threat[56]. Things appeared to have improved though the terrorists still had their hideouts in the Valley. Commenting on the general situation in Kashmir born out of the newly started diplomacy and strict military vigilance, India's Chief of Army Staff, Gen. J. J. Singh said, "there is smile on the face of the common man, they are speaking out and there are visible signs of prosperity" and expressed the hope that "the region will soon become the centre of South-East Asia".

But, despite all the media hype of the bus launch as a "historic moment" and a great step among the latest Confidence Building Measures, some crucial issues remained unsolved. Because, this bus service did not evoke any warmth from Pakistan as it did in India. Indeed it was India alone that became over-jubilant over it. Comparing to the over-enthusiasm shown at the function arranged to celebrate the bus service, which was marked by the presence of India's Prime Minister, Dr. Manmohan Singh and the Chairperson of India's ruling United Progressive Alliance, Mrs. Sonia Gandhi and the carnival-like atmosphere it created in Srinagar, the arrival and departure of the bus was not a high profile affair in Muzaffarabad. Neither the Pakistan President, nor Prime Minister, nor even its Foreign Minister was present to flag off the bus. India achieved nothing diplomatically, politically, culturally or economically from this venture. Thinking it right, one can only say that it was one more addition to the bunch of follies India has been committing over the years in respect of Indo-Pakistan relations. Indeed in an adolescent joy, everyone seemed to have forgotten that as far as India was concerned Muzaffarabad formed a part of India under Pakistani occupation. Having made too much of the bus service, India was only strengthening the claim of Pakistan over 'Pakistan Occupied Kashmir'. By describing the Srinagar-Muzaffarabad bus service as India-Pakistan bus service India was inadvertently affirming that Muzaffarabad as well as the entire PoK is Pakistani territory. One may hereafter naturally doubt India's propriety in calling this area as 'Pakistan Occupied' any more. It would only strengthen the aggressor's claim to a piece of territory it had unlawfully grabbed from India and continues to occupy. Besides, by allowing the passengers to come only on the strength of scant travel documents, India has made it easy for terrorists to cross over. There was no way of checking whether the passengers are bonafide citizens of PoK. Especially in a state where the control of the Government of India has often been in a paralyzed state, where almost all its administrators with their scant pro-Indian credence could only remain mute spectators to the terrorists ruling the roost, all the rigours on the terrorists' spree in crossing the LoC could only go loosened. These were facts, which the usual run of Indian political leadership found it difficult to digest.

Closely following the launch of the bus service was the visit of Gen. Pervez Musharraf on 16 April 2005. In his first visit after the failure of the Agra summit of 2001 India once again rose from her somber mood to welcome the General. "For India", as an expert on Indo-Pakistan relations commented, "the external environment has never been so good for pursuing a vigorous peace process with Pakistan"[57]. True, Pakistan's policy of patronizing terrorism against India and its people had not been given up. However, it appeared that the over-all situation had much changed owing to many developments. Islamabad's attempt to masquerade as the global level fighter on terrorism in the company of the US government and simultaneously sponsoring terrorist activities in Kashmir had been successfully exposed by India soon after the attack on Parliament in December 2001. Besides, India's status had steadily risen, especially in her relations with China and the US. The fact that China, which was an ally of Pakistan, changed her stand disheartened Pakistan very much. Her call to forge a CPC-BJP relation along with the government-to-government contact proved path breaking. True, by 2005 the BJP has gone from power, but the Indo-Chinese goodwill started during the rule of Vajpayee's National Democratic Alliance did not die out. It may be noted that just days before

Musharraf's arrival in India there was signed the Indo-Chinese accord on some guiding principles to resolve the boundary dispute with China. This achieved considerable gains in bilateral trade and the promotion of strategic partnership with Beijing. The Washington visit of India's External Affairs Minister in the third week of April 2005 with blueprints to create a new strategic partnership with the United States was certainly a new development. This visit, which Mr. Natwar Singh termed as constructive and positive received a warm welcome in Washington. It was indeed a great acceptance India got when the US Secretary of States Ms. Condoleezza Rice acknowledged that, "...international organizations in general will have to take into account India's growing role in the world in order to be updated and to be effective"[58]. India was soaring high in US opinion. "The message from Beijing and Washington" was thus "unlikely to be lost on Gen. Pervez Musharraf"[59]. Naturally India, as its Foreign Secretary Mr. Syam Saran said, looked forward to the friendly visit of the Pakistan President, which it hoped would be "constructive" with "forward-looking results"[60].

In a moment of high emotion Musharraf touched down at the Sanganer airport of Jaipur, Rajasthan's capital city on his way to pay homage at the Mausoleum of the Sufi saint Khwaja Moinuddin Chisti. Describing his India visit as "historic", he expressed his confidence that there were chances of optimism in boosting up the neighbourly relations as there was a change in the environment, which had become more congenial and friendly than that which had prevailed in Agra during his last visit. "We have come here with a message of peace and unity... We have prayed that in times to come, all differences between India and Pakistan are resolved and peace returned", he said. The visiting delegation that accompanied the General who was in India to watch the final one-day cricket match between India and Pakistan at Ferozeshah Kotla on 17 April included Pakistan's First Lady, Begum Sheba Musharraf, the Information Minister, Sheik Rashid Ahmad, Foreign Minister, Khurshid Mehmud Kasuri, the Minister of State for Religious Affairs, Amir Liaqat Hussain, Minister of State for Education, Gulam Bibi Bharvana, Advisor to Prime Minister on Women's Welfare, Nilofer Bhaktiar, the Foreign and Information Secretaries and other dignitaries.

The talks between Gen. Musharraf and India's Prime Minister Dr. Man Mohan Singh were marked with all cordiality and friendship, which according to reports, sent a clear message across the world that the two nations born of the common tradition are out to cut the long drawn ice. Both the leaders agreed that their army had required acting in close cooperation so that differences over implementing Confidence Building Measures might well be addressed, especially in regard to Siachen issue and maritime boundary in Sir Creek. Gen. Musharraf and Dr. Singh had a 40-minute one-to-one dialogue after a two-hour-long delegation level meet during which they came up with a broad vision to cooperate more effectively to promote cross border exchanges along the Line of Control as well. At the meeting held in Hyderabad House, Singh zeroed in on the responsibility of both the countries to project themselves as role models for the entire region in opening up trade routes and adding transport links that would expedite economic cooperation.

The discussions led to emergence of ideas regarding a range of possible steps desirable to improve bilateral amity. These included Kashmir centred CBMs leading to a more porous LoC like the suggestion of seven meeting points for the relatives, cross-LoC trade, increasing transport linkages and establishing more communication links, reviving the joint commission on trade and business and setting up a joint business council to improve contacts between private sectors on both sides, giving top priority to Iran-Pakistan-India gas pipeline proposal along with looking at other energy resources in the region, and developing appropriate transit facilities to improve trade relations with Central Asian and West Asian regions[61]. Dr. Singh however reminded the Pakistan President that all these steps could be expedited if only Pakistan would stick to and honour its commitment to curb terrorism and that it was the duty of both the countries to ensure that no terrorist elements thwart positive movements and ambience.

Friendship seemed at its emotional heights with the Pakistan President having met his Indian counterpart Dr. A.P.J. Abdul Kalam who waxed on the need of maintaining fraternal relation between the two countries. Dr. Kalam, India's top philosopher-scientist thus put it in his usually imaginative diction: "It is essential for India and Pakistan to place all their acts [CBMs] in one incubator or basket and then watch the eggs nurture in this basket of goodwill and also see that no one kicks it over". "We should harness or direct all our energy to nurture this goodwill and no third party should be allowed to enter and damage it", he said[62].

Gen. Musharraf found this a good occasion to share pleasantries with L K Advani, Leader of Opposition in Lok Sabha. He presented the BJP leader with an album containing photographs from Advani's school days till his last visit to Pakistan. Along with this, which Advani termed a "precious gift" Musharraf extended his nation's invitation to India's rightist Hindu wing leader to visit Pakistan. Advani accepted it and hinted at his probable visit likely to take place in June 2005 itself. Later, expressing satisfaction at the outcome of the talks between Gen. Musharraf and Dr. Singh, Advani hoped that it would lead to "concrete measures". To him it was a matter of gratification that "the whole process which was initiated by the previous National Democratic Alliance government and the joint statement in 2004 are moving forward". He described the talk as another step in the fulfillment of the 2004 Islamabad agreement signed between Gen. Musharraf and India's former Prime Minister, Mr. A B Vajpayee wherein the former had agreed that, "he would not allow Pakistani soil to be used for anti-India terrorist activities". It is desirable that "we should continue talks like this to resolve our mutual differences" since "one of the reasons for the growth of terrorism is the mutual mistrust between the two countries", Advani said, appreciating the Musharraf-Singh meeting[63].

Musharraf invited Mrs. Sonia Gandhi too, Chairperson of the ruling United Progressive Alliance, and in his thirty-minute meeting with her he discussed various aspects of the bilateral relations. She accepted the invitation, and the meeting was marked with great fondness and enthusiasm.

He also called on former Prime Minister, Atal Behari Vajpayee with whom he struck a personal rapport and developed a lot of respect despite the failure of the Agra summit. Vajpayee was all admiration of the General who sought support for carrying forward the peace process and there were exchange of pleasantries and gifts.

But as usual Kashmir continued to be a hard nut to crack. True, both Gen. Musharraf and Dr. Singh agreed that there could not be any time bound solution to Kashmir. But differences arose with the Pakistani leader having raised the possibility of including Kashmiris in the dialogue process and the Indian Prime Minister pointing out the Kashmir issue as one India was committed to address and that it did not take Kashmiri Muslim outfits into account. The Kashmiri Muslim separatist organizations have urged Gen. Musharraf to include them in the ongoing talks relating to the Kashmir imbroglio. The meeting between President Musharraf and Kashmiri Muslim organizations held at Pakistan House on 17 April was attended by moderate Hurriat leader Mirwaiz Umar Sheik, hardliner Syed Ali Shah, Democratic Freedom Party Chief Shabir Shah, Jammu and Kashmir Liberation Front's Yaseen Malik and Jammu and Kashmir Liberation Forum chief, Javeed Mir. "Any talk between India and Pakistan are incomplete without the involvement of the people of Jammu and Kashmir, who are a primary party to the dispute. So we asked Gen. Musharraf to press India to include the true representatives of the people in the ongoing dialogue process", said Mirwaiz Umar Farooq, the Hurriyat Chairman. They said that they have apprised the General of their views on the situation in Jammu and Kashmir. Mr. Syed Ali Shah Geelani in his 90-minute meeting with Musharraf told him that the current confidence building measures were meaningless unless human rights violations and killings were stopped in Jammu and Kashmir. To bring about a "just and amicable" solution India should take some tangible steps in line with the spirit of the UN Security Council resolutions, he said. In a three-paged memorandum to Musharraf detailing the alleged killings and human rights violations in Jammu and Kashmir, Geelani demanded that India withdraw its military, central forces and release all "freedom fighters" detained in jails. He unrolled before Musharraf the allegedly sad plight of the people of Jammu and Kashmir as if to some one in whom he saw the saviour expected to help the so-called "freedom fighters" to bail Kashmir out of the hell into which India had put it[64]. And naturally this helped Musharraf to act in the best interest of Pakistan by using the Kashmiri separatist organizations as a cat's paw in continuing his country's proxy war with India. But for this, the government of India is to be blamed since its having played into the hands of Pakistan by letting the ball of Kashmir issue roll into the enemy's court. Because Kashmir issue, exclusively India's national question, is something to be decided by India alone without allowing Pakistan to thrust its oars into it. Besides, a nation's interference in the neighbouring country's internal affairs is against all accepted canons of international relations. As Kashmir issue was India's internal affair, India should not have approved of Musharraf's talk with the Kashmir separatists, nor have given them permission to go to Pakistan with a memorandum of their grievances against Indian security forces. Indeed India should have ensured that the General behave as an honoured guest. She should not have helped him contribute to the worsening of Kashmir situation. By allowing Musharraf to do so India was committing another blunder. If Jawaharlal Nehru committed the blunder of taking the Kashmir issue to the United Nations what the present governments were doing was more foolish than what Nehru did. It is as if they were seeking the help of an alien and enemy nation and its virtual agents, the secessionist outfits of Kashmir to resolve the dispute. And the General returned making the Kashmir as well as all issues concerning Indo-Pakistan relations more messy than earlier. Consequently, the talks could only end in utter failure. Even the warmth and goodwill generated by India's Leader of Opposition's visit in June 2005 failed to ensure better relations with Pakistan. Advani's pointing out that Muhammad Ali Jinnah was highly secular though he happened to fall into the rut of communalism, and that he wanted the nation he fathered to follow the secular credentials, as could be expected, could not lead to any positive improvement in Indo-Pak relations.

That the road towards Indo-Pakistan amity abounds in insurmountable obstacles is the only lesson one could draw from the experience over the years. It may not be an exaggeration to state nothing useful would emerge from holding any kind of peace negotiations with the self-installed ruler of a nation whose life and position is unmistakably shaky. As noted elsewhere it appears useless for a democratic nation to hold peace negotiation with a neighbouring country where usurpers seize power after sabotaging the democratically elected rulers. Considering the trend of developments in bilateral relations during the last half a century or more, it may not be wrong to think that no positive and concrete results would come out of any talk with a nation in which there was no likelihood of any elected government remaining in power for long. Friendship could be possible only with nations with democratic governments enjoying stability and respecting its obligations. It should not be with someone who debases the lofty principles of governance and makes it a joke.

References

1. Sri Aurobindo, *Essays on the Gita*, Pondicherry, 1987, p. 45.
2. Surjit Mansingh, *India's Search for Power: Indira Gandhi's Foreign Policy 1966-1982*, New Delhi, 1984, pp. 98-99.
3. India's nuclear detonation had brought worldwide criticisms and adverse responses. The US suspended the transfer of fuel to the nuclear power plant at Tarapur. Canada called off all its nuclear cooperation with India. See Brahma Chellaney, *Nuclear Proliferation: The US Conflict*, New Delhi, 1993.
4. A P J Abdul Kalam, *Wings of Fire*, Hyderabad, 2002, p. 117.
5. *Ibid.*, p. 136.
6. *Ibid.*, pp. 144-145.
7. *Ibid.*, pp. 153-154.
8. J N Dixit, 'India's Nuclear Future', *Hindustan Times*, 2 March 1999.
9. *From Surprise to Reckoning – The Kargil Committee Report*, New Delhi, 2000, p. 205.
10. 'Nuke-haves asked to disarm', Reuters' report, *The New Indian Express*, 3 May 2005.
11. C Raja Mohan, 'Orbiting the NPT', *The New Indian Express*, 3 May 2005.
12. It has been well on the agenda of the Bharatiya Janata Party, which later proved to be a very feeble reincarnation of the one time leonine patriotic outfit, the Bharatiya Janasangh guided by leaders like Dr. Syama Prasad Mukherji, all noted for their pugnacious patriotism and uncompromising principles, to fight against Islamic terrorism generating from across the Indo-Pak borders. It was indeed the BJP leaders' pledge to uphold the idea of Hindu nationalism against the Islamic fundamentalism in India, which identified itself with Pakistani nationalism that popularized them and elected them to power. But all their pledges vanished into thin air no sooner than they were elected. Again their promise to creatively act for the *Ramajanmabhumi* cause too favoured

their coming to power. It was the Hindu majority of the Indian voters, mesmerized by Mr. L K Advani's glittering *rathayathra* (chariot procession), who voted state after state and finally the Centre too into the BJP basket. Thinking on these lines one can only conclude that the BJP as a government could not do what BJP as a party could prior to its coming to power at the Centre. Those who recited *Ramamantra* thus far and celebrated the fall of the *Babri Masjid* at Ayodhya left Rama on the wayside for a newly convenient secularism, which they thought would earn them the votes of the non-Hindus too in the future gamble for power. They forgot Ayodhya when they crossed Delhi! A bus to Pakistan, they might have thought, would help them cross over to the hearts of the Pakistan fans in India. Certainly as was well known, no goodwill and friendly gestures from India would befriend the Pak tyrants. Interestingly when the Vajpayee's National Democratic Alliance Government started regular bus service to Lahore with Indian Prime Minister himself as the first passenger, his Pakistani counterpart who was only a puppet of the military, received the bus. Gen. Parvez Musharraf, the then Army Chief of Pakistan had refused to salute the Indian Prime Minister. Indeed to the military leader who was the de-facto ruler of Pakistan Indian Prime Minister was only an uninvited guest. Yet the Indian government of Vajpayee and his BJP fraternity still went ahead celebrating these types of non-events, which were of no avail to the nation. Consequently what the Hindus could do under the Congress government of Narasimha Rao could not be done under the Vajpayee's BJP government. The Hindutva agenda proved mere eyewash. And the alienation of at least a right thinking patriotic Hindu minority resulted in BJP's failure to continue in power for another five more years.

13. *The Economist*, 26 June 1999.
14. Rahul Bedi, 'A Dismal Failure', *Guns and Yellow Roses*, Delhi, 1999, p. 141.
15. *Ibid.*, p. 144.
16. *Ibid.*, p. 147.
17. Ranjit Bhushan, 'Kargil, Post Mortem', *Outlook India*, 26 July 1999.
18. Rahul Bedi, *Op. Cit.*, p. 150.
19. Maj. General Ashok Krishna, 'The Kargil War', *Kargil: The Tables Turned*, (Ed. Ashok Krishna), New Delhi, 2001, p. 105; Also see The War in Kargil, *Frontline*, 5-18 June 1999.
20. Barry Bearak, 'India jets strike Guerilla Force Now in Kashmir' *The New York Times*, 27 May 1999.

21. *The New York Times*, 28 May 1999.
22. Moti Dar, 'Blundering Through', *Guns and Yellow Roses*, p. 176.
23. *The Pioneer*, 21 June 2005.
24. D N Dhar, *Op. Cit*, p. 245.
25. *Straits Times*, 16 June 1999.
26. Gaurav C. Sawant, *Dateline Kargil: A Correspondent's Nine-Week Account from the Battleground*, New Delhi, 2000, p. 285.
27. *Washington Post*, 26 June 1999.
28. *The Hindu*, 31 May 1999.
29. *The Hindu*, 6 June 1999.
30. *Pioneer*, 30 May 1999.
31. Sumit Ganguly, *Op. Cit*, p. 118.
32. *New York Times*, 9 June 1999.
33. Maj. Gen. Ashok Krishna, *Op. Cit*, pp. 126-129.
34. *Ibid.*, p. 118-120.
35. *Indian Express*, 28 June 1999.
36. *The New York Times*, 15 July 1999.
37. K R Malkani, 'India taken for a ride in Agra', *Organiser*, 19 August 2001, p. 10.
38. Mervyn M Dymally, 'Pakistan still has a finger in the wind', *Los Angeles Times*, 10 April 2002.
39. Sumit Ganguly, *Op. Cit*, p. 140.
40. N. S. Rajaram, 'Beyond bin Laden: Pakistan's double game', *Organiser*, 2 December 2001, pp. 7-8.
41. *New York Times*, 6 November 2001.
42. Inder Malhotra, 'Post-Agra message from Pakistan', *Organiser*, 19 August 2001, pp. 24-25.
43. Seshadri Chari, 'Target Democracy', *Organiser*, 23 December 2001.
44. Shyam Khosla, 'Fight Decisively', *Organiser*, 23 December 2001.
45. Syam Khosla, 'In True Colours', *Organiser*, 17 February 2002.
46. *The New Indian Express*, 14 June 2003.
47. *The New Indian Express*, 19 June 2003.
48. *Organiser*, 22 September 2002.
49. *The New Indian Express*, 6 August 2004.
50. Report of PTI, *The New Indian Express*, 5 September 2004.
51. *The Times*, London, 6 December 2004; report of PTI, *The New Indian Express*, 7 December 2004.
52. *The New Indian Express*, 10 December 2004.

53. Report of UNI, *The New Indian Express*, 5 December 2004.
54. *The New Indian Express*, 5 April 2005.
55. *The New Indian Express*, 8 April 2005.
56. *Ibid.*, 8 April 2005.
57. C. Raja Mohan, 'New Delhi relaxed about General's second coming', *The New Indian Express*, 16 April 2005.
58. *The Hindu*, 17 April 2005.
59. C. Raja Mohan, 'New Delhi relaxed about General's second coming', *The New Indian Express*, 16 April 2005.
60. *Ibid*, 17 April 2005.
61. *Ibid*, 18 April 2005.
62. *The Hindu*, 18 April 2005.
63. *The New Indian Express*, 19 April 2005.
64. *The Hindu*, 18 April 2005.

9

Conclusion

Born out of bloodshed and nourished down the decades by anti-India feelings, Pakistan has been without a political or patriotic ideology that could provide it a solid national foundation. All the successive leaders knew how to play upon this anti-Indian feeling to sustain their positions of authority in Pakistan's politics. As such, it could not leave aside its animosity to India. The Pakistani clique who sabotaged Zulfiqar Ali Bhutto and all the later administrators had quiet artfully carried down the decades this artificially created animosity with India. It is also true that despite all these foul means every Pakistani leader could not escape from the military coup and assassination by their successors, the cases of Bhutto or Gen. Zia Ul Huq being the best examples. Yet none of these ill-fated ones would learn anything from their past history. Interestingly, soon after the hanging of Bhutto, the military dictator Gen. Zia Ul Huq started his tirade against India and even had gone up to the extent of exhorting Indian Muslims to support the Pakistan army in case of a Pakistani invasion against India. True, there was the 'Nishan-I-Pakistan' awarded to the Indian Prime Minister, Morarji Desai and the frequent exchanges of goodwill, which went to make the international community feel that the two nations were on good terms. But the fact that even more powerful and popular leaders could not hold any longer in Pakistan without an agenda for the internal progress of their nation did not occur to Gen. Zia. Haunted by fear on all the sides, this General who could well be counted as one among the murderers of the Pakistani democracy had no other alternative than to resort to usual gimmick his predecessors depended on and pursue the 'Hate-

India' campaign. Yet Pakistan's internal feuds and military and political intrigues outbalanced the top military security Zia moved amidst. Killed in an air crash with even his mortal remains failing to help the officials identify him, except for the jumping moustache and the long teeth, he left leaving room for the later unscrupulous leaders who too did not learn from the life and fate of their predecessors. Benazir Bhutto, Nawas Sharif and the present Gen. Pervez Musharaf also went on with the time old tactics to keep themselves in power. Whether it was democracy or military rule, the unpopular rulers sedulously pursued the anti-India tirades. It was in the logic of Pakistani politics that if a ruler was to keep himself in power he was required to keep the anti-India feeling alive in Pakistan. It is interesting to note the recent statement of the Pakistan President, Pervez Musharaf. Asked of his readiness to settle the issues with India, he said if he were to settle the problems with India it would be better for him to purchase his ancestral property and live a happy life in India than return to Pakistan. Like all his predecessors, he too knows well that the only thing that keeps him in power is his baseless allegation that India is the foremost problem confronting Pakistan. If it is once realized by innocent Pakistani people that India is not their enemy but it is the innumerable and unsolved domestic problems that have been the real enemies of their nation, these irresponsible and power hungry politicians would be left with no chance to continue in power.

The successive governments, which ruled Pakistan since its birth, had never cared to meet the needs of its people as mentioned in the former chapters. Indeed Pakistan cannot be considered as a nation but only a ruthless military engine that bridles together a conglomeration of different unyielding national and ethnic groups like the Beluchis, Sindhis and the Punjabis. Bengal had already broken away from Pakistan owing to the impolitic and dictatorial dealings of the latter who colluded with the military. Almost all the cheap political tricks and the dirty diplomacy Pakistan had been practising had only boomeranged upon her. Kashmir issue, the artfully groomed child of Pakistan has turned to kick rebelliously at its own mother. It has been backfiring on Pakistan with the Jammu and Kashmir Liberation Front crying for an independent Kashmir. More notable is the changing global politics. The USA which so far used Pakistan as a cat's paw against the USSR and whose beneficiary Pakistan has been in the Security Council is no more interested in helping her. The recent Pakistani operation against India through the Kargil did not get the Chinese support too which the Musharaf administration was hoping for. The tirades Musharaf has been making lately against India, accusing her with many baseless complaints did not attract as much international attention as was expected though he is still going ahead with the same. The utterance he made in September 2003 that Osama Bin Laden, the terrorist whom the USA is chasing in connection with the September 11 tragedy, is somewhere in Pakistan, would only further aggravate the anti-Pakistani feeling in the States. The complaint of the Afghan President that Pakistan is breeding terrorism in its areas bordering with Afghanistan has also proved an eye opener. Also it is interesting to remember that years ago India's Minister of Home Affairs, L K Advani requested the international community including the USA, to declare Pakistan a terrorist state, a request he is making still. It is the breeding ground of all terrorist activities, which can subvert attempts for peace in the Asiatic region. Finding it difficult to control the terrorist elements within the state, Pakistan usually selects to support the outfits, which make the call for 'Jihad'. The recent statement of the Pakistani President Musharaf that Pakistan's military operation in Kargil "was a decision taken by the Mujahideen and we got involved in it because of the action taken by the Indian troops" brings out the bare fact that often the decision for war is taken by terrorist outfits whom the government of Pakistan cannot control[1]. It means that if Indian troops resort tc arms against the intrusion of any Pakistani outfit, unauthorized though it is, the Pakistan and its army would have to fight against India. This exposes the collusion between the Pakistan Government and the terrorist outfits and the helplessness of the former against the latter's hooliganism. But so long as the leaders of Pakistan are not prepared to look into the real problems ailing their state rather than getting on with clownish tactics to retain their power, Pakistan can never escape from its final doom. Its picture is of a state falling into the grave, which it is digging. But without realizing this it shouts and hisses at others.

In the meantime India too had been suffering from so many troubles though not as severe as those of Pakistan. India's impotent pacifism, the foolish Nehruvian scheme that took the Kashmir dispute to the UN instead of solving it in a judicious manner, the ceasefire at the points of victory, and the signing away of victory at the negotiating table have been only jeopardizing the national interests and adding to the enemy's audacity. If Nehru, instigated by Mountbatten, put the issue of the Pakistan Occupied Kashmir on the chessboard of international politics by taking it to the UN, that portion of Kashmir which still is in Indian hands has been a source of unending troubles. The Delhi agreement between Jawaharlal Nehru and Sheik Abdullah made Kashmir a mess by envisaging special citizenship rights for that 'state's subjects', flying of a separate flag for the state along with the national flag, and the extension of the provisions of the Indian Constitution in respect of the fundamental rights, emergency powers of the President and the jurisdiction of the Supreme Court subjecting them to certain limitations and restrictions. Kashmiris themselves objected to this step. Spearheaded by the Praja Parishad, they raised slogans that "in one country, two constitutions; in one country, two flags; in one country, two Prime Ministers" should not be tolerated. When Dr. Syama Prasad Mukherjee proceeded to Jammu to protest against this antinational scheme he was arrested on 11 May 1953. Tortured in Jail, this brave son of India died in custody on 23 June. The emotional attachment almost amounting to fraternal would not allow Nehru to move against the Sheik even when the latter remarked on 10 July 1953 that "Time will therefore, come when I will bid them (Indians) goodbye". Again on 13 July he commended, "It is not necessary that our state should become an appendage of either India or Pakistan". The Sheik was no doubt dreaming of becoming an independent ruler of an independent Sheikdom, a dream which evidently got the support of the Western powers including Britain whose Prime Minister Atlee, notwithstanding the fact that his own cabinet passed the Indian Independence Act, stated that "Kashmir should belong neither to India nor to Pakistan but be independent"[2]. The whole problem was thus the creation of the first Prime Minister of India whose successors too neglected the nationalist demand to abrogate Article 370 of the Indian Constitution, which envisages special status to Kashmir. The Kashmir problem thus remained unsolved all these days. And as Jag Mohan, former Minister of the Indian Union and the

Governor of Kashmir rightly pointed out, "it will go on in future also – unless Indian leaders stop building castles in the air".

India's nonalignment, as already noted was an added misfortune, which earned for Pakistan the support of the UK and USA. Indeed India's neutralism would not have saved her had she been truly nonaligned. For, the nonalignment movement embracing within it all the third world consisting the undemocratic and fanatic elements could not help its members in finding peace even among themselves, leave alone helping any of its own members against its enemy. It was indeed an undesirable conglomeration of the nations like Iran whose leaders were specialists in fanning the flames of fanaticism or Pakistan where murder of democracy has been a continuing scenario or India which saw the dynastic rule that spanned over a period of more than forty years since its independence. And as one of India's noted writers has sarcastically commented some time before, had Idi Amin of Uganda been in power he too would surely have chaired the NAM. The NAM never helped India in her foreign relations. It is interesting to notice that even Sri Aurobindo, rising from his seclusion and saint-life at Pondicherry came out heavily against the Nehru Government's appeasing policy. Even as early as in 1950 he said that India would be the Chinese target of attack unless she "precipitately" be on the side of the Communist nations, and urged the Indian leadership to be in close friendship with America, including the military alliance to check the impending attack of "Mao's mechanized millions"[3]. Indeed whenever India became the target of attacks both in war and international fora, she was helped either by the USA or the USSR. The NAM could not help her in such critical times. Even the help the USA gave India against the Chinese incursion of 1962 was the part of her anti-Communist policy while the support the U S S R extended to India in 1971 against the Pakistani attack and the Western intervention, could be taken as an expression of the anti-capitalist stand of the Communist nation. In both the cases the help was negative. Yet the early Prime Ministers of India would not take leave of the NAM, lest it should do away the image they had been having among the third world nations. Of course, the disappearance of the U S S R was thought to have brought about some changes in Indo-American relations of which the Pressler amendment was construed as a signal. It has to be borne in mind however that throughout its history USA had no permanent friend in Asia. To pursue her economic interests she would resort either to friendly gestures or military exercise with Asiatic powers.

The categorical rejection by the former UN Secretary General Mr. Boutros Boutros Ghali of the UN's unilateral intervention in the Kashmir dispute on the basis of the old Security Council resolution as demanded by Pakistan, had indeed frozen the Pakistan's bullying tactics on Kashmir. Another eyewash was the pretended willingness of the former Pakistan President Nawaz Sharif to envisage a new option on Kashmir. An independent Kashmir was needed as an essential and desirable link in the chain of important incidents relating to Indo-Pakistan issues, he opined. He was presumably floating the trial balloon to know the Pakistani reaction when in an interview to the BBC in February 1992 he said that he had an open mind about the need of an independent Kashmir. No doubt it evoked much criticism from the extremist politicians of Jamat-i-Islami variety. In any way both India and Pakistan are forced to agree on one thing, that there cannot be an independent Jammu and Kashmir. There are other problems of Himalayan proportions, which haunt both the nations. It is high time that casting aside their enmity they seek avenues of economic development for which the Simla Agreement, despite its many shortcomings, has left open the doors for mutual consultations.

It is necessary that something entirely new which the U N or its members could not so far think of should be devised in such a way as to turn the bilateral relations cordial and enduring. The solution is so simple and surprising, though it has not presented itself to our modern generation of politicians. It is a confederation between India and Pakistan, an idea that had dawned as early as 1956 to Deen Dayal Upadhyaya and Ram Manohar Lohia. The idea did not get acceptance then, for at that time politicians were not ready to accept it. This is not of course a backdoor method, but not an idea the blood thirsty Pakistani Generals would readily consent to. But there is no other way out. The Kashmiri demand for independence will best be resolved once Pakistan and India bury their hatchet and agree that for the greater good of all the people in the South Asian Sub-Continent we need a common market and an economic community that would switch over to constructive activities. This is the most and only desirable alternative. This concept of confederation goes beyond the South Asian Association for Regional Cooperation, which asks only for cooperation, and the Simla Agreement, which speaks only of consultation. It calls upon the two nations for mutual trust, mutual reduction of armed forces, the cessation of all physical and emotional hostility, and a willingness to build a new society[4].

But a government that comes to power through military coup or the one led by people without any national vision, to save their country from its economic disasters would not suffice any more for peace between the two nations. What is needed is the replacement of the proverbial 'government of, by and for the President' of Pakistan with a popular government, which can dedicate itself for the cause of national progress and prosperity. Pakistan must think of the need of an enlightened leader who is free from the temptations of power and position and most bothered about her peoples' welfare. There must be somebody who loves his people, the principle of universal humanism and the highest ideal of a ruler who believes in what Plato envisioned centuries ago, the idea of a philosopher king.

The people too of Pakistan are indeed desirous of freeing themselves from the ruthless military dictatorship, which they think is the only panacea for the long-standing enmity between India and Pakistan. After all what is the content behind the argument of the Pakistani leaders regarding the traditional enmity between the two nations? What enmity the ordinary Pakistani has towards an Indian whom he does not know? In fact all what is called the Pakistani enmity to India, if there is anything like that, is only the creation of the power hungry Pak politicians. It is interesting to notice that the ordinary people of Pakistan are not averse to their nation living in friendship with India. This popular trend has never vanished to these days from Pakistan. A report from Islamabad says that the members of the Indian delegation visiting Pakistan were surprised at the change in public mood against *jihad* and the craving of the people for friendship and good relations with India[5]. Shahid Siddiqi, who was on the delegation pointed out this discernable change in the Pakistanis' attitude towards Indians. He says, "In the past I used to hear a lot about *jihad*. This time I have not heard this in a single meeting anywhere. Even in private conversation nobody mentions this word. There seems to be a change in attitude in the ruling elite in Pakistan". He mentions that "In the past whenever I mentioned Indian Muslims I was not allowed to speak. This time not only people are listening to me but they are appreciating my point of view that Indian Muslims are the crucial part of the Indian secular fabric. And Indian secular fabric is inextricably linked to the solution of the Kashmir issue". This smacks of a great change, which has not so far been experienced in the attitude of the Pakistani people to the Indians. This Pakistani perception about India has its source perhaps in the realization about the futility of mutual conflict both nations have been engaged in for the past fifty or more years. Kuldip Nayar who led an Indian Parliamentary delegation in the middle of 2003 was indeed jubilant over the warm reception the team got from the Pakistanis. He wrote, "We, the nine parliamentarians were swept off our feet by love and affection showered upon us at Lahore, Islamabad and Karachi. It was almost a people's war against the age-old prejudice and hatred against India". At Lahore Nayar and his team was surprised at the rousing reception accorded to them and the warmth with which they were entertained at the dinner hosted by the India-Pakistan Soldiers Initiative for Peace (IPSIP). The Jamate-e-Islami, which too did not seem to be averse to the move for peace, has given their first ever reception since the birth of Pakistan. Indeed many of the people and organizations in Pakistan are for shedding all differences with India and they are finding fault with the military set up for its abhorrence to find a solution to Indo-Pak problem. "Never before had I heard in Punjab such a barrage of unprintable words against the military", writes Nayar. Ms. Seema Mustafa who accompanied one of the early Parliamentary Delegations to Pakistan opined:

> There is an upsurge for peace in Pakistan. From the shopkeeper to the taxi-driver to the retired civil servant there is only one question on everybody's lips: are the two governments serious about peace? Kashmir is lost somewhere in the middle of this overwhelming demand for peace. Pakistani analysts admit that it is something that they have never really witnessed before. It is as if the rhetoric of war and confrontation has created a sense of fatigue and the people of Pakistan want to be free.

This columnist of the *Asian Age* adds further that "in discussions with retired government servants, army officers, journalists and others, the word "Kashmir" barely figured". The enthusiastic response to the visit of the Indian MPs in particular was tempered with a desire to see more of such exchanges with speaker after speaker dwelling at length on the need to restore facilities for the people in both countries[6]. According to Saeed Naqvi the dominant message was "an all pervasive desire in both the sides to put an end to the 'misunderstandings' of the past 57 years". In fact the Pakistani attitude towards India is fast changing for the better. What one may learn from this change of situation is the growing aversion to the daily dose of hatred the Pakistani Army has been feeding the people and the killing of the innocent peoples of Jammu and Kashmir, which has fallen very heavily on the Pakistani collective conscience. "Yet another reason" as M V Kamath very rightly puts it "may be the realization that Pakistan can never get Jammu and Kashmir whether through war, terrorism or third party mediation and it is more sensible to come to terms with that fact than to carry on an interminable proxy war". Coupled with this is the strong wave against the United States, which is sweeping through Pakistan. Probably they have by now started to realize that the USA was hitherto playing the Pakistani card to undo the stability of the Asiatic nations and the likelihood of their unity which may adversely affect the prospects of American economic imperialism. It is also possible that "the public has come to realize that their country's abject dependence on the United States has robbed it of its self-respect and self-confidence"[7]. The strong American armed contingent stationed on the Pakistani soil during the Afghan war was also beyond their tolerance.

But the problem is still the military rule, which has been the curse of Pakistan throughout its history. It always stands as a hindrance for the people finally coming into their own to forget all about the two-nation theory and live in peace and contentment with India. The situation indeed calls for a people's war against the military dictatorship of Pakistan. A longstanding and stable democracy totally independent of the military forces alone can help Pakistanis establish a friendly link with India, which is ready to shower its love on them by opening its doors to them and showing them that India cares for her neighbours who were once her own kith and kin. Therefore it is desirable if the military vultures of Pakistan are thrown out, something that only the people of Pakistan can do. But it is also to be noticed that the state of Pakistan, sliding into corruption and economic ruin, is surely on the verge of collapse, which in all probability is not very long in coming. It may not have even a quarter century of existence and quite automatically the Pakistani problem would shortly come to an end. Nonetheless what is desirable is not the collapse of a state but an overall growth of that land, which can help its own people as well as its neighbours to progress on the path of peace and self-sufficiency. But this requires a determined approach and the willingness to undergo many hardships the kind the East Pakistanis endured for the freedom from the military vultures of the West Pakistan. Indeed this depends on the popular will of the Pakistanis.

References

1. *The New Indian Express*, Kochi, 14 June 2003.
2. Jag Mohan, "The Kashmir Tragedy", *Indian Express*, Kochi, 11 March 1992.
3. V B Kulkarni, *Problems of Indian Democracy*, Bombay, 1977, p. 175.
4. M V Kamath, "Solutions and Non-Solutions", *Organiser*, 15 April 1990.
5. The report of the PTI, 24 June, 2003.
6. M V Kamath, "The Irrelevance of Musharaf in Pakistan", *Aseemaa*, Mangalore, September, 2003.
7. *Ibid.*

Appendix - I

Indian Independence Act–1947

An Act to make provision for the setting up in India of two independent Dominions, to substitute other provisions for certain provisions of the Government of India Act, 1935, which apply outside those Dominions, and to provide for other matters consequential on or connected with the setting up of those Dominions.

Be it enacted by the King's most Excellent Majesty, by and with the advice and consent of the Lord's Spiritual and Temporal, and Commons, in this present Parliament assembled, and by the authority of the same, as follows:

1. The New Dominions

1. As from the fifteenth day of August, nineteen hundred and forty seven, two independent Dominions shall be set up in India, to be known respectively as India and Pakistan.
2. The said Dominions are hereafter in this act referred to as 'the new Dominions' and the said fifteenth day of August is hereafter in this Act referred to as 'the appointed day'.

2. Territories of the New Dominions

1. Subject to the provisions of sub-section (3) and (4) of this section, the territories of India shall be the territories under the sovereignty of His Majesty which, immediately before the appointed day, were included in British India except the territories which, under sub-section (2) of this section, are to be the territories of Pakistan.
2. Subject to the provisions of sub-sections (3) and (4) of this section, the territories of Pakistan shall be

(a) the territories which, on the appointed day, are included in the Provinces of East Bengal and West Punjab as constituted under the two following sections;

(b) the territories which, at the date of the passing of this Act, are included in the Province of Sind and the Chief Commissioner's Province of British Baluchistan; and

(c) if whether before or after the passing of this Act but before the appointed day, the Governor-General declares that the majority of the valid votes cast in the referendum which, at the date of the passing of this Act, is being or has recently been held in that behalf under his authority in the North West Frontier Province are in favour of representatives of that province taking part in the Constituent Assembly of Pakistan, the territories which, at the date of the passing of this Act, are included in that Province.

3. Nothing in this section shall prevent any area being at any time included in or excluded from either of the new Dominions, so, however, that

   (a) no area not forming the part of the territories specified in sub-section (1) or, as the case may be, sub-section (2), of this section shall be included in either Dominions without the consent of that Dominion; and

   (b) no area which forms part of the territories specified in the said sub-section (1) or, as the case may be, the said sub-section (2) or which has after the appointed day been included in either Dominion, shall be excluded from that Dominion without the consent of that Dominion.

4. Without prejudice to the generality of the provisions of sub-section (3) of this section, nothing in this section shall be construed as preventing the accession of Indian states to either of the new Dominions.

3. Bengal and Assam

1. As from the appointed day

   (a) the Province of Bengal, as constituted under the Government of India Act, 1935, shall cease to exist; and

(b) there shall be constituted in lieu thereof two new Provinces, to be known respectively as East Bengal and West Bengal.

2. If whether before or after the passing of this Act, but before the appointed day, the Governor General declares that the majority of the valid votes cast in the referendum which, at the date of the passing of this Act, is being or has recently been held in that behalf under his authority in the District of Sylhet are in favour of that District forming part of the new Province of East Bengal then, as from that day, a part of the new Province of Assam shall, in accordance with the provisions of sub-section (3) of this section, form part of the new Province of East Bengal.

3. The boundaries of the new Provinces aforesaid and, in the event mentioned in the sub-section (2) of this section, the boundaries after the appointed day of the Province of Assam, shall be such as may be determined, whether before or after the appointed day, by the award of a boundary commission appointed or to be appointed by the Governor General in that behalf, but until the boundaries are so determined,

(a) The Bengal Districts specified in the First Schedule to this Act, together with, in the event mentioned in sub-section (2) of this section, the Assam District of Sylhet, shall be treated as the territories which are to be comprised in the new Province of East Bengal; and

(b) The remainder of the territories comprised at the date of the passing of this Act in the Province of Bengal shall be treated as territories which are to be comprised in the new Province of West Bengal; and

(c) In the event mentioned in sub-section (2) of this section, in the District of Sylhet shall be excluded from the Province of Assam.

4. In this section, the expression 'award' means, in relation to a boundary commission, the decisions of the chairman of that commission contained in his report to the Governor-General at the conclusion of the commission's proceedings.

4. The Punjab

1. As from the appointed day.
   (a) the Province of the Punjab, as constituted under the Government of India Act, 1935, shall cease to exist; and
   (b) there shall be constituted two new Provinces to be known respectively as West Punjab and East Punjab.
2. The boundaries of the said new Provinces shall be such as may be determined, whether before or after the appointed day, by the award of a boundary commission appointed or to be appointed by the Governor-General in that behalf, but until the boundaries are so determined –
   (a) the District specified in the second schedule to this Act shall be treated as the territories to be comprised in the new Province of West Punjab; and
   (b) the reminder of the territories comprised at the date of the passing of this Act in the Province of the Punjab shall be treated as the territories which are to be comprised in the new Province of East Punjab.
3. In this section, the expression 'award' means, in relation to a boundary commission, the decisions of the chairman of that commission contained in his report to the Governor-General at the conclusion of the commission's proceedings.

5. The Governor-General of the New Dominions

For each of the new Dominions, there shall be a Governor-General who shall be appointed by His Majesty for the purposes of the Government of the Dominion:

Provided that, unless and until provision to the contrary is made by a law of the Legislature of either of the new Dominions, the same person may be Governor-General of both the new Dominions.

6. Legislation for the New Dominions

1. The Legislature of each of the new Dominions shall have full power to make laws for that Dominion, including laws having extra-territorial operation.
2. No law or no provision of any law made by the Legislature of either of the new Dominions shall be void or inoperative

on the ground that it is repugnant to the law of England, or to the provisions of this or any existing or any future Act of Parliament of the United Kingdom, or to any order, rule or regulation made under any such Act, and the powers of the Legislature of each Dominion include the power to repeal or amend any such Act, order, rule or regulation in so far as it is part of the law of the Dominion.

3. The Governor General of each of the new Dominions shall have full power to assent in His Majesty's name to any law of the Legislature of that Dominion and so much of any Act as relates to the disallowance of laws by His Majesty's or the reservation of laws for the signification of His Majesty's pleasure thereon or the suspension of the operation of the laws until the signification of His Majesty's pleasure thereon shall not apply to laws of the Legislature of either of the new Dominions.

4. No Act of Parliament of the United Kingdom passed on or after the appointed day shall extend, or be deemed to extend, to either of the new Dominions as part of the law of that Dominion unless it is extended thereto by a law of the Legislature of that Dominion.

5. No Order in Council made on after the appointed day, or no order, rule or other instrument made on or after the appointed day under any such Act by any United Kingdom Minister or authority, shall extend, or be deemed to extend, to either of the new Dominions as part of the law of that Dominion.

6. The power referred to in sub-section (1) of this section extends to the making of laws limiting for the future the powers of the Legislature of that Dominion.

7. Consequences of the setting up of the new Dominions

1. As from the appointed day
   (a) His Majesty's Government in the United Kingdom have no responsibility as respects the government of any of the territories which, immediately before that day, were included in British India.
   (b) the suzerainty of His Majesty over Indian states lapses, and with it, all treaties and agreements in force at the

date of the passing of this Act between His Majesty and the rulers of Indian States, all functions exercisable by His Majesty at that date with respect to Indian States, all obligations of His Majesty existing at that date towards Indian States or the rulers thereof, and all powers, rights, authority or jurisdiction exercisable by His Majesty at that date in or in relation to Indian States by treaty, grant, usage, sufferance or otherwise; and

(c) there lapse also any treaties or agreements in force at the date of the passing of this Act between His Majesty and any persons having authority in the tribal areas, any obligations of His Majesty existing at that date to any such persons or with respect to the tribal areas, and all powers, rights, authority or jurisdiction exercisable at that date by His Majesty in or in relation to the tribal areas by treaty, grant, usage, sufferance or otherwise;

Provided that, notwithstanding anything in paragraph (b) or paragraph (c) of this sub-section, effect shall, as nearly as may be, continue to be given to the provisions of any such agreement as is therein referred to which relate to customs, transit and communications, posts and telegraphs, or other like matters, until the provisions in question are denounced by the ruler of the Indian States or person having authority in the tribal areas on the one hand, or by the Dominion or Province or other part thereof concerned on the other hand, or are superseded by subsequent agreements.

2. The assent of the Parliament of the United Kingdom is hereby given to the omission from the Royal Style and Titles of the words 'Indiae Imperator' and the words 'Emperor of India' and to the issue by His Majesty for that purpose of His Royal Proclamation under the Great Seal of the Realm.

8. Temporary provision as to Government of each of the new Dominions

1. In case of each of the new Dominions, the powers of the Legislature of the new Dominion shall, for the purpose of making provision as to the constitution of the Dominion,

be exercisable in the first instance of the Constituent Assembly of that Dominion, and references to this Act to the Legislature of the Dominion shall be construed accordingly.

2. Except in so far as other provision is made by or in accordance with a law made by the Constituent Assembly of the Dominion under sub-section (1) of this section, each of the new Dominions and all Provinces and other parts thereof shall be governed as nearly as may be in accordance with the Government of India Act, 1935; and the provisions of that Act, and of the Orders in Council, rules and other instruments made thereunder, shall, so far as applicable, and subject to any express provisions of this Act, and with such omissions, additions, adaptations and modifications as may be specified in orders of the Governor-General under the next succeeding section, have effect accordingly:

Provided that:

(a) the said provision shall apply separately in relation to each of the new Dominions and nothing in this sub-section shall be construed as continuing on or after the appointed day any Central Government or Legislature common to both of the new Dominions;

(b) nothing in this sub-section shall be construed as continuing in force on or after the appointed day any form of control by His Majesty's Government in the United Kingdom over the affairs of the new Dominions or of any Province or other part thereof;

(c) so much of the said provisions as requires the Governor-General or any Governor to act in his discretion or exercise his individual judgment as respects any matter shall cease to have effect as from the appointed day;

(d) as from the appointed day, no Provincial Bill shall be reserved under the Government of India Act, 1935, for the signification of His Majesty's pleasure, and no Provincial Act shall be disallowed by His Majesty thereunder; and

(e) the powers of the Federal Legislature or Indian Legislature under that Act, as in force in relation to each Dominion, shall, in the first instance, be exercisable by the Constituent Assembly of that Dominion in addition to the powers exercisable by that Assembly under sub-section (1) of this section.

3. Any provision of the Government of India Act, 1935, which, as applied to either of the new Dominions by sub-section (2) of this section and the orders therein referred to, operates to limit the legislature of that Dominion shall, unless and until other provision is made by or in accordance with a law made by the Constituent Assembly of the Dominion in accordance with the provision of sub-section (1) of this section, have the like effect as a law of the Legislature of the Dominion limiting for the future the powers of that Legislature.

9. Orders for bringing this Act into force

1. The Governor General shall by order make such provision as appears to him to be necessary or expedient–
   (a) for bringing the provisions of this Act into effective operation;
   (b) for dividing between the new Dominions, and between the new Provinces to be constituted under this Act, the powers, rights, properties, duties and liabilities of the Governor-General in Council, or as the case may be, of the relevant Provinces which, under this Act, are to cease to exist;
   (c) for making omissions from, additions to, and, adaptations and modifications of, the Government of India Act, 1935, and the Orders in Council, rules and other instruments made thereunder, in their application to the separate new Dominions;
   (d) for removing difficulties arising in connection with the transition to the provisions of this Act;
   (e) for authorizing the carrying on of the business of the Governor General in Council between the passing of this Act and the appointed day otherwise than in accordance with the provisions in that behalf of the ninth schedule of the Government of India Act, 1935;
   (f) for enabling the agreements to be entered into, and other acts done, on behalf of either of the new Dominions before the appointed day;
   (g) for authorizing the continued carrying on for the time being on behalf of the new Dominions or on behalf of

any two or more of the said new Provinces, of service and activities previously carried on on behalf of the British India as a whole or on behalf of the former Provinces which those new Provinces represent;

(h) for regulating the monetary system and any matters pertaining to the Reserve Bank of India; and

(i) so far as it appears necessary or expedient in connection with any of the matters aforesaid, for varying the Constitution, powers and jurisdiction of any Legislature, court or other authority in the new Dominions and carrying new Legislatures, courts or other authorities therein.

2. The powers conferred by this section on the Governor-General shall, in relation to their respective Provinces, be exercisable also by the Governors of the Provinces which, under this Act are to cease to exist; and those powers shall, for the purpose of the Government of India Act, 1935, be deemed to be matters as respects which the Governors are, under that Act, to exercise their individual judgment.

3. This section shall be deemed to have had effect as from the third day of June, nineteen hundred and forty seven, and any order of the Governor General or any Governor made on or after that date as to any matter shall have effect accordingly, or any order made under this section may be said so as to be retrospective to any date not earlier than the said third day of June:

Provided that no provision shall be deemed to be guilty of an offence by reason of so much of any such order as makes any provision thereof retrospective to any date before the making thereof.

4. Any orders made under this section, whether before or after the appointed day, shall have effect–

(a) up to the appointed day, in British India;

(b) on and after the appointed day, in the new Dominion or the Dominion concerned; and

(c) outside British India, or as the case may be, outside the new Dominion or Dominions concerned, to such extent, whether before, on or after the appointed day, as a law of the Legislature of the Dominion or Dominions concerned, would have on or after the appointed day, but shall, in case of each of the Dominions, be subject to the same powers of repeal and amendment as laws of the Legislature of that Dominion.

5. No order shall be made under this section, by the Governor of any Province, after the appointed day, or, by the Governor-General, after the thirty-first day of March, nineteen hundred and forty eight, or such earlier date as may be determined, in case of either Dominion, by any law of the Legislature of that Dominion.

6. If it appears that a part of the Province of Assam is, on the appointed day, to become part of the new Province of East Bengal, the preceding provisions of this section shall have effect as if, under this Act, the Province of Assam was to cease to exist on the appointed day as a new Province.

10. Secretary of State's services etc.

1. The provisions of this Act keeping in force provisions of the Government of India Act, 1935, shall not continue in force the provisions of that Act relating to appointments to the civil services of, and civil posts under, the Crown in India by the Secretary of State, or the provisions of that Act, relating to the reservation of posts.
2. Every person who
   (a) having been appointed by the Secretary of State, or Secretary of State in Council, to a civil service of the Crown in India continues on or after the appointed day to serve under the Government of either of the new Dominions or of any Province or part thereof, or
   (b) having been appointed by His Majesty before the appointed day to be the judge of the Federal Court or of any court which is a High Court within the meaning of the Government of India Act, 1935, continues on and after the appointed day to serve as a judge in either of the new Dominions, shall be entitled to receive from the Governments of the Dominions and Provinces or parts which he is from time to time serving or as the case may be, which are served by the courts in

which he is from time to time a judge, the same conditions of service as respects remuneration, leave and pension, and the same rights as respects disciplinary matters, or, as the case may be, as respects the tenure of his office, or rights as similar thereto as changed circumstances may permit, as that person was entitled to immediately before the appointed day.

3. Nothing in this Act shall be construed as enabling the rights and liabilities of any person with respect to the family pension fund vested in Commissioners under section two hundred and seventy three of the Government of India Act, 1935, to be governed otherwise than by Orders-in-Council made (whether or after the passing of this Act or the appointed day) by His Majesty-in-Council and the rules made (whether before or after the passing of this Act or the appointed day) by a Secretary of State or such other Minister of the Crown as may be designated in that behalf or Order-in-Council under the Ministers of the Crown (Transfer of Functions) Act, 1946.

11. Indian Armed Forces

1. The orders to be made by the Governor-General under the preceding provisions of this Act shall make provision for the division of the Indian armed forces of His Majesty between the new Dominions and for the command and governance of those forces until the division is completed.
2. As from the appointed day, while any member of His Majesty's forces, is attached to or serving with any of His Majesty's Indian forces
   (a) he shall, subject to any provision to the contrary made by a law of the Legislature of the Dominion or Dominions concerned or by any order of the Governor-General under the preceding provisions of this Act, have, in relation to the Indian forces in question, the powers of command and punishment appropriate to his rank and functions; but
   (b) nothing in any enactment in force at the date of the passing of this Act shall render him subject in any way to the law governing the Indian forces in question.

12. British Forces in India

1. Nothing in this Act affects the jurisdiction or authority of His Majesty's Government in the United Kingdom, or of the Admiralty, the Army Council, or the Air Council or of any other United Kingdom authority, in relation to any of His Majesty's forces which may, on or after the appointed day, be in either of the new Dominions or elsewhere in the territories which, before the appointed day, were included in India, not being Indian forces.

2. In its application in relation to His Majesty's forces, other than Indian forces, the Army Act shall have effect on or after the appointed day
   (a) as if His Majesty's Indian forces were not included in the expressions 'the forces' and the 'regular forces'; and
   (b) subject to the further modifications specified in Parts I and II of the Third Schedule to this Act.

3. Subject to the provisions of the sub-section (2) of this section, and to any provisions of any law of the Legislature of the Dominion concerned, all civil authorities in the new Dominions, shall in those Dominions and in the other territories which were included in India before the appointed day, perform in relation to His Majesty's military forces, not being Indian forces, the same functions as were, before the appointed day, performed by them, or by the authorities corresponding to them, whether by virtue of the Army Act or otherwise, and the matters for which provision is to be made by orders of the Governor-General under the preceding provisions of this Act shall include the facilitating of the withdrawal from the new Dominions and other territories aforesaid of His Majesty's military forces, not being Indian forces.

18. Provision as to Existing Laws etc.

1. In so far as any Act of Parliament, Order in Council, order, rule, regulation or other instrument passed or made before the appointed day operates otherwise than as part of the law of British India or the new Dominions, references therein to India or British India, however worded and whether by name or not, shall, in so far as the context permits and

expects so far as Parliament may hereafter otherwise provide, be construed as, or as including, references to the new Dominions, taken together, or taken separately, according as the circumstances and subject matter may require.

Provided that nothing in this sub-section shall be construed as continuing in operation any provisions in so far as the continuance thereof as adapted by this sub-section is inconsistent with any of the provisions of this Act other than this section.

2. Subject to the provisions of sub-section (1) of this section and to any other express provision of this Act, the Orders in Council made under sub-section (5) of section three hundred and eleven of the Government of India Act, 1935 for adapting and modifying Acts of Parliament shall, except so far as Parliament may hereafter otherwise provide, continue in force in relation to all Acts in so far as they operate otherwise than as part of the law of British India or the new Dominions.

3. Save as otherwise expressly provided in this Act, the law of British India and of the several parts thereof existing immediately before the appointed day shall, so far as applicable and with necessary adaptations continue as the law of each of the new Dominions and the several parts thereof until other provision is made by laws of the Legislature of the Dominion in question or by any other Legislature or other authority having power in that behalf.

4. It is hereby declared that the Instruments of Instructions issued before the passing of this Act by His Majesty to the Governor General and the Governors of Provinces lapse as from the appointed day, and nothing in this Acts shall be construed as continuing in force any provision of the Government of India Act, 1935, relating to such Instruments of Instructions.

5. As from the appointed day, so much of any enactment as requires the approval of His Majesty in Council to any rules of court shall not apply to court in either of the new Dominions.

19. Interpretations, etc.

3. Reference in this Act to the Constituent Assembly of a Dominion shall be construed as references

(a) in relation to India, to the Constituent Assembly, the first sitting whereof was held on the ninth day of December, nineteen hundred and forty six, modified

(i) by the exclusion of the members representing Bengal, the Punjab, Sind and British Baluchistan; and

(ii) should it appear that the North-West Frontier Province will form part of Pakistan, by the exclusion of the members representing that Province; and

(iii) by the inclusion of members representing West Bengal and East Punjab; and

(iv) should it appear that, on the appointed day, a part of the Province of Assam is to form part of the new Province of East Bengal, by the exclusion of the members heretofore representing the Province of Assam, and the inclusion of members chosen to represent the remainder of that Province;

(b) in relation to Pakistan, to the Assembly set up or about to be set up at the date of the passing of this Act under the authority of the Governor General as the Constituent Assembly for Pakistan:

Provided that nothing in this sub-section shall be construed as affecting the extent to which representatives of the Indian States take part in either of the said Assemblies, or as preventing the filling of casual vacancies in the said Assemblies or as preventing the participation, in either of the said Assemblies in accordance with such arrangements as may be made in that behalf, of representatives of the tribal areas on the borders of the Dominion for which that Assembly sits, and the powers of the said Assemblies shall extend, and be deemed always to have extended, to the making of provision for the matters specified in this provision.

20. This Act may be cited as Indian Independence Act, 1947.

First Schedule

Bengal districts provisionally included in the new Province of East Bengal.

In the Chittagong division, the districts of Chittagong, Noakhali and Tipera.

In the Dacca division, the districts of Bakarganj, Dacca, Faridpur and Mymensingh.

In the Presidency division, the districts of Jessore, Murshidabad and Nadia.

In the Rajshahi division, the districts of Bogra, Dinajpur, Malda, Pabna, Rajshahi and Rangpur.

Second Schedule

Districts provisionally included in the new province of West Punjab.

In the Lahore division, the districts of Gujranwala, Gurdaspur, Lahore, Sheikhupura and Sailkot.

In the Rawalpindi Division, the districts of Attock, Gujrat, Jhelum, Mianwali, Rawalpindi, and Shahpur.

In the Multan Division, the districts of Dera Ghazi Khan, Jhang, Lyallpur, Montgomery, Multan and Muzaffargarh.

Appendix - II

The Instrument of Accession

Whereas the Indian Independence Act, 1947, provides that as from the fifteenth day of August, 1947, there shall be set up an independent dominion known as India, and the Government of India Act of 1935, shall, be with such omission, additions, adaptations and modifications as the Governor General may by order specify, be applicable to the Dominion of India.

And whereas the Government of India Act, 1935, as so adapted by the Governor General provides that an Indian state may accede to the Dominion of India by an Instrument of Accession executed by the ruler thereof:

Now, therefore, I Sriman Inder Mahender Rajarajeswar Maharajadhiraj Sri Hari Singhji Jammu and Kashmir Naresh Tatha Tibbet adi Deshadhipathi, Ruler of Jammu and Kashmir State, in the exercise of my sovereignty in and over my said state do hereby execute this Instrument of Accession and

1. Thereby declare that I accede to the dominion of India with the intent that the Governor General of India, the Dominion Legislature, the Federal Court and any other Dominion authority established for the purpose of the Dominion shall, by virtue of this my Instrument of Accession but subject always to the terms thereof, and for the purpose only of the Dominion, exercise in relation to the state of Jammu and Kashmir (herein afterwards referred to as "this state") such functions as may be vested in them by or under the Government of India Act, 1935, as in force in the Dominion of India, on the 15th Day of August 1947, (which Act as so in force is hereafter referred to as "the Act").

2. I do hereby assume the obligation of ensuring that the due effect is given to provisions of the Act within this state so far as they are applicable therein by virtue of this my Instrument of Accession.

3. I accept the matters specified in the schedule hereto as the matters with respect to which the Dominion Legislature may make laws for the state.

4. I do hereby declare that I accede to the Dominion of India on the assurance that if an agreement is made between the Governor General and the ruler of this state whereby any function in relation to the administration in this state of any law of the Dominion Legislature shall be exercised by the Ruler of this state, then any such agreement shall be deemed to form the part of this Instrument and shall be construed and have effect accordingly.

5. The terms of this my Instrument of Accession shall not be varied by any amendment of the Act or the Indian Independence Act 1947, unless such is accepted by me by Instrument supplementary to this Instrument.

6. Nothing in this Instrument shall empower the Dominion Legislature to make any law for this state authorizing the compulsory acquisition of for any purpose, but I hereby undertake that should the Dominion for the purpose of a Dominion law which applies in this state deem it necessary to acquire any land, I will at their request acquire the land at their expense, or if the land belongs to me transfer it to them on such terms as may be agreed, or, in default of agreement, determined by an arbitrator to be appointed by the Chief Justice of India.

7. Nothing in this Instrument shall be deemed to commit in any way to acceptance of any future Constitution of India or to fetter any discretion to enter into agreement with the Government of India under any such future constitution.

8. Nothing in this instrument affects the continuance of my sovereignty in and over this state, or, save as provided by or under this Instrument, the exercise of any powers, authority and rights now enjoyed by me as ruler of this state or the validity of any law at present in force in this state.

9. I hereby declare that I execute this Instrument on behalf of this state and that any reference in this Instrument to me or to the ruler of this state is to be construed as including a reference to my heirs and successors.

Given under my hand this 26th day of October, nineteen hundred and forty seven.

Hari Singh

Maharajadhiraj of
Jammu and Kashmir State.

Appendix–III

Text of The Simla Summit Agreement

1. The Government of India and the Government of Pakistan are resolved that the two countries put an end to the conflict and confrontation that have hitherto marred their relations and work for the promotion of friendly and harmonious relationships and the establishment of durable peace in the subcontinent, so that both countries may henceforth devote their resources and energies to the pressing task of advancing the welfare of their people.

In order to achieve this objective, the Government of India and the Government have agreed as follows:

(i) That the principles and purposes of the charter of the United Nations shall govern the relations between the two countries;

(ii) That the two countries are resolved to settle their differences by peaceful means through bilateral negotiations or by any other peaceful means mutually agreed upon between them. Pending the final settlement of any of the problems between the two countries, neither side shall unilaterally alter the situation and both shall prevent the organization or encouragement of any acts detrimental to the maintenance of peaceful and harmonious relations;

(iii) That the prerequisites for reconciliation, good neighbourliness and durable peace between them is a commitment by both the countries to peaceful coexistence, respect for each other's territorial integrity and sovereignty, and noninterference in each other's internal affairs; on the basis of equality and mutual benefit;

(iv) That the basic issues and causes of conflict which have bedeviled the relations between the two countries for the last 25 years shall be resolved by peaceful means;

(v) That they shall always respect each other's national unity, territorial integrity, political independence and sovereign equality;

(vi) That in accordance with the charter of the United Nations, they will refrain from the threat or use of force, against the territorial integrity or political independence of each other.

2. Both Governments will take steps within their power to prevent hostile propaganda directed against each other. Both countries will encourage the dissemination of each information as would promote the development of friendly relations between them.

3. In order to progressively restore and normalize relations between the two countries step by step, it was agreed that:

(i) Steps shall be taken to resume communications, postal, telegraphic, sea, land, including border posts and air links, including over-flights;

(ii) Appropriate steps shall be taken to promote travel facilities for the nationals of the other country;

(iii) Trade and cooperation in economic and other agreed fields will be resumed as far as possible;

(iv) Exchange in the fields of science and culture will be promoted. In this connection delegations from the two countries will meet from time to time to work out the necessary details.

4. In order to initiate the process of the establishment of durable peace, both the Governments agree that:

(i) Indian and Pakistani forces shall be withdrawn to their side of the international border;

(ii) In Jammu and Kashmir, the line of control resulting from the ceasefire on 17 December 1971, shall be respected by both the sides with out prejudice to the recognized position of either side. Neither side shall seek to alter it unilaterally, irrespective of mutual differences and legal interpretations. Both sides further undertake to refrain from the threat or the use of force in violation of this line;

(iii) The withdrawals shall commence upon entry of this agreement and shall be completed within a period of thirty days thereof.

5. This agreement will be subject to ratification by both countries in accordance with their respective constitutional procedures and will come into force with effect from the date on which the instruments of ratification are exchanged.

6. Both Governments agree that their respective heads will meet again at a mutually convenient time in the future and that, in the meanwhile, the representatives of the two sides will meet to discuss further the modalities and arrangements for the establishment of durable peace and normalization of relations, including the question of repatriation of prisoners of war and a civilian internees, a final settlement of Jammu and Kashmir and the resumption of diplomatic relations.

Sd/(Indira Gandhi)
Prime Minister
Republic of India.

Sd/ (Zulfikar Ali Bhutto)
President
Islamic Republic of
Pakistan.

Appendix–IV

Kashmir Accord–1974

1. The State of Jammu and Kashmir, which is a constituent unit of the Union of India, shall, in its relations with the Union, continue to be governed by Article 370 of Constitution of India.
2. The residuary powers of legislation shall remain with the State; however, Parliament will continue to have power to make laws relating to the prevention of activities directed towards disclaiming, questioning or disrupting the sovereignty and territorial integrity of India or bringing about cession of a part of the territory of India or secession of a part of the territory of India from the Union or causing insult to the Indian National Flag, the Indian National Anthem and the Constitution.
3. Where any provision of the Constitution of India had been applied to the State of Jammu and Kashmir with adaptations and modifications, such adaptations and modifications can be altered or repealed by an order of the President under Article 370, each individual proposal in this behalf being considered on its merits; but provisions of the Constitution of India already applied to the State of Jammu and Kashmir without adaptation or modification are unalterable.
4. With a view to assuring freedom to the State of Jammu and Kashmir to have its own legislation on matters like welfare measures, cultural matters, social security, personal law, and procedural laws, in a manner suited to the special conditions in the State, it is agreed that the State Government can review the laws made by Parliament or extended to the State after 1953 on any matter relatable

to the Concurrent List and may decide which of them, in its opinion, needs amendment or repeal. Thereafter, appropriate steps may be taken under Article 254 of the Constitution of India. The grant of President's assent to such legislation would be sympathetically considered. The same approach would be adopted in regard to laws to be made by Parliament in future under the Proviso to clause 2 of that Article. The State Government shall be consulted regarding the application of any such law to the State and the views of the State Government shall receive the fullest consideration.

5. As an arrangement reciprocal to what has been provided under Article 368, a suitable modification of that Article as applied to the State should be made by Presidential order to the effect that no law made by the Legislature of the State of Jammu and Kashmir, seeking to make any change in or in the effect of any provision of the Constitution of the State of Jammu and Kashmir, seeking to make any change in or in the effect of any provision of the Constitution of the State of Jammu and Kashmir relating to any of the undermentioned matters, shall take effect unless the Bill, having been reserved for the consideration of the President, receives his assent; the matters are:

   (a) the appointment, powers, functions, duties, privileges and immunities of the Governor; and

   (b) the following matters relating to Election, namely, the superintendence, direction and control of elections by the Election Commission of India, eligibility for inclusion in the electoral rolls without discrimination, adult suffrage and composition of the Legislative Council, being matters specified in sections 138, 139, 140, and 50 of the Constitution of the State of Jammu and Kashmir.

6. No agreement was possible on the question of nomenclature of the Governor and the Chief Minister and the matter is therefore remitted to the Principals.

(sd) Mirza Mohammad Afzal Beg (sd) G. Parthasarthi

Appendix–V

Article 370 of the Indian Constitution

Temporary Provision with Respect to the State of Jammu and Kashmir

1. Notwithstanding anything in this Constitution,
   - (a) the provisions of Article 238 shall not apply in relation to the State of Jammu and Kashmir,
   - (b) the power of Parliament to make laws for the said State shall be limited to,
     - (i) those matters in the Union List which, in consultation with the Government of the State are declared by the President to correspond to matters specified in the Instrument of Accession governing the accession of the State to the Dominion of India as the matters with respect to which the Dominion Legislature may make laws for that State; and
     - (ii) such other matters in the said list, with the concurrence of the Government of the State, the President may by order specify.

       Explanation for the purposes of this article, the Government of the State means the person for the time being recognized by the President as the Maharaja of Jammu and Kashmir acting on the advice of the Council of Ministers for the time being in office under the Maharaja's proclamation dated the fifth day of March, 1948:
   - (c) the provisions of Article I and of this article shall apply in relation to that State;

(d) such of the other provisions of this Constitution shall apply in relation to that State subject to such exceptions and modifications as the President may by order specify:

Provided that no such order, which relates to the matters specified in the Instrument of Accession of the State referred to in paragraph (i) of sub-clause (b) shall be issued except in consultation with the Government of the State:

Provided further that no such order which relates to the matters other than those referred to in the last preceding proviso shall be issued except with the concurrence of that Government.

2. If the concurrence of the Government of the State referred to in paragraph (ii) of sub-clause (b) of clause (1) or in the second proviso to sub-clause (d) of that clause be given before the Constituent Assembly for the purpose of framing the Constitution of the State is convened, it shall be placed before such Assembly for such decision as it may take thereon.

3. Notwithstanding anything in the foregoing provisions of this article, the President may by public notification, declare that this article shall cease to be operative only with such exceptions and modifications and from such date as he may specify:

Provided that the recommendation of the Constituent Assembly of the State referred to in clause (2) shall be necessary before the President issues such a notification

In exercise of the powers conferred by Article 370 the President, on recommendation of the Constituent Assembly of the State of Jammu and Kashmir, declared that as from the 17th Day of November, 1952, the said Article 370 shall be operative with the modification that for the explanation in Cl. (1) thereof, the following explanation is substituted namely.

"*Explanation*–For the purpose of this article, the Government of the State means the person for the time being recognized by the President on the recommendation of the Legislative Assembly of the State as the *Sadr-I-Riyasat* (now Governor) of Jammu and Kashmir, acting on the advice of the Council of Ministers of the State for the time being in office". (Ministry of Law order No. C.O. dated 15th November 1952).

Bibliography

Abdul Kalam, A. P. J., *Wings of Fire*, Hyderabad, 2002.

Akbar, M. J.., *Kashmir: Behind the Vale*, New Delhi, 2003.

Akbar, M. K., *Kargil–Cross Border Terrorism*, New Delhi, 1999.

Anand, Mulk Raj (Ed.), *V K Krishna Menon's Marathon Speech on Kashmir at the Security Council*, Allahabad, 1992.

Anil Maheshwari, *Crescent Over Kashmir,* New Delhi, 1993.

Anthony Hyman, Muhammed Ghayur and Naresh Kaushik., *Pakistan: Zia and After*, New Delhi, 1989.

Anwar Shaik, *Islam*, Cardiff (UK), 1994, *Vedic Civilization*, Cardiff, 2003. *Islam: Sex and Violence*, Cardiff, 1999.

Maj. Gen. Ashok Krishna and P R Chari (Ed.) *Kargil: The Tables Turned*, New Delhi, 2001.

Aurobindo, Sri, *Bande Mataram*, Pondicherry, 1973.

The Human Cycle–The Ideal of Human Unity–War and Self-Determination, Pondicherry, 1985. *Essays on the Gita, Pondichery, 1987*

Azad Abdul, Kalam, *India Wins Freedom*, Madras, 1988.

Bajaj, Prem Nath, *Kashmir in the Crucible*, Bombay, 1969.

Bhattacharjea, Ajit, *Count Down to Partition*, New Delhi, 1997.

Bindra, S. S., *Indo-Pak Relations*, New Delhi, 1981.

Birdwood, Christopher, *Two Nations and Kashmir*, London, 1956.

Brahma Chellaney, *Nuclear Proliferation: The US Conflict*, New Delhi, 1993.

Brecher, Michael, *Nehru: A Political Biography*, London, 1959.

Callard, Keith, *Pakistan: A Political Study*, London, 1957.

Campbell, Johnson Alan, *Mission with Mountbatten*, London, 1957.

Chakravartty, Nikhil, *India-Pakistan–Themes Beyond Borders*, Delhi, 2004.

Chand, Tara, *History of the Freedom Movement in India*, Delhi, 1983.

Chagla, MC, *Roses in December*, Bombay, 1994.

Chatterji, Bankim Chandra, *Anandamath* (Trans. B K Roy), Delhi, 2000.

Chaudhury, Khaliquzzaman, *Pathway to Pakistan*, Lahore, 1961.

Chopra, Maharaj K., *India: The Search for Power*, Bombay, 1969.

Chopra, V D, *Pakistan and Asian Peace*, New Delhi, 1985. *Studies in Indo-Pakistan Relations*, New Delhi, 1984.

Colridge H J. (Ed.), *Life and Letters of Francis Xavier*, London, 1861.

Coupland, Reginald, *India: A Restatement*, London, 1945.

Danino, Michel, *The Invasion that Never Was*, Mysore, 1966.

David, Lelyveld, *Aligarh's First Generation*, Princeton, 1977.

Dhar, D N, *Dynamics of Political Change in Kashmir*, New Delhi, 2001.

Dixit, J. N., *Anatomy of a Flawed Inheritance*, Delhi, 1995.

Dogra, Ramesh C., *Jammu and Kashmir*, New Delhi, 1986.

Fischer, Louis, *The Life of Mahatma Gandhi*, Bombay, 1983.

Gaurav C. Sawant, *Dateline Kargil: A Correspondent's Nine-Week Account from the Battleground*, New Delhi, 2000.

Gibb, H. A. R., *Modern Trends in Islam*, Chicago, 1945.

Godse, Nathuram, *May it Please Your Honour* (Ed. Gopal Godse), Delhi, 1989.

Gupta, Karunakar, *India in World Politics*, Calcutta, 1969.

Gupta, Sisir, *India and International System*, New Delhi, 1981.

Gurumukh, Nihal Singh, *Landmarks in Indian Constitutional and National Development*, Banaras, 1933.

Heinman, Charles H and Mansingh Surjeet, *A Diplomatic History of Modern India*, Calcutta, 1971.

Hodson H. V., *The Great Divide*, London, 1969.

Huntington, Samuel, P., *The Clash of Civilizations and the Remaking of World Order*, New Delhi, 1996

Ismay H. L., *Memoirs of Lord Ismay*, London, 1960.

Iyengar, K.R. Srinivasa, *Sri Aurobindo – A Biography and History*, Pondicherry, 1985.

Jagmohan, *My Frozen Turbulence in Kashmir*, New Delhi, 1991.

Jha D. C., *Indo-Pakistan Relation*, Patna, 1972.

Jai Singh, Hari, *Kashmir a Tale of Shame*, New Delhi, 1996.

Jog N. G., *Lokamanya Bala Gangadhara Tilak*, New Delhi, 1979.

Kalhana, *Rajatarangini* (Trans &Ed. R S Pandit), New Delhi, 1977.

Karnik V. B., *Chinese Invasion: Background and Sequel*, Bombay, 1966.

Kasyap, Subhash C., *Bangladesh: A Study in International Legal Norms and Permissive Conscience*, Bombay, 1972. *Bangladesh, Background and Perspective*, Delhi, 1971.

Kersten, Holger, *Jesus Lived in India*, New Delhi, 2001.

Ketelbey C. D. M., *A History of Modern Times*, Bombay, 1979.

Khan, Aga., *Memoirs of Aga Khan*, London, 1954.

Khan, Wali, *Facts are Facts – The Untold Story of India's Partition*, New Delhi, 1988.

Kulkarni S. D., *The Story of Hindu Supremacy*, Bombay, 1992.

Kulkarni V. B., *British Dominion in India and After*, Bombay, 1964. *India and Pakistan: A Historical Survey of Hindu-Muslim Relations*, Bombay, 1973. *M.R. Jayakar*, New Delhi, 1976. *Pakistan: Its Origin and Relations with India*, New Delhi, 1988 *Problems of Indian Democracy*, Bombay, 1977.

Larry Collins and Dominique Lapierre, *Mountbatten and Independent India*, Delhi, 1998.

Montague, Edwin, *An Indian Diary*, London, 1930.

Majumdar, A. K., *Advent of Independence*, Bombay, 1963.

Majumdar, R., *Pakistan: Jinnah to the Present Day*, New Delhi, 1988, Vol. II.

Majumdar R. C., *History of the Freedom Movement in India*, Calcutta, 1975.

Menon, V. P., *Montague Chelmsford Reforms*, Bombay, 1965. *Transfer of Power*, Madras, 1988.

Moon, Penderel, *Divide and Quit*, London, 1961.

Mosely, Leonard, *The Last Days of the British Raj*, Bombay, 1971.

Mugal, Rafique M., 'Recent Archaeological Research in Cholistan Desert', *Harappan Civilisation* (Ed. G Possehl), Delhi, 1993.

Muhammad Shah, *Writings and Speeches of Sir Syed Ahmed Khan*, Bombay, 1972.

Munshi, K. M., *Indian Constitutional Documents*, Vols. 2, Bombay, 1967.

Mukherjee, Amitava, *India's Policy Towards Pakistan*, New Delhi, 1989.

Nanda, B. R., *Gandhi–Pan-Islamisn, Imperialism and Nationalism in India*, Bombay, 1989.

Noorani, A. G., *India, the Super Powers and the Neighbours*, New Delhi, 1985.

Palit, D. K., *The Lightening Campaign: Indo-Pakistan war– 1971*, New Delhi, 1972.

Panikker, K. M., *Asia and Western Dominance*, Bombay, 1999.

Peter, J.S.Duncon, *The Soviet Union and India* (New York: Council of Foreign Relations).

Pillai, Arjunan M., *Ancient Indian History*, New Delhi, 1988.

Pyarelal, *Mahatma Gandhi: The Last Phase*, Ahmadabad, 1958

Ramgopal, *Indian Muslims – A Political History*, Bombay, 1964.

Russel Andrews & Azizali F. Mohammad, *The Economy of Pakistan*, London, 1958.

Salman Khurshid, *Beyond Terrorism*, New Delhi, 1995.

Salunke S. P., *Pakistani Prisoners of War*, New Delhi, 1987.

Saxsena, Ajay, *India and Pakistan*, New Delhi, 1987.

Sayed, Khalid B., *The Political system of Pakistan*, Boston, 1967.

Seshadri H. V., *The Tragic Story of Partition*, Bangalore, 1982.

Sumit Ganguly, *Conflict Unending: India-Pakistan Tensions Since 1947*, New Delhi, 2002.

Surjit Mansingh, *India's Search for Power: Indira Gandhi's Foreign Policy 1966-1982*, New Delhi, 1984.

Tendulkar D. G., *Mahatma*, Delhi, 1988.

Tyabji, Husain B., *Badarudiin Tyabji: A Biography*, Bombay, 1952.

Verma P. S., *Jammu and Kashmir at the Political Crossroads*, New Delhi, 1994.

Victoria Schefield, *Kashmir in Conflict*, New Delhi, 2004.

Newspapers (NP), Journals, Periodicals and Government Publications

Amrit Bazar Patrika (NP), Calcutta.

Aseemaa, Mangalore.

Asian Recorder, Karachi.

Bande Mataram (NP), Calcutta.

Bhavan's Journal, Bombay.

Current History Magazine, March, 1992.

Dawn (NP), Karachi.

Eastern Economist, New Delhi.

The Economist (NP) London.

Facets of a Proxy War, Government of India, New Delhi, 1993.

Far Eastern Economic Review, 8 February, 1990.

Foreign Affaires Report, New Delhi.

From Surprise to Reckoning–The Kargil Committee Report, New Delhi, 2000.

Guns and Yellow Roses: *Essays on the Kargil war*, (Harper Cillins) Delhi, 1999.

The Hindu (NP), Madras.

A Hundred Years of the Hindu, Madras, 1985.

Hindustan Standard (NP), Calcutta.

The Hindustan Times (NP), Calcutta.

The Hindustan Times Weekly, Calcutta.

Himalayan and Central Asian Studies, New Delhi, April-June, 1988.

Illustrated Weekly of India, New Delhi.

Indian Defence Review, April-June 1999, Vol.14 (2).

Indian Express (NP), Kochi &Thiruvananthapuram.

India Quarterly, New Delhi.

India Today, New Delhi

Indu Prakash, Bombay.

Indian and Foreign Review, New Delhi.

International Studies, New Delhi.

Journal of Indian History, Thiruvananthapuram.

The Journal of Industry and Trade, New Delhi.

Manchester Guardian (NP), Manchester.

New York Times (NP), New York.

Observer (NP), London.

Organiser, New Delhi.

Pakistan Horizon, Karachi.

Pakistan Observer (NP), Dacca.

Pakistan Times (NP), Lahore.

The Pioneer.

Profile of Terrorist Violence – in Jammu and Kashmir, Ministry of Home Affairs, New Delhi, January 1996.

Profile of Terrorist Violence, Government of India, New Delhi, 1999.

Review of International Affaires, Belgrade.

The Statesman (NP), Calcutta.

Sunday Times (London).

Swiss Review of World Affaires, Zurich.

The New Indian Express, Kochi and Thiruvananthapuram.

The Times (NP), London.

Time, New York.

Times of India (NP), New Delhi.

The Tribune (NP), Ambala.

Vichara Bharathi, Thiruvananthapuram.

Voice of Jammu and Kashmir, Jammu.

Index

C

J

K

N

O

P

V

W

Y

Z